TECHNIQUES OF FINANCIAL ANALYSIS

TECHNIQUES OF
FINANCIAL ANALYSIS

by

ERICH A. HELFERT, D.B.A.

Internal Consultant
Crown Zellerbach Corporation
San Francisco, California

formerly Assistant Professor
Graduate School of Business Administration
Harvard University

Revised Edition · 1967
RICHARD D. IRWIN, INC.
Homewood, Illinois

Revised Edition

First Printing, April, 1967
Second Printing, July, 1967
Third Printing, February, 1968
Fourth Printing, September, 1968
Fifth Printing, March, 1969
Sixth Printing, November, 1969
Seventh Printing, June, 1970
Eighth Printing, February, 1971

Library of Congress Catalog Card No. 67–17045

Printed in the United States of America

PREFACE

This book contains a collection of what are known as "technical notes" on tools and techniques of analysis as well as other institutional background information being used in the first year of the M.B.A. program at the Harvard Graduate School of Business Administration, as supplements to case books and materials. Such notes are written to provide the student with the basic skills and knowledge required to analyze case situations for class discussion in preparation for a business career. Together with selected readings these materials help to build up the student's proficiency in analysis by introducing him to accepted techniques and a basic structure of institutional information.

The materials in this book form a set of the more important techniques of financial analysis commonly used, to provide a source for study, reference, and practice apart from the wider subject of financial management. The acquisition of most technical skills requires some practice, and for this reason the book contains with each chapter a variety of problems and exercises to accompany the descriptions and discussions of the various analytical techniques.

The first edition of this book contained selected materials that, with the exception of Chapter 6, had been used for at least two years in the finance curriculum of the Harvard Business School. For the new edition, all materials were completely updated, both in text and examples, and Chapters 2, 5 and 7 were newly written in view of the wide use the book has found since its first publication and in the light of developments in the finance field.

At this point I should like to express my appreciation to Professors Pearson Hunt, Frank L. Tucker, and Charles M. Williams of the Harvard Business School, and to Professor

Alan B. Coleman (now at Stanford University) and Professor
James E. Walter (now at the Wharton School of Commerce
and Finance), who as a teaching group or individually contributed ideas or materials to the original edition, or gave me
the benefit of their suggestions. Likewise I should like to express my appreciation to the many colleagues at universities
here and abroad, too numerous to mention individually, who
encouraged the development of an updated edition.

My thanks also go to the President and Fellows of Harvard
College who have granted me permission to use those materials which bear their copyright, and to Dean George P. Baker
and the administration of the Harvard Business School for
having provided me with the opportunity to develop many of
the materials in this volume.

San Francisco, California   ERICH A. HELFERT
March, 1967

TABLE OF CONTENTS

COMMON REFINEMENTS: Profits and Dividends. Depreciation as a "Source." FURTHER REFINEMENTS: The Earned Surplus Account (Retained Earnings). The Net Property Account. PRESENTATION.

Effects of Operations on Profits. Effects of Operations upon Cash.

RATIOS MEASURING A COMPANY'S LIQUIDITY AND INDEBTEDNESS: The Current Ratio. The Liquidity Ratio or "Acid Test." Debt Ratios. RATIOS APPRAISING FUNDS MANAGEMENT ("TURNOVER" RELATIONSHIPS): Accounts Receivable. Accounts Payable. Inventories. Fixed Assets. RATIOS REFERRING TO PROFITABILITY: Profitability as Related to Investment. Profitability as Related to Sales ("Profit Margin"). Relationships between Ratios. Other Comments.

Pro Forma Operating Statements and Balance Sheets. Cash Budgets. Reconciliation of Cash Budget with Pro Forma Statements.

The Point of View. The Cost of Debt. Operating Debt. Debt in the Capital Structure. The Cost of Preferred Stock. The Cost of Common Stock. Graphic Analysis of Earnings Fluctuations. The Choice among the Alternatives. Cost of Capital in Composites.

The Nature of Capital Budgeting. Components of Investment Analysis. Measures of Relative Desirability. Some Complications.

INTRODUCTION

THIS BOOK introduces the basic framework of financial analysis and presents a series of concepts and tools which are helpful to the financial manager or the financial analyst confronted with the task of interpreting financial statements and other operating data of a business.

The accompanying problems and caselets provide an opportunity to practice in relatively simple situations understanding and mastery of the material. It must be emphasized, however, that apart from acquiring the technical ability to *work* these tools, it is vital that the student look upon the *selection* of given tools in a situation as the important art to be mastered. Thus an understanding of what each tool can and can't do is necessary, analogous to the selectivity a craftsman applies to the tools of his trade.

In this connection, it should be noted that the main purpose of financial analysis is to provide reasonable clues and answers to *specific questions* posed by problems of interest to the analyst. It cannot be overemphasized that financial analysis (the use of analytical tools) is not an automatic or standardized process; rather, it is a flexible approach tailored to the needs of the specific situation. Some have called one of the key attributes of effective management "the art of asking significant questions." Likewise, the work of financial analysis will become much more meaningful and efficient if the financial manager or outside analyst practices this art to *focus* his investigation.

For instance, in the discussion of analytical tools which follows, numerous refinements are introduced together with the basic concepts. Depending on the kind of investigation desired, refinements of the tools chosen may substantially add to the insights gained into the financial picture of a company, or they may simply be waste motion spent on belaboring obvious or irrelevant facts.

1

It is strongly suggested, therefore, that any financial analysis be preceded by sober questions as to what factors, relationships and trends might be useful in helping to solve the problem at hand, be it to appraise the merits of extending credit, or to appraise the relative profitability of a company, or any other problem calling for the interpretation of financial data. Selection of the relevant tools as well as the relevant factors and time periods for investigation will do much to reduce the amount of detail work to be done and will increase the yield of the efforts expended. When used in this framework, financial analysis helps the manager or outside analyst appraise management performance, corporate efficiency, financial strengths and weaknesses, credit worthiness and other aspects of a company, division, or other financial unit, based upon its past performance.

At the same time, there are obvious limitations to the usefulness and reliability of the analytical tools, partly because of the form and reliability of the information available and partly because of the need to use past performance as a guide to future expectations and decisions. The discussions in this book will take into account the limitations as well as the uses of financial analysis.

Chapter 1

FUNDS FLOW CONCEPTS

ONE OF THE most basic and continuous series of decisions facing business management in general, and the financial manager in particular, is of a dual nature: "Where shall we put our present funds (capital employed in the firm) to best use in the interest of the owners of the enterprise, or, where shall we obtain additional resources (new capital added to the firm) to apply to the unfulfilled needs and opportunities we see in the enterprise?" It is the uncommon case where a business has more resources or means than it can profitably employ; generally much effort and deliberation is spent on proper allocation of available funds, and on raising additional capital for the opportunities within the firm, in line with its risk and profit objectives.

The continuous process of deciding on the best uses and best sources of funds is reflected in transactions such as the purchase of machinery, the buildup of the bank account or an accumulation of inventories, all of which represent commitments of funds. These investments are based upon management decisions to put to use in these areas corporate funds which might have been shifted to other uses as well. Conversely, the sale of stock, profits from operations, borrowing from a bank, or credit extended by suppliers all are sources of funds, for they provide or increase the means for investment. Investments on one hand, and capital raised for investment on the other, however, are not the only funds decisions possible. Management actions often result in the reduction of assets, or "disinvestments," such as the sale of a building or reduction in inventories or accounts receivable, which represent a release (source) of funds for other purposes. Also, management may decide to apply (use) funds to a reduction of liabilities or other claims against the firm, or to payment of cash dividends to stockholders.

It is obvious that each use or application of funds, as an investment decision, must be offset by one or more sources of funds, since one cannot invest funds one does not have available in one form or another. Thus, the funds for the purchase of a new plant may be provided in part by a reduction of the cash account (cash payment) and in part by an increase in debt. Similarly, a given source must have offsetting uses. Funds raised from an issue of capital stock may be committed to increases in the cash account, inventories and machinery, or to reductions of current or long-term liabilities. Profits, as inflows (sources) of funds, increase the total funds available to the firm and are committed to a variety of uses, while losses, as outflows (uses) decrease the total capital of the firm and must be covered by sources such as the reduction of assets and increases in liabilities or capital accounts.

The net effect of management decisions regarding investment and disinvestment, raising and repayment of funds is a continuous day-to-day flow of funds back and forth between the investment uses and the generating sources, with the aim of achieving liquidity and profitability objectives.

In the normal course of business the flow of funds is pictured as a circular movement (see Figure 1–1). This movement begins with the use of funds for the purchase of goods or materials. The sources of these funds could be the capital contributed by the owners, a reduction of cash or other forms of investments already owned, or credit extended to the firm by the suppliers of materials and goods. At the same time, additional funds are committed to the costs and expenses of production and operation, and finished goods are produced. The next step is the sale of the goods. If the firm sells for cash, funds will flow back into the cash account. If sales are on credit, the immediate effect will be a shifting of funds from inventory to accounts receivable, and it is not until the time when customers' remittances arrive that funds begin to flow back into the cash account, only to be committed again to new uses. Profitable operations will result in an inflow of funds greater than the original funds commitments to production and operations, while unprofitable opera-

Figure 1-1

FUNDS FLOW
(Manufacturing Company)

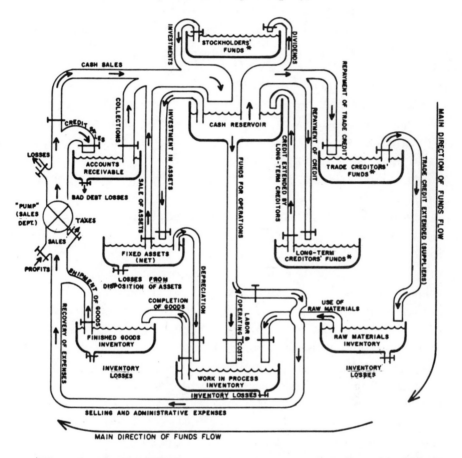

* These are *not* the firm's *obligations*, rather, the "tubs" represent the funds owned by the firm's creditors. These "reservoirs of credit" are available to the firm as needed, and are replenished by repayment. The outstanding liabilities of the firm have an inverse relationship to the level of funds in the "tubs." Full tubs mean low liabilities (accounts payable, notes payable or ownership claims), while empty tubs mean full use of the credit available, i.e., large liabilities or ownership claims.

tions will result in a reduced inflow relative to the original commitments. This normal cycle of funds flows is augmented by major investments or borrowings, new stock issues, changes in credit terms, inventory reductions, acquisition or disposal of fixed assets, and other management decisions.

The financial manager and the analyst both are interested in this flow because it helps them appraise the impact and quality of the management decisions made in the business during a given period of time. An analysis of funds flows for a year, a month, a week, or any other relevant period will show where management decided to commit funds (uses), where to reduce its investments (sources), where to acquire additional funds (sources), or where to reduce claims against the firm by giving up funds in payment (uses). Through an arrangement of these changes in a meaningful way the manager or analyst can judge whether the decisions made in the firm resulted in "normal" movements, as reflected in past experience of the company, in its forecasts or in comparative industry data, or if there were abnormal or at least interesting flows of funds which invite closer scrutiny.

Before beginning with a demonstration of this type of analysis, it must be emphasized that there are many different ways in which to define funds and various useful ways of approaching the analysis. Some define funds as *cash,* and concern themselves only with the movements in the cash account. This approach is useful to the financial officer who wishes to watch closely the cash receipts and disbursements for a given period and their effect on the firm's availability of cash. Chapter 4 deals with this problem. Others look upon funds in a broader sense as *economic values,* or *investments and claims,* the latter being concepts used earlier in this chapter. Flows in the cash account are only a part of the wider funds movements under this definition, and many of these movements do not involve cash, such as the purchase of merchandise on credit, or the sale of an asset on account. Consequently, the manager or analyst who subscribes to the wider definition of funds turns his attention to the firm's balance sheet, which is the statement of financial condition (or "funds condition"), and which reflects a picture of the firm's investments (assets) and the claims (liabilities, net worth) against these investments. Thus, the asset side of the balance sheet summarizes the net funds uses, while the liability side summarizes the net funds sources. We refer to *net* uses and sources, since the balance of each of the accounts on the balance sheet, such as the cash account or accounts payable, represents the net effect of the many individual transactions that preceded the balance sheet date, each of which affected the funds picture of the firm.

Depending on the aims of the manager or analyst, then, the definition of funds can be widened or narrowed, and the scope of the funds flow analysis focused on one type of funds, such as cash, or extended to cover all of the net sources and uses of funds as shown on the balance sheet. There are even situations where greater insights can be obtained from selective analysis of individual transactions behind the net changes on the balance sheet. This chapter will demonstrate such refinements at a later point. Chapter 2 deals with the specific analysis of operating cash flows.

More specifically, now, the process of analysis under the broad definition of funds utilizes a comparison of the balance sheets of the business at the beginning and the end of the relevant period under examination. The differences in the individual accounts of the two balance sheets represent the various net funds flows resulting from the management decisions during the period. The manager or analyst looks at the *changes* in the accounts and attempts to interpret their meaning. For instance, he may discover a major use of funds in a sizable increase of the inventory account. He may become concerned if the only major source of these funds were the profits for the period. This could mean that management had applied the funds generated from profitable operations to one place, possibly out of proportion to the other requirements of the firm. A further check through analysis of significant relationships between the inventory account and other operating and financial data of the firm, through industry comparisons and consideration of prevailing economic conditions, may help answer the question which was posed by the funds flow picture.

Another example is a major increase in the plant and equipment account. Offsetting this use of funds as the only major source could be a considerable buildup of current obligations, such as accounts payable, tax accruals, and so forth. The analyst asks the question whether it was wise to commit funds to a long-term application by using current short-term credit as a source. Will this result in problems for the company when the time comes to meet these current obligations? Should the source of funds for plant expansion have been one that more nearly

CROWN ZELLERBACH CORPORATION

CONDENSED BALANCE SHEETS AND CHANGES*

December 31, 1964 and 1965
(millions of dollars)

Assets	1965	1964	Change
Cash	$ 27.9	$ 26.0	+$ 1.9
Short-term investments	15.2	.5	+ 14.7
Accounts receivable (net)	83.2	75.8	+ 7.4
Inventories	118.0	108.2	+ 9.8
Prepaid expenses	11.1	11.0	+ 0.1
Total Current Assets	$255.4	$221.5	+$ 33.9
Properties: Timberlands,† buildings, machinery and equipment	$818.7	$725.5	+ 93.2
Less: Accumulated depreciation	298.7	275.3	+ 23.4
Net Properties	$520.0	$450.2	+$ 69.8
Investments in affiliated companies	$ 15.0	$ 7.7	+$ 7.3
Other investments and receivables	14.6	14.4	+ 0.2
Deferred charges	1.7	1.4	+ 0.3
Total Assets	$806.7	$695.2	+$111.5
Liabilities			
Trade accounts payable	$ 65.5	$ 64.2	+$ 1.3
Accrued U.S. and Canadian taxes	10.3	23.1	− 12.8
Dividends payable	7.6	7.6	0
Long-term debt due in one year	5.1	5.0	+ 0.1
Total Current Liabilities	$ 88.5	$ 99.9	−$ 11.4
Long-term debt due after one year	$171.3	$ 76.9	+$ 94.4
Deferred income taxes	49.1	40.9	+ 8.2
Reserve for self-insurance‡	8.9	6.4	+ 2.5
Minority interests—Canadian subsidiaries	7.9	5.9	+ 2.0
Cumulative preferred stock	24.7	25.3	− 0.6
Common stock	76.5	76.4	+ 0.1
Other surplus	96.2	95.6	+ 0.6
Income retained in business	283.6	267.9	+ 15.7
Total Liabilities and Net Worth	$806.7	$695.2	+$111.5

* Adapted from 1965 annual report.
† Included net of depletion allowances.
‡ So-called surplus reserves are not counted as part of the capitalization or net worth of the company. As a general rule only surplus items not specifically set aside for a definite purpose are so counted, which includes most "contingency" reserves.

matched the long-term character of the funds use, such as a term loan, an increase in equity capital, or continuing ample profits?

For a very quick appraisal, a scanning of the balance sheets laid side by side will often suffice, as the main changes in the accounts are obvious. A more exacting interpretation requires formal steps, however, and a start is made with the tabulation of balance sheet changes from the two balance sheets under review. The accompanying condensed statements of the Crown Zellerbach Corporation will serve as the basis for the illustrations throughout this chapter. (See pages 8 and 12.)

This tabulation of changes in the two balance sheets, more elaborate than a simple scanning, becomes the basis for sorting out which of the funds flows (reflected by increases or decreases of assets and liabilities) are sources and which are uses of funds. As stated before, commitments of capital to increase assets or decrease liabilities are *uses* of funds, while the freeing of capital through decreases in assets, or the addition of new capital through increases of liabilities or net worth are *sources* of funds. The statement on page 10, often called a "where-got, where-gone" statement, is a rearrangement of the balance sheet changes of Crown Zellerbach according to these principles.

The decisions of Crown Zellerbach management and the economic conditions of 1965 resulted in three major sources of funds for the corporation during the year. First, the company was committed to a sizable increase of $94.5 million in its long-term debt. Second, earnings retained in the business amounted to $15.7 million. Third, deferred income taxes which did not have to be paid during 1965 contributed $8.2 million because of differences in the treatment of expenses for financial accounting and tax accounting. In addition, about $6.2 million came from minor additions to the company's obligations to creditors and stockholders.

What did Crown Zellerbach do with these funds? By far the largest use was the increase in net property of $69.8 million, because of the company's largest expansion program in its history. In addition to this particular funds use, the company com-

CROWN ZELLERBACH CORPORATION

STATEMENT OF BALANCE SHEET CHANGES
(1964–1965)

("Where-Got, Where-Gone" Statement)
(millions of dollars)

Sources of Funds

Increase in trade accounts payable	$ 1.3
Increase in long-term debt°	94.5
Increase in deferred income taxes	8.2
Increase in reserves for self-insurance	2.5
Increase in minority interests	2.0
Increase in common stock	0.1
Increase in other surplus	0.6
Increase in retained income	15.7
Total Sources	$124.9

Uses of Funds

Increase in cash	$ 1.9
Increase in short-term investments	14.7
Increase in accounts receivable (net)	7.4
Increase in inventories	9.8
Increase in prepaid expenses	0.1
Increase in properties (net)†	69.8
Increase in investments in affiliated companies	7.3
Increase in other investments and receivables	0.2
Increase in deferred charges	0.3
Decrease in accrued income tax	12.8
Decrease in cumulative preferred stock	0.6
Total Uses	$124.9

° Net of "long-term debt due in one year" and "long-term debt."
† It is common to reflect changes in the *net* fixed assets rather than to show the components of this account (gross fixed assets, accumulated depreciation).

mitted $7.3 million to an increase in its investments in affiliated companies. Next in importance was the increase in working capital due to growing sales and production: Inventories required an additional $9.8 million and accounts receivable (net) rose by $7.4 million. Cash and short-term investments rose $16.6 million, as the expansion program had not yet fully required the funds borrowed and generated for this purpose. Scheduled tax payments reduced accrued income taxes by $12.8 million. Finally, about $1.3 million was absorbed in minor changes in prepaid expenses, other investments and receivables, deferred charges, and preferred stock.

The only major question that one might raise at this point is on the relationship of the net property investment to the sources available. Later it will be illustrated how a *selective* investigation of some of the net flows on the where-got, where-gone statement yields further insights into funds movements. Generally, these net flows are made up of both sources and uses that balance out to the net amount shown. It is a matter of practical convenience how much detail is included. For example, in the item "inventory change," theoretically one should substitute the main component funds flows, such as the total of additions to inventory (uses) and the total of withdrawals (sources). Similarly, one might substitute all sales on account and all collections for the net change in accounts receivable. Little, if anything, would be gained by these actions, and time and effort would have been wasted. We are more interested in the investment status of these two assets, which would be obscured by such details.

COMMON REFINEMENTS

There are two common refinements which financial analysts make in the net flows as presented by the simple where-got, where-gone statement. These refinements will be discussed now, while more complex adjustments will be treated under a separate heading. The first of the refinements is the individual recognition of profits (or losses) from operations on the one hand and dividends paid on the other. The second refinement is concerned with the idea of showing depreciation as a "source of funds," based on the argument that profits were understated in a funds sense through the depreciation charge, which is a "book entry" causing no funds changes.

a) *Profits and Dividends*

One of the most significant funds flows is the amount of net profit (income) or net loss provided by operations. Profits are one of the first sources to which the businessman turns for his investment needs or for repayment of obligations incurred. Consequently, it is desirable (but not essential) on many occasions to show net profit as a source or net loss as a use on the funds flow analysis.

The where-got, where-gone statement, however, only reflects the *net* change in the earned surplus account, of which net profit (or loss) is only one component. Among the factors partially or wholly offsetting profits, we most commonly find dividends. These arise from management decisions to distribute part of the profits for the period, and they may represent a significant funds commitment. Therefore, it is often desirable to reflect separately the use of funds for dividends. If the net change in earned surplus consists of net profit and dividends paid, we simply substitute these components for the net change by listing net profit as a source, and dividends as a use on the where-got, where-gone statement. The detailed figures necessary for this adjustment are usually found on the operating statement (income

CROWN ZELLERBACH CORPORATION

CONDENSED OPERATING STATEMENTS*

Years Ending December 31, 1964 and 1965
(millions of dollars)

	1965	1964
Sales (net)	$709.4	$662.2
Cost of goods sold†	$541.9	$496.7
Selling and administrative costs	66.7	62.3
Taxes, other than on income	21.2	20.4
Operating costs	$629.8	$579.4
Operating profit	$ 79.6	$ 82.8
Other income	5.9	13.2‡
Total income	$ 85.5	$ 96.0
Other expenses	8.8	5.0
Income before U.S. and foreign income taxes	$ 76.7	$ 91.0
Provision for income taxes	29.3	34.3
Net income	$ 47.4	$ 56.7
Cash dividends	31.7	30.1
Income retained in business§	$ 15.7	$ 26.6

* Adapted from 1965 annual report.
† Includes depreciation amortization of $35.0 in 1965 and $30.9 in 1964.
‡ Includes special item—$10.1 million gain on sale of St. Helens paper mill.
§ To earned surplus.

statement) or on a separate reconciliation statement of earned surplus.

In the case of Crown Zellerbach, we observe that the net increase in retained earnings of $15.7 million was composed of $47.4 million net profit, and dividends paid of $31.7 million (see operating statement on page 12).

The net effect of substituting the profit and dividend details would be as before, a net funds source of 15.7 million:

Source: Net profit	$47.4
Use: Dividends paid	(31.7)
Net source	$15.7

b) Depreciation as a "Source"

The sum of after-tax profits and depreciation is commonly called "cash flow," "internally generated funds," or "cash throw-off," a significant measure of the funds generating ability of an enterprise. Consequently, it is often useful in a funds flow analysis to show the amount of depreciation for the period as a source. Questions are often raised on the propriety of this point, however. We remember that depreciation charges are an allocation to period income of the past cost of the fixed assets in question. We should argue that the only time a funds flow took place was when the asset was acquired in the past and that current depreciation charges are simply bookkeeping entries recording a decrease in value, but not reflecting any capital movements. If we observe closely the effect of depreciation charges on profits and the balance sheet, we find that they in fact *conceal the full funds flow*, since they form at least a partial offset to the profits from operations.

A simple illustration clarifies this problem. If we assume an operating statement of a firm to appear as follows, we see that no profit for the period was made:

	Period
Sales	$1200
Cost of sales	1050
Depreciation charges	150
Profit	0

Yet, on a simple balance sheet we observe that with all other things equal the cash account has increased by $150, just as accumulated depreciation has grown by $150:

	Beginning of Period	End of Period	Change for Period
Assets			
Cash	$ 100	$ 250	+$150
Inventory	500	500	0
Gross plant and equipment	1000	1000	0
Less: Accumulated depreciation	(200)	(350)	+(150)
Net plant and equipment	$ 800	$ 650	−$150
Total Assets	$1400	$1400	0
Liabilities			
Liabilities	$ 400	$ 400	0
Net worth	1000	1000	0
Total Liabilities and Net Worth	$1400	$1400	0

In spite of the fact that *no* profit was made, the cash account has shown an increase of $150, offset by a growth in accumullated depreciation, or better, by a drop in the recorded value of fixed assets. The operations for the period have resulted in an exchange of value: capital equipment for cash. In a way one can say that the firm is no better off than it was before; yet funds have definitely flowed because receipts exceeded disbursements, even though the depreciation charge (a "noncash charge") canceled out this cash profit.

Some will call depreciation a source of funds; others will say with respect to operations that sales is the only real source and that depreciation, being a noncash charge, falsely offsets and reduces the funds flow from profits. To record the correct flow it must therefore be added back (*in effect* as an additional source) to profit. Whichever interpretation is used, the amount of depreciation charged against operations should be *reflected* as a source. The offsetting use will be an increase of the original "change in net plant and equipment" by the same amount. This is necessary since the period charge for depreciation also reduced the net plant and equipment account, and if we add depreciation as a source on one side, we must show an equal increase in uses on the other.[1] In the case of Crown Zellerbach we would show depreciation of $35 million as a source (from operating statement on page 12), and list an offsetting use of $35 million by raising the item "increase in net property" from $69.8 million to $104.8 million, thus balancing the statement and showing the amount of plant and equipment outlays for the year.

The accompanying revised funds flow statement for Crown Zellerbach takes into account the two refinements described.

CROWN ZELLERBACH CORPORATION

FUNDS FLOW STATEMENT
(millions of dollars)

Sources of Funds

Increase in long-term debt	$ 94.5
Income earned	47.4
Funds from depreciation and amortization	35.0
Increase in deferred income taxes	8.2
Increase in reserve for self-insurance	2.5
Increase in minority interests	2.0
Increase in trade accounts payable	1.3
Increase in other surplus	0.6
Increase in common stock	0.1
Total Sources	$191.6

Uses of Funds

Increase in properties	$104.8
Dividends paid	31.7
Increase in short-term investments	14.7
Decrease in accrued income tax	12.8
Increase in inventories	9.8
Increase in accounts receivable	7.4
Increase in investment in affiliated companies	7.3
Increase in cash	1.9
Decrease in cumulative preferred stock	0.6
Increase in deferred charges	0.3
Increase in other investments and receivables	0.2
Increase in prepaid expenses	0.1
Total Uses	$191.6

---

[1] Some analysts, in an effort to obtain a "clean" funds flow statement, will likewise add back as a source of funds any other so-called noncash charges which were made against income. Thus, if any assets such as patents are amortized against current income, they will "reverse," that is, add back the amortization as a source, and also add back (as a use) the same amount to the asset being amortized. This latter action eliminates the original change in the assets concerned, unless there have been additional investments or disinvestments.

FURTHER REFINEMENTS

In many cases, the simple refinements in the previous section will suffice. There may, however, be situations in which more detailed and significant funds flows took place. The subsequent comments deal with such additional and more complex refinements.

a) The Earned Surplus Account (Retained Earnings)

Profits and dividends are only two of many possible components of the earned surplus change. It is quite common to find adjustments of asset values, or the establishment (or elimination) of so-called surplus reserves to provide against contingencies. If we have decided to show separately the components of the change in earned surplus, it may be necessary also to reflect such adjustments in the funds flow analysis as was done with profits and dividends. If there are several of these items, a judgment must be made as to the relevance of listing each separately. Usually these adjustments are relatively minor in importance and may be lumped together into an item "other increases in earned surplus" (a source) or "other decreases in earned surplus" (a use). Again, the total of the separate recording of profits, dividends, and other surplus adjustments must obviously net out to equal the former single net change in earned surplus.

There is an additional consideration regarding the surplus adjustments. Many analysts and accountants argue the theory that some transactions resulting in surplus adjustments do *not* constitute funds flows in the sense of capital movements, but rather are mere bookkeeping entries. Consequently, these authorities wish to eliminate such transactions altogether from the funds flow analysis. Without entering the argument about the propriety of the distinction between funds flows and nonfunds transactions, a hypothetical example of eliminating "nonfunds" surplus adjustments is presented as follows:

In the balance sheet of Crown Zellerbach we find an account "Reserve for self-insurance" of $8.9 million in 1965. This account represents provision against possible claims, accidents and losses which would arise in the future. Over the years these reserves were built up through charges against the profits for the period. Let us *assume* now that Crown Zellerbach re-examined this reserve during 1965 and found it to be too large. It was decided, therefore, to write off $3 million of this reserve into earned surplus, and thereby to reduce the reserve to $5.9 million. The where-got, where-gone statement, under this assumption, would have reflected an *additional use* of funds of $3 million (decrease in reserves) and an *additional source* of funds of $3 million (increase in earned surplus). Our analysis of the change in earned surplus would have appeared as follows:

Source:	Net income	$47.4
	"Other increases"	3.0
Use:	Dividends paid	(31.7)
Net change in earned surplus	...	$18.7

The argument of some would now be that the "other increases" of $3 million did not represent a funds flow in the "pure" sense of their definition, and should not be shown at all on the funds flow analysis. Consequently, they eliminate *both* the use of $3 million, as reflected in the decrease of the reserves account, *and* the source of $3 million, as reflected in the increase in earned surplus. We observe that the balance of sources and uses has been maintained, since the same amount was canceled on both sides of the funds flow analysis.

Other examples where many analysts adjust for these "bookkeeping entries," and thereby cancel both the source and the use, are write-ups or write-downs of inventories and fixed assets, or the write-off of goodwill, patents, or organization expense (as contrasted to regular amortization of assets against operating income, which will be discussed later), and the payment of *stock* dividends. In all of these transactions, charges or credits are made to earned surplus, and corresponding credits or charges to the respective asset or capital accounts. Usually these adjustments are attempts to reflect changes in economic value, or to show "conservatism" in the recording of asset worth. After due consideration of the theoretical and practical advantages gained, it is permissible either to eliminate such transactions from the funds flow analysis by canceling both the source and the use, or leave them in the picture as before. Again, the additional insights gained thereby are the key to this decision.

The main effect of the more detailed analysis of the change in earned surplus in the case of Crown Zellerbach was to point up the fact that profits from operations were a more significant source of funds ($47.4 million) than at first glance, and that management chose to use the larger part of these funds to pay dividends. The question about the relative size of the property investment, asked earlier, has still not been fully answered, however.

b) *The Net Property Account*

As shown on the balance sheets on page 8, the net property account summarizes the changes in property and accumulated depreciation (reserve for depreciation). Apart from the simple adjustment for depreciation demonstrated above, additional insight into the quality of corporate funds management can be gained in many cases through an analysis of these components of the change in net property. Generally, the main movements of funds summarized in this net change are the investments in new fixed assets, the funds freed by the disposal of existing fixed assets, and the effect of the depreciation charges and adjustments for the period. If it is considered worthwhile to investigate these individual changes, an analysis of the main movements in the accounts must be made. Many times the published financial statements do not provide the outside analyst with all the details necessary to make a complete analysis, and certain assumptions must suffice. For most practical purposes, however, the ultimate refinements available to the financial manager will not yield many more insights than the assumptions made by the outside analyst.

Assuming the role of the outsider who has no more information about Crown Zellerbach than is given on pages 8 and 12, we use as our starting point the balances and changes in the three accounts which constitute the fixed asset action of the balance sheet:

	Balances		Change
	12/31/65	*12/31/64*	*1964/1965*
Gross property	$818.7	$725.5	+$93.2
Less: Accumulated depreciation ...	298.7	275.3	+ 23.4
Net property	$520.0	$450.2	+$69.8

It is our task to find the relevant sources and uses of funds, which netted out make up the increase in net property of $69.8 million. An immediate observation would be that gross property increased by $93.2 million, representing a net investment (funds use) in fixed assets, while accumulated depreciation was an off-setting source of $23.4 million. To some analysts this finding is a sufficient approximation of the gross movements which may be hidden behind the account balances. For a more detailed analysis, however, three questions arise: (*a*) What was the amount of new investment in land, plant and equipment, and what was the amount of any "dis-investments," or asset retirements, which netted out would amount to $93.2 million? (*b*) What were the components of the change in the accumulated depreciation account? (*c*) How did each component in (*a*) and (*b*) affect funds flows?

The answer to the first question is reached most easily via answering the second one, since at least one of the components of the depreciation account balance is readily available. Under the simplest circumstances, one expects the normal depreciation charges for the period (as a reflection of the deterioration in usefulness and value of the assets) to appear both in the operating statement as a charge against income for the period, and on the balance sheet as an increase in the balance of accumulated depreciation. This was the assumption made for the simple adjustment described on page 14. If no other transactions affecting these accounts took place, accumulated deprciation would increase by the *same amount* as the depreciation charge shown on the operating statement. A quick check on page 12 yields the depreciation charge for 1965 of $35 million. This is the amount by which accumulated depreciation should have increased, if no other transaction took place. Thus, as shown here, the December 31, 1965 balance of accumulated depreciation should have been $310.3 million:

Accumulated depreciation, 12/31/64	$275.3
Add: Depreciation charges for 1965	35.0
Expected balance, 12/31/65	$310.3

In fact, however, we find that the balance of accumulated depreciation was $298.7 million. The question now arises as to the kind of transaction which must have taken place to reduce the account balance by the difference of $11.6 million. The financial manager who has access to the books of Crown Zellerbach could readily obtain this information. As outsiders, however, we *now* must make an important assumption: To us, the drop of $11.6 million reflects the retirement and *scrapping of fully depreciated* assets. It is quite possible that in reality all of the assets retired were not fully depreciated, or that at least some of these assets were sold for a consideration. We do not know from the information at hand about these facts, but are satisfied that our assumption approximates the truth. It is almost certain that assets were *retired* and this, for most practical purposes, is sufficient. (The effect of additional information is described on pages 22 and 23.)

Whenever fully depreciated assets are retired, a bookkeeping entry is made to reflect the full decrease in *both* the property account (cost) *and* the accumulated depreciation account (depreciation). Under our assumption we therefore state that the accompanying components make up the change in the accumulated depreciation account:

Accumulated depreciation, 12/31/64	$275.3
Add: Depreciation charges for 1965	35.0
	$310.3
Less: Accumulated depreciation on retired, fully depreciated assets	11.6
Accumulated depreciation, 12/31/65	$298.7

or shown differently:

Depreciation charges for 1965	$ 35.0
Less: Depreciation accumulated on retired assets	11.6
Change in accumulated depreciation, 1964/1965	$ 23.4

To answer question (*a*) on the components of the gross property change, we now utilize the fact that we assumed an asset retirement of $11.6 million. If no other transaction had taken place, the gross property account would have been reduced by this amount:

Gross properties—12/31/64	$725.5
Less: Cost of fully depreciated assets retired	11.6
Expected balance, 12/31/65	$713.9

Obviously, we know that the balance of the account rose to $818.7 million by December 31, 1965, and this must have been due to investments in fixed assets in the amount of the difference of $104.8 million. Again, this figure is the result of the asset retirement assumption made earlier, but it usually provides a fair approximation of the real detailed facts.

We now have a picture of the components of the gross property account change:

Gross property—12/31/64	$725.5
Add: New investments	104.8
	$830.3
Less: Cost of fully depreciated assets retired ...	11.6
Gross property—12/31/65	$818.7

or shown differently:

Investments in land, plant and equipment—1965 .	$104.8
Less: Cost of retired assets	11.6
Change in gross property	$ 93.2

Having answered questions (*a*) and (*b*), we possess the raw material to answer question (*c*), the effect of these components on the funds flow picture. An arrangement of all components in the accompanying table provides a convenient summary:

	(1) 12/31/64	(2) Addi- tions	(3) Deduc- tions	(4) 12/31/65	(5) Change 1964/1965
Gross property	$725.5	$104.8	$11.6	$818.7	+$93.2
Less: Accumulated depreciation	275.3	35.0	11.6	298.7	+ 23.4
Net property	$450.2	$ 69.8°	0	$520.0	+$69.8°

° Must be equal since deductions (3) cancel out.

The problem now remaining is to sort out from the components of the change in net property ($69.8 million) the proper
items which should be substituted for this amount on the where-
got, where-gone statement. Beginning with column (2), we find
that investments of $104.8 were made in land, plant and equip-
ment. Clearly, this commitment of funds represents a use of
corporate capital, and will therefore appear on the use side of the
where-got, where-gone statement. The other component in
column (2), $35 million of depreciation for the period, must be
an offsetting source, and will appear on the source side of the
where-got, where-gone statement, as indicated before. Column
(3) shows two further components of $11.6 million each, which
cancel out since one appears as a source (reduction in assets)
while the other appears as a use (reduction in an offset-to-assets
account). The question can be raised whether these components
should be put on the where-got, where-gone statement. It is con-
ceivable that some might wish to do so, but for most purposes
little would be gained. We remember that these figures reflect
the assumed write-off of *fully depreciated* assets, which involved
no capital movements but simply was a recognition on paper
that worn-out assets were scrapped.

A final problem arises if we have information to the effect that
assets retired during a period were not fully depreciated, and
were sold at a loss or at a gain. If these factors are significant to
us in terms of relative size or interest, we no longer have to
assume a write-off of fully depreciated assets (as was done on
page 20). For example, we may know from detailed company
information the total investments made, the gain on the sale of
assets, the proceeds received for the assets sold, and the amount
of depreciation taken during the period and on the assets retired.

The table below contains all of the relevant data for a hypotheti-cal company, which reported a change in net plant and equip-ment of $125.

	Beginning of Period	Addi-tions	Deduc-tions	End of Period	Change for Period
Gross property	$1000	$250	$100°	$1150	+$150
Less: Accumulated depreciation ...	200	100	75°	225	+ 25
Net property	$ 800	$150	$ 25	$ 925	+$125

° Assets which cost $100 and had a book value of $25 were sold for $50, a gain of $25. The gain was shown on the operating statement as part of the net profit for the period.

The components of the change in net property ($125) could be substituted as follows: Obviously, the investment of $250 is to be recorded as a use of funds, just as the depreciation charges of $100 for the period are a source of funds. There are two ways of reporting the remaining $25 source needed to achieve the net use of $125. First, some simply record a $25 source and call it gain from sale of assets. This is not quite correct, since we know that the net profit for the period already contains the $25 gain. The second, to many the more precise way, is to call the proceeds of the assets ($50) a source of funds, and also to reduce the profits for the period by $25 to eliminate the recorded gain as a "book-keeping" profit. This latter step is based on the same reasoning as any other elimination ("reversals") of noncash or "book" charges to profits discussed earlier. As a simple rule it can be remembered that all proceeds from the sale of fixed assets are sources of funds (just as all purchases of assets are uses of funds), and any loss or gain on such a sale should be eliminated from the funds flow analysis. If the latter was recorded as a decrease or increase of net profits, elimination is made by respectively rais-ing or decreasing the profits figure. The components of the sub-stitution would appear as follows:

Uses:	Investment in property	$250
	Decrease of net profit°	25
Sources:	Depreciation charges	(100)
	Proceeds from sale of assets	(50)
Net use (change in net property)		$125

° Gain was recorded as part of net profit for the period.

If the gain or loss was recorded in the earned surplus account, it is eliminated simply by omission from the funds flow statement (just as other "nonfunds" transactions—inventory valuation, patent write-off) were eliminated (see page 17).

Returning now to the Crown Zellerbach example, we shall see that the combined sources of net profits, depreciation, and the bonds floated for this purpose provided more than sufficient funds for the investment in plant and equipment.

The resulting funds flow statement is identical to the one shown on page 15, since according to our assumptions no complicating detail was unearthed by our refined analysis.

PRESENTATION

The statement on page 15 is only one form in which funds flow analysis can be presented. Essentially, it is a refined where-got, where-gone statement. Depending on the needs and the focus of the analysis, many variations can be introduced. One of the commonest shortcuts is to summarize the changes in current assets and current liabilities into one "change in working capital." This method obscures many of the individual movements in the current accounts, yet it provides a focus on the more basic capital movements of the firm. The analyst must decide the nature of the presentation according to the purposes he wishes to achieve and the kinds of specific questions he wishes to answer. Exhibits 1–1 and 1–4 contain several examples of funds flow statements included by major companies in their annual reports to stockholders.

Shown on page 25 is Crown Zellerbach's presentation of its funds flow analysis (1965 Annual Report; footnotes omitted). Crown Zellerbach preferred to show a funds flow analysis in the form of additions and substractions to working capital. Most of the figures agree readily with our statement on page 15, with the exception of several items, where the insider's knowledge becomes apparent.

Among the sources is an item of $5.5 million which represents the proceeds from sale of assets. Not knowing this detail we

CROWN ZELLERBACH CORPORATION AND ITS
SUBSIDIARIES

STATEMENTS OF SOURCES AND USES OF WORKING CAPITAL

(thousands of dollars)

	Year Ended December 31, 1965	Year Ended December 31, 1964
Sources of Working Capital:		
Net income	$ 47,426	$ 46,593
Expenses which did not require current cash outlay:		
Depreciation, amortization and depletion	34,956	30,910
Net book value of assets sold or abandoned	5,473	3,029
Provision for decline in conversion of Canadian assets	2,400	1,600
Provision for deferred income taxes	8,099	5,162
Cash flow from operations	$ 98,354	$ 87,294
Increase in long-term debt	100,000	—
Stock issue by Canadian subsidiary to acquire S. M. Simpson, Ltd.	1,878	—
Proceeds from sale of common stock under Selected Employees Stock Option Plan	600	694
Net proceeds from sale of St. Helens properties less portion receivable ($6,000,000) in subsequent years	—	14,472
Timberland purchase commitments	—	3,978
Miscellaneous, net	(169)	801
	$200,663	$107,239
Uses of Working Capital:		
Additions to properties	110,195	95,916
Dividends declared	31,641	30,108
Long-term debt currently maturing	5,610	5,516
Investments in affiliated companies	7,335	565
Preferred stock redemptions	589	344
	$155,370	$132,449
Net Increase (Decrease) in Working Capital During Year	$ 45,293	($25,210)

had understated our own figure for new plant investment by that amount, because of our assumption that assets retired were fully depreciated and scrapped. A check of Crown Zellerbach Corporation's figure for plant investment also shows a difference of $5.5, as expected. Further, we did not have the insider's knowledge on the proceeds from the sale of stock under the stock option plan.

An important decision which must be made prior to the funds

flow analysis is the choice of the time period to be covered. The examples presented here were based on annual statements, but it is often useful to make funds flow analyses for shorter periods, or over annual dates other than the firm's fiscal year. The reason for such selectivity lies in the seasonal or secular swings of activity which may be characteristic of a firm. Some analysts desire to place their funds flow periods to reflect some or all of the ups and downs in assets and liabilities connected with the operational pattern of the firm. The purpose of the analysis will dictate the choice of dates.

Exhibits 1–1 through 1–4 (pp. 27–29) show a variety of funds flow statements as prepared by major U.S. corporations. We observe differences in focus, format, and time span covered, as well as elements typical of the different industries illustrated.

Owens-Illinois prefers to show a five-year period of funds flows, prepared to analyze the difference in working capital at the beginning and end of each period (Exhibit 1–1).

A relatively brief treatment of only the major items is shown by W. R. Grace & Co., in Exhibit 1–2.

United States Steel Corporation again uses the format of additions to and subtractions from working capital, with no emphasis provided for particular items (Exhibit 1–3).

Finally, the statement shown by R. H. Macy & Co., Inc. (Exhibit 1–4) is a fairly standard funds flow statement, giving considerable detail for the special transactions which took place during the two-year period covered.

Exhibit 1-1

OWENS-ILLINOIS

SOURCE AND APPLICATION OF WORKING CAPITAL

(thousands of dollars)

	1965	1964	1963	1962	1961
Working Capital Provided by:					
Operations:					
Net earnings	$ 52,155	$ 42,661	$ 35,116	$ 33,160	$ 34,359
Charges against earnings not requiring an outlay of working capital in the current period:					
Depreciation and depletion	23,130	28,227	26,791	25,987	22,726
Retirements of fixed assets ...	2,248	1,098	1,098	1,055	1,214
Increase in furnace rebuilding reserve, deferred taxes, etc.	8,985	4,333	5,638	2,668	965
Cash flow	$ 86,518	$ 76,319	$ 68,643	$ 62,870	$ 59,264
Sale of six forest products plants	22,169	—	—	—	—
Consolidation of German and Italian subsidiaries .	9,231	—	—	—	—
Gain on sale of Continental Can Company, Inc., stock	—	—	4,412	—	—
Exchange of fixed and other noncurrent assets of Colombian branch for a foreign investment ..	—	—	—	3,358	—
Sales of common shares— stock options	1,560	1,740	1,258	515	736
Other	620	—	—	—	—
	$120,098	$ 78,059	$ 74,313	$ 66,743	$ 60,000
Working Capital Applied:					
Dividends	22,154	20,902	21,519	21,551	21,536
Additions to fixed assets ..	80,546	35,948	34,632	34,769	45,774
Additions to foreign investments	2,732	5,136	7,818	10,603	1,861
Increase in other assets ...	1,440	3,066	1,583	1,475	2,237
Decrease in long-term debt	416	1,177	1,952	1,851	(303)
Acquisition of preferred shares	2,000	10,020*	3,225	924	—
	$109,288	$ 76,249	$ 70,729	$ 71,173	$ 71,105
Increase in working capital .	$ 10,810	$ 1,810	$ 3,584	$ (4,430)	$(11,105)
Working capital at beginning of year	160,757	158,947	155,363	159,793	170,898
Working capital at end of year	$171,567	$160,757	$158,947	$155,363	$159,793

* Includes cost of Monsanto Company shares exchanged for preferred shares—$6658.

Exhibit 1–2

W. R. GRACE & CO.
AND SUBSIDIARY COMPANIES

CONSOLIDATED STATEMENT OF SOURCE AND APPLICATION
OF FUNDS

Source	1965	1964
	(in thousands)	
Net income	$ 45,348	$ 42,740
Provision for depreciation and depletion	41,906	37,542
Provision for deferred income taxes	2,505	3,156
Increase in long-term debt	125,154	33,780
Proceeds from—		
Liquidation of Texas Gulf Producing Company	—	10,652
Exercise of stock options, etc.	2,667	4,153
Other transactions	20,158	21,604
	$237,738	$153,627
Application		
Cash dividends	$ 19,903	$ 17,560
Capital expenditures and increase in investments	168,095	112,768
Increase in working capital	49,740	23,299
	$237,738	$153,627

Exhibit 1–3

UNITED STATES STEEL CORPORATION

SUMMARY OF 1965 FINANCIAL OPERATIONS
(millions of dollars)

Additions to Working Capital:

Income		$275.5
Add: Wear and exhaustion of facilities		324.5
Deferred investment tax credit		12.5
Proceeds from sales and salvage of plant and equipment		8.0
Proceeds from sale of common stock under stock option incentive plans		0.4
Miscellaneous additions		1.5
Total Additions		$622.4

Deductions from Working Capital:

Expended for plant and equipment	$353.6	
Increase in miscellaneous investments	30.8	
Reduction in long-term debt due after one year	40.3	
Dividends declared on preferred and common stocks	133.5	
Total Deductions		$558.2
Increase in Working Capital		$ 64.2

Working Capital per Consolidated Statement of Financial Position:

December 31, 1965	$890.6
December 31, 1964	826.4
	$ 64.2

Exhibit 1–4

R. H. MACY & CO., INC.
AND CONSOLIDATED SUBSIDIARIES

CONSOLIDATED STATEMENT OF SOURCE AND APPLICATION
OF FUNDS
(thousands of dollars)

	Year (52 weeks) Ended	
	July 30, 1966	July 31, 1965
Source of Funds:		
Net earnings	$18,179	$15,432
Noncash items:		
Depreciation and amortization	9,285	7,752
Increase in deferred federal income tax	1,458	2,506
Increase in other deferred credits	776	264
Other non-cash charges	452	818
Net proceeds from sale of shopping center (leased		
back from buyer)	4,283	–
Additions to long-term debt	9,654	35,921
Exchange of common shares in acquisition of		
subsidiary	1,411	–
Proceeds from sales of common shares under options .	640	410
	$46,138	$63,103
Application of Funds:		
Additions to property	$30,658	$29,929
Dividends on common and preferred shares	7,024	6,191
Increase in equity in Macy Credit Corporation	1,624	1,873
Reduction in previously existing long-term debt	3,584	2,349
Miscellaneous—net	206	503
Increase in working capital	3,042	22,258
	$46,138	$63,103

SELECTED REFERENCES

ANTHONY, ROBERT N. *Management Accounting.* 3rd ed. Homewood, Ill.: Richard D. Irwin, Inc., 1964, chap. 12.

DORIS, LILLIAN (ed.). *Business Finance Handbook.* Englewood Cliffs, N.J.: Prentice-Hall, Inc., 1953, pp. 487–91.

HORNGREN, CHARLES T. *Cost Accounting, A Managerial Emphasis.* Englewood Cliffs, N.J.: Prentice-Hall, Inc., 1962.

HOWARD, BION B., AND UPTON, MILLER. *Introduction to Business Finance.* New York: McGraw-Hill Book Co., 1953, chap. 5.

HUNT, PEARSON; WILLIAMS, CHARLES M.; AND DONALDSON, GORDON. *Basic Business Finance.* 3rd ed. Homewood, Ill.: Richard D. Irwin, Inc., 1964.

MOORE, CARL L., AND JAEDICKE, ROBERT K. *Managerial Accounting.* Cincinnati, Ohio: South-Western Publishing Company, 1963, chap. 7.

PROBLEMS AND EXERCISES

1. From the following financial statements prepare a funds flow statement showing separately the sources and applications of funds for the ABC Company during 1965–1966. Comment on your findings.

ABC COMPANY

CONDENSED BALANCE SHEETS
December 31, 1965 and 1966

	1966	1965
Current assets:		
Cash	$ 18,500	$ 17,000
Marketable securities	—	5,000
Accounts receivable	39,500	28,500
Inventories	98,000	113,000
Total Current Assets	$156,000	$163,500
Plant and equipment (net)	275,000	290,000
Other assets	3,000	8,000
Total Assets	$434,000	$461,500
Current liabilities:		
Accounts payable	$ 34,500	$ 18,000
Note payable	20,000	25,000
Accrued expenses	18,500	11,500
Total Current Liabilities	$ 73,000	$ 54,500
Mortgage payable	20,000	30,000
Common stock	200,000	200,000
Earned surplus	141,000	177,000
Total Liabilities and Net Worth	$434,000	$461,500

ABC COMPANY

CONDENSED OPERATING STATEMENTS
Years 1965 and 1966

	1966	1965
Sales	$330,000	$395,000
Cost of sales*	265,000	280,000
Gross profit	$ 65,000	$115,000
Selling and administrative	$ 95,000	$ 88,000
Other expense	4,000	3,500
Interest	2,000	3,000
Total Expense	$101,000	$ 94,500
Profit (loss) before taxes	($ 36,000)	$ 20,500
Federal income tax	—	10,500
Net profit (loss)†	($ 36,000)	$ 10,000

* Includes depreciation of $15,500 in 1965, and $15,000 in 1966.
† No dividends were paid in 1966.

2. Work out the following problems:

a) For purposes of a funds flow analysis for the year 1966, the following additions were made to the funds flow statement of a company:

Funds from depreciation $33,500
Investment in fixed assets 29,300

The balance of the gross fixed asset account was $622,600 on 12/31/65 and $622,700 on 12/31/66. The accumulated depreciation on 12/31/65 was $139,000. What was the amount of the change in *net* fixed assets between the two balance sheet dates? (Stipulate your assumptions.)

b) On the funds flow statement and on the various financial statements of a company for 1966 we find the following items:

Write-off of goodwill $10,000
Depreciation—1966 15,600
Write-down of inventory 25,000
Investment in fixed assets 45,000
Net profits after taxes 37,000
Common dividends paid 10,000

The balance of the earned surplus account (the only surplus account of the company) at 12/31/65 was $139,500. Which of the items listed above are components of the surplus balance at 12/31/66, and what is this balance? Apart from this question, which of the above items are sources, and which are uses of funds?

c) The following transactions in the fixed assets section of the balance sheet of a company took place during 1966:

Sold assets originally recorded at $100,000 for $25,000. Accumulated depreciation on these assets was $60,000. (The loss was recorded as a charge to earned surplus.)

The account accumulated depreciation increased by $14,500 from 1965 to 1966.

1966 depreciation charges were $86,500.

The *gross* fixed assets account at 12/31/65 was $963,400 and $1,011,200 at 12/31/66.

What was the amount of the new investment in fixed assets to be shown on the funds flow statement? What other items shown above should appear on that statement? What was the amount of *change* in the *net* fixed assets account?

3. Prepare a funds flow statement for XYZ Corporation, netting out changes in working capital accounts into one figure and making any adjustments you deem necessary. Comment on your findings.

THE XYZ CORPORATION

BALANCE SHEETS

December 31, 1965 and 1966

(thousands of dollars)

	1966	1965	Change
Cash	$ 22	$ 19	+$ 3
Government bonds	9	4	+ 5
Accounts receivable	123	134	− 11
Inventories	168	215	− 47
Total Current Assets	$322	$372	−$50
Property, plant and equipment	$433	$401	+$32
Less: accumulated depreciation	208	203	+ 5
Net property, plant and equipment	$225	$198	+$27
Other assets	23	36	− 13
Total Assets	$570	$606	−$36
Accounts payable	$ 99	$ 73	+$26
Notes payable	66	77	− 11
Accrued expenses and taxes	28	16	+ 12
Total Current Liabilities	$193	$166	+$27
Long-term liabilities	—	80	− 80
Preferred stock	50	—	+ 50
Reserve for inventory valuation	10	25	− 15
Capital surplus	10	10	—
Earned surplus	157	175	− 18
Capital stock	150	150	—
Total Liabilities and Net Worth	$570	$606	−$36

THE XYZ CORPORATION

OPERATING STATEMENTS

Years 1965 and 1966

(thousands of dollars)

	1966	1965
Sales	$1,435	$1,246
Less: Cost of sales		
Material	$ 593	$ 501
Labor	266	196
Depreciation	41	35
Overhead	127	113
Total	$1,027	$ 845
Gross profit	$ 408	$ 401
Selling and administrative	$ 353	$ 321
Interest	3	9
	$ 356	$ 330
Profit before taxes	$ 52	$ 71
Income taxes	25	32
Net Profit	$ 27	$ 39

THE XYZ CORPORATION

STATEMENT OF EARNED SURPLUS
Years 1965 and 1966
(thousands of dollars)

Balance 12/31/65		$175
Additions:		
Net profit from 1966 operations	$27	
Gain from sale of fixed assets	10	37
		$212
Deductions		
Preferred dividends	$ 3	
Common dividends	20	
Inventory valuation reserve adjustments	20	
Write-down of other assets	12	55
Balance 12/31/66		$157

Other Facts:

Fully depreciated machinery sold for $10.
Inventory written down by $35 to reflect more realistic value.

4. Prepare a funds flow statement for the All Genius Company, after adjusting for nonfunds transactions. A set of balance sheets, operating statements, and a statement of earned surplus are provided for this purpose. Comment on your findings.

THE ALL GENIUS COMPANY

BALANCE SHEETS
December 31, 1965 and 1966
(thousands of dollars)

	1966	1965	Change
Cash	$ 2	$ —	+$ 2
Accounts receivable	68	75	− 7
Inventory	172	139	+ 33
Total Current Assets	$242	$214	+$28
Fixed assets	$ 63	$ 39	+$24
Accumulated depreciation	18	17	+ 1
Net fixed assets	$ 45	$ 22	+$23
Patents	35	42	− 7
Organization expense	10	15	− 5
Total Assets	$332	$293	+$39
Overdraft—bank	$ —	$ 4	−$ 4
Notes payable—bank	45	30	+ 15
Chattel mortgage	30	18	+ 12
Accounts payable	49	45	+ 4
Taxes payable	22	15	+ 7
Accruals	18	21	− 3
Total Current Liabilities	$164	$133	+$31

Total Current Liabilities carried over	$164	$133	+$31
Loan from officers (subordinated) ..	30	30	—
Total Liabilities	$194	$163	+$31
Common stock	50	50	—
Surplus	88	80	+ 8
Total Liabilities and Net Worth	$332	$293	+$39

THE ALL GENIUS COMPANY

OPERATING STATEMENTS

Years 1965 and 1966

(thousands of dollars)

	1966	1965
Net sales	$431	$396
Less: Cost of goods sold°	261	240
Gross profit	$170	$156
Selling and administration expense	$135	$134
Amortization of patents	7	7
	$142	$141
Profit before taxes	$ 28	$ 15
Taxes	9	5
Net Profit after Taxes	$ 19	$ 10

° Includes depreciation of $5 for 1966 and $4 for 1965.

THE ALL GENIUS COMPANY

STATEMENT OF EARNED SURPLUS

Years 1965 and 1966

(thousands of dollars)

Earned surplus, 12/31/65		$80
Net profit for 1966 operations		19
		$99
Less: Write-off of organization expenses	$5	
Loss on sale of assets	6	11
Earned surplus, 12/31/66		$88

During 1966, the company sold fixed assets originally recorded at $20 for $10. Depreciation accumulated on these assets amounted to $4.

5. The King-Kan Company, a fruit cannery, had a pronounced seasonal character which dominated its financial planning as well as its physical operations. Shown on page 35 are nine quarterly balance sheets covering a period of two years. From this information, construct a funds flow analysis which will best reflect the extent and character of the funds movements in the company.

KING-KAN COMPANY

QUARTERLY BALANCE SHEETS
9/30/64–9/30/66
(thousands of dollars)

	9/30/66	6/30/66	3/31/66	12/31/65	9/30/65	6/30/65	3/31/65	12/31/64	9/30/64
Cash	$ 2	$ 1	$ 47	$ 23	$ 4	$ 15	$ 19	$ 31	$ 6
Accounts receivable	79	34	128	214	98	46	137	226	84
Inventories	430	389	113	218	493	402	124	251	406
Net plant and equipment	137	144	151	158	165	172	132	137	142
Total Assets	$648	$568	$439	$613	$760	$635	$412	$645	$638
Accounts payable	$159	$126	$ 42	$ 98	$183	$133	$ 56	$115	$166
Notes payable	78	51	—	114	190	171	25	207	168
Mortgage payable	37	38	39	40	41	42	43	44	45
Preferred stock	75	75	75	75	75	50	50	50	50
Common stock	150	150	150	150	150	150	150	150	150
Earned surplus	149	128	133	136	121	89	88	79	59
Total Liabilities and Net Worth	$648	$568	$439	$613	$760	$635	$412	$645	$638

Other Information:
Depreciation per quarter: $5 through 6/30/65, $7 thereafter.
Fixed assets: purchased $45 of machinery in June 1965.
Dividends paid per quarter: $10 through 6/30/65, $12 thereafter.

Chapter 2

PROFITS, BREAK-EVEN ANALYSIS AND CASH FLOWS

THE PURPOSE of this chapter is to discuss the factors which affect the size of corporate profits and to trace the influence of variations in operations upon the cash position of the firm. Chapter 1 examined funds flows in broad terms; now we must look behind the figures to view the effect of changes which invariably occur as corporate fortunes fluctuate with, or independent of, the industry and the economy as a whole.

The ability to generate *cash flows*—the narrowest type of funds flow but the most important as far as meeting obligations is concerned—is related to, but not quite the same as, the ability to generate *profits*. The importance of cash flows will again be demonstrated in later chapters, as we discuss investment analysis and the financing of operating and capital budgets. While firms often can resort to outside sources of funds, they depend heavily upon *internally generated cash flows* to meet interest and principal payments on debt outstanding and to finance expansion and cash dividends. Access to outside funds, moreover, depends —among other factors—upon the level of internally generated cash flows, which are measured as one criterion of sound management.

Effects of Operations on Profits

Profits are generally defined as the difference between periodic gross revenue and the costs and expenses incurred in obtaining it. Gross revenue typically consists of receipts from sales attributable to the accounting period, plus other income items such as interest earned, rental income, and so on. Costs and expenses are normally broken down at least into cost of goods or services sold, selling and administrative expense, and other expenses such as interest paid and losses from value adjustments. While state and local taxes of various types are included as an element of selling and administrative expense, and often find their way into cost of goods sold, federal income taxes are shown separately in most income statements. Opinions differ as to whether federal income taxes should be regarded as an expense item or as a distribution of profits, but apart from this they are important enough to warrant a separate setting. The key figure of interest for analysis is normally the net profit *after* federal income taxes, as the residue from profitable operations accruing to the owners of the corporation, the stockholders.

Accounting practices followed by a company can materially affect the magnitude and interrelationship of the various elements of profit. Without going into the many aspects of the interpretation of generally accepted accounting principles, suffice it to say that such problems as the recognition of income from long-term contracts, amortization and depreciation, the choice between expensing or capitalizing research and development outlays, the treatment of differences arising from tax accounting versus book accounting, and other equally significant issues affect the net profit from period to period and the ability to compare the results of one company against those of others. Even though accounting principles should be consistently applied, there is enough room for variation to introduce distortions. The discussion of valuation concepts in Chapter 7 will return to these issues, as profit is one key element in establishing economic values.

All elements of gross revenue, cost and expense are relevant to the overall analysis of a company's profitability. For the purpose at hand, however, it will be useful to exclude such items as income and expense of a nonoperating nature, such as gains and losses from sales of capital items, interest on indebtedness, as well as federal and state taxes on income. Instead, the focus will be upon *profits from operations*, that is, the relationship between sales revenues, cost of goods sold (including depreciation, amortization, and so on) and selling and administrative expenses, *before* federal income taxes. These major elements are sufficient to demonstrate the principles involved.

In a very basic sense, operating profits are determined by costs and expenses on the one hand, and volume and prices on the other. For this purpose we can consider costs and expenses as one element, and in order to make a proper analysis we must concentrate on the behavior of this element during changes in the volume of operations. It is customary to distinguish at least in theory between two kinds of cost: *Fixed costs*, which are constant in amount irrespective of operating volume, and *variable costs*, which vary in close proportion to changes in operating volume. In practice, of course, many costs are fixed or partly fixed under certain conditions, and variable under others, and it is difficult to categorize them as simply as our definition implies. Again, further detailed consideration of the detailed aspects would tend to obscure rather than to clarify the main issues.

A graphic demonstration of the interrelationship of costs, volume and prices will serve as a useful aid in discussing their implications. Figure 2–1 sets forth the cost, volume and price structure of a hypothetical company, the ABC Corporation. As shown by the horizontal line, ABC has fixed costs amounting to $100,000. Selling price and variable costs per unit in turn are set at $100 and $50 respectively, and are reflected in the sloping lines of the graph. Total revenue (sales) is the product of selling price and unit volume, while total cost are the sum of fixed and variable cost, that is, $100,000 plus $50 times the number of units. The two lines representing sales revenue and variable costs at various operating levels intersect at a *volume break-even point* of 2000 units. This indicates that ABC Corporation must sell 2000 units in order to break even, since at this point total revenue just offsets the total of fixed and variable costs. At a higher sales volume, operations are profitable, as indicated by the crosshatched area, while at a lower sales volume operations are unprofitable, as indicated by the dotted area.

All other factors being equal, operating profits will increase as volume increases. For example, operating profits amount to

Figure 2-1

ABC CORPORATION

VOLUME BREAK-EVEN CHART
(Initial Example)

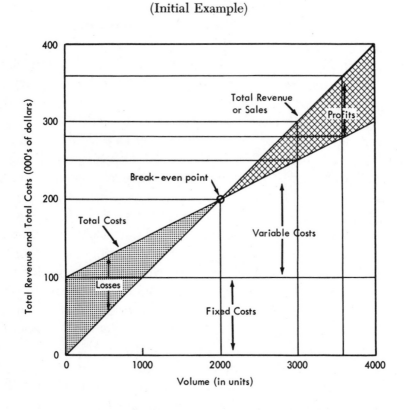

PROFITS AT VARIOUS VOLUME LEVELS:

		Percent Increase from Previous Level:	
Volume	Profit	Volume	Profit
2,000	0	-	-
2,500	$25,000	25%	infinite
3,000	50,000	20	100%
3,600	80,000	20	60
4,320	116,000	20	40

$25,000 at a sales volume of 2500 units, and $50,000 at a volume of 3000 units. Note that a sales increase of 20 percent (500 units) has produced an increase of 100 percent! This phenomenon of a more than proportional increase in profit with increasing volume is known as *operating leverage*. In simple terms, operating leverage works because fixed costs remain unchanged, and once these are covered by the profit contribution from the units sold, each additional unit sold adds pure profit to the results for the period. The principle, however, operates in the opposite direction as well. The student should observe the impact of a *decline* in volume on profitability by tracing it on the graph, and carry the analysis also into the *loss* area. Again, more than proportional decreases in profit result from declines in operating volume.

The effects of operating leverage diminish at higher levels of sales, as shown in the tabulation under Figure 2–1. For example, a 20 percent increase in volume from 3000 units to 3600 units will produce a change in operating profits of $30,000, which is only a 60 percent change. We must observe that the *relative* increase in profits diminishes as volume increase, even though the *absolute* increase in dollars is greater. In short, companies operating near their break-even points will have more volatile profits for a given percentage change in volume than those operating well above (or below) their break-even levels—assuming a comparable price-volume-cost relationship.

Volume changes are, of course, not the only factor affecting profitability, and profits can be improved by *reducing fixed costs*, for example. Figure 2–2 traces the effect upon operating profits of a decrease in fixed charges from $100,000 to $80,000. Profits are raised—or losses reduced—by $20,000 at all levels of sales volume. The operating leverage characteristics of ABC Corporation also change because the company's volume break-even point has dropped from 2000 to 1600 units. Profits now will rise only 43 percent with a 20 percent increase in volume from 3000 units, as seen in the tabulation under the chart.

Changes in variable cost further affect profitability. For example, as shown in Figure 2–3, profits would rise to $65,000 at

Figure 2–2

ABC CORPORATION

VOLUME BREAK-EVEN CHART
(Decreased Fixed Charges)

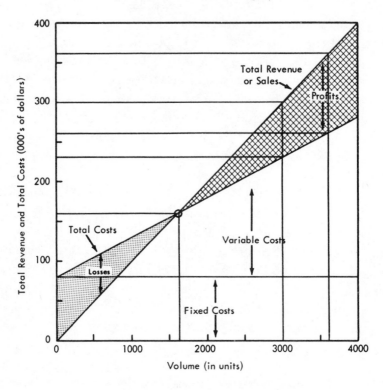

Volume (in units)

PROFITS AT VARIOUS VOLUME LEVELS:

Volume	Profit	Percent Increase from Previous Level: Volume	Profit
1,600	0	–	–
2,000	$ 20,000	25%	infinite
2,500	45,000	25	125%
3,000	70,000	20	56
3,600	100,000	20	43
4,320	136,000	20	36

a volume of 3000 units if ABC Corporation were able to reduce
its variable costs to $45 per unit. Such a reduction would, of
course, raise the "contribution margin" per unit to $55. The
volume break-even point therewith declines to approximately

1800 units and the operating leverage characteristics are changed. Now a 20 percent increase in volume from 3000 units will produce a profit increase of only 50.5 percent, since the position relative to the break-even point has been shifted.

This point is worth noting. There are many who believe that

Figure 2–3
ABC CORPORATION
VOLUME BREAK-EVEN CHART
(Reduced Variable Costs)

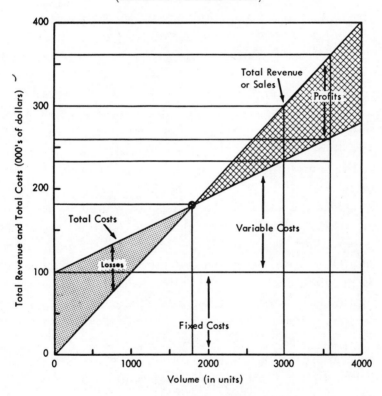

PROFITS AT VARIOUS VOLUME LEVELS:

		Percent Increase from Previous Level:	
Volume	Profit	Volume	Profit
1,820	0	-	-
2,000	$ 10,000	10%	infinite
2,500	37,500	25	275%
3,000	65,000	20	73
3,600	98,000	20	51
4,320	137,600	20	40

changes in fixed costs *alone* can result in changes in operating leverage characteristics, but this analysis clearly demonstrates that changes in the contribution margin—attributable to changes in variable costs per unit (or selling price, as will be seen)—are also influential.

Changes in price per unit have a similar though opposite effect upon profitability, as is demonstrated in Figure 2–4. Again the contribution margin is altered and a shift in operating characteristics occurs. An increase in price per unit to $105 will raise profits again to $65,000 at a volume of 3000 units, the same level as in the previous example since the contribution margin has been raised to $55 per unit as before. Again, changes in the operating leverage characteristics and the volume break-even point are the result.

In the foregoing analysis, cost, volume, and price implications for profitability were analyzed one at a time. In practice, numerous pressures develop to affect these variables simultaneously. Costs, volume, and prices for a single product may all be changing at the same time in subtle, and often unmeasurable ways. Where several products are involved, the analysis is further confused by changes in the product sales mix. Moreover, we have so far not distinguished between sales operations on the one hand, and production operations on the other hand. In a manufacturing company, these two processes can be widely out of phase, that is, production may be greater than sales and vice versa, with inventories absorbing the differences. This possibility introduces further complications in measuring the specific impact upon profits of fluctuations in operations.

The application of these concepts is by no means simple, even when the analyst has the vantage point of being within the company and has access to unpublished data concerning fixed and variable costs, unit volumes of sales and production, and prices of specific products. Yet the understanding of the relationships is crucial to the appraisal of past performance and judgments about future profits, for interested parties both within the company and in the financial community. From a financial viewpoint, another concept which builds upon the effect of fixed

Figure 2–4

ABC CORPORATION

VOLUME BREAK-EVEN CHART
(Increased Price)

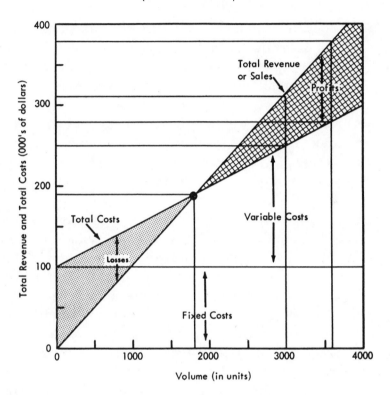

PROFITS AT VARIOUS VOLUME LEVELS:

		Percent Increase from Previous Level:	
Volume	Profit	Volume	Profit
1,820	0	–	–
2,000	$ 10,000	10%	infinite
2,500	37,500	25	275%
3,000	65,000	20	73
3,600	98,000	20	51
4,320	137,600	20	40

costs is important, as will be seen in Chapter 5. This is *financial leverage* which affects profits in an analogous way through the introduction of capital sources with fixed costs into the capital structure of a company. Operating leverage and financial leverage together must be taken into account—even in a highly simplified framework—to study the behavior of corporate profits for financial analysis.

Effects of Operations upon Cash

Profits constitute an important source of capital for expansion, the payment of dividends, the reduction of debt obligations used to finance past expansion programs, and so on. Only cash, however, not book profits, pays bills! As we examine the ability of a company to finance expansion programs or other major outlays, we must have some idea of the effects of operations on cash since these need not be the same as the impact upon profits. An understanding of operating cash flows is important for this reason, and this analysis ties into and extends the concepts treated in Chapter 1.

Net operating cash flows represent the difference between cash receipts from the sale of goods or services and cash outlays associated with the production of these goods or services. Profits differ from net operating cash flows in that (1) certain expense items—for example, depreciation—do not involve the outlay of cash; (2) income and expense items commonly accrue before they are reflected in cash flows—that is, they are reported in the operating statement before they affect the bank account; (3) profits are reported net of interest expense even though the latter is a financial charge and is excluded from net operating cash flows; and (4) sales need not be equated with production in any period—that is, inventories may rise or fall.

Despite the distinction between profits and net cash flows from operations, modified cash flow statements can be readily derived from comparative balance sheets and operating statements. Generally, cash receipts from operations are approximately equal to sales less the increase (or plus the decrease) in accounts receivable. To the extent that sales are *credit* sales, actual cash receipts *lag behind* the sales themselves, and this fact is taken into account when we include the change in receivables. Other income and changes in other current assets (excluding cash items and inventories) also enter the picture, but their effect is usually minor.

Operating cash outflows consist of cost of sales (omitting depreciation charges), selling and administrative expenses, federal income taxes, and the change in inventories. Depreciation is omitted from cost of sales (cost of goods sold) because it does not involve the outlay of cash, as was demonstrated in Chapter 1. To take account of accruals in our cash flow picture, we must deduct an increase in current liabilities (from operations) or add a decrease. The change in inventories must be included since the cash outflows caused by the expenses of operating are governed by the volume of production carried out, rather than by the prevailing level of sales. It should be noted that an increase in inventories *adds* to the operating cash outflows for the period, while a decrease in inventories reduces them. The student will recognize that we are applying the funds flow principles of Chapter 1 in a specific form, by sorting the funds flows into cash flows from operations and other cash and funds flows. The same reasoning about increases and decreases in assets, liabilities, revenues and expenses holds as before, and if there are problems of understanding the funds flow diagram on page 5 in Chapter 1 should be consulted.

It will be useful to present an illustration of the principles just presented, and we shall use for this purpose the 1964/65 fiscal year performance of SCM Corporation (formerly Smith–Corona Marchant Inc., manufacturers of office equipment and electronics devices). Exhibits 2–1 and 2–2 provide the balance sheets and operating statement of the company, while Exhibit 2–3 shows the modified statement of cash flows which focuses on the discussion of the material in this section.

The modified statement of cash flows shown below indicates that operations provided a total cash inflow of about $152 million, which was offset by an operating cash outflow of about $145 million. There was very little change in current operating liabilities or in inventories, so that we find a close correspondence between the figures in the income statement and our

Exhibit 2-1

SCM CORPORATION
BALANCE SHEETS AS OF JUNE 30, 1964 AND 1965
(thousands of dollars)

	1965	1964	Change
Assets			
Cash and cash items	$ 2,138	$ 1,250	+$ 888
Accounts receivable—net	28,019	24,900	+ 3,119
Inventories	40,996	40,719	+ 277
Other current assets	485	521	− 36
Total Current Assets	$71,638	$67,390	+$4,248
Investments	—	100	− 100
Property, plant and equipment°	36,238	33,756	+ 2,482
Accumulated depreciation	17,334	16,230	+ 1,104
Net property, plant and equipment	$18,904	$17,526	+$1,378
Other assets	6,388	6,512	− 124
Total Assets	$96,930	$91,528	+$5,402
Liabilities			
Notes payable	$ 2,000	$ 500	+$1,500
Accounts payable	7,282	6,535	+ 747
Accrued wages, taxes, etc.	4,683	4,015	+ 668
Federal and foreign income tax	986	1,166	− 180
Customer prepayments	4,286	4,330	− 44
Current portion of long-term debt	1,407	1,424	− 17
Total Current Liabilities	$20,644	$17,970	+$2,674
Long-term debt	21,913	23,104	− 1,191
Deferred income tax	1,375	520	+ 855
Reserve for retirement fund	50	49	+ 1
Preferred stock ($50)†	3,706	12,002	− 8,296
Common stock ($5)	13,471	10,217	+ 3,254
Capital surplus	16,982	10,329	+ 6,653
Earned surplus	18,789	17,337	+ 1,452
Total Liabilities and Net Worth	$96,930	$91,528	+$5,402

° Capital expenditures for the year were $3972. This amount is not entirely reflected in the balance sheet account due to unspecified adjustments which also affected capital surplus. (See Chapter 1.)

† During the fiscal year, $8296 par value of preferred stock was converted into common stock, which resulted in a credit to capital surplus of $5466. The remainder of the preferred stock was retired by the corporation on 7/8/65 at $52.50 per share plus dividends. Stock options exercised during the year added $44 to capital surplus.

modified cash flow analysis. The biggest single item resulting from accounting differences was the increase in accounts receivable of $3.1 million, which reflects the fact that collection for sales made during the period will not take place until the following year—a current drain on SCM's resources.

The framework of analysis just presented can be used for a

Exhibit 2-2

SCM CORPORATION
OPERATING STATEMENT
Year Ending June 30, 1965
(thousands of dollars)

Net sales	$149,657
Cost of sales*	99,916
Gross profit	$ 49,741
Selling and general expense	41,425
Net profit from operations	$ 8,316
Other income	54
	$ 8,370
Other deductions:	
Interest	1,664
	$ 6,706
Provision for income tax:	
U.S.	$ 2,250
Canadian and foreign	641
	$ 2,891
Net profit after taxes	$ 3,815
Retained earnings on June 30, 1964	17,337
	$ 21,152
Dividends:	
Cash	$ 660
Stock	1,703
	$ 2,363
Retained earnings on June 30, 1965	$ 18,789

* Includes depreciation of $2477.

variety of insights in the cash flow picture of SCM Corporation, and the detail can be expanded considerably, depending on the amount of inside information available. For example, federal and foreign income taxes are a sizable factor in any corporation's cash flows. The full impact of federal and foreign taxes was $180,000 more than shown on the operating statement, since the corporation reduced its short-term liability for taxes by that amount. Our cash flow analysis buries this amount in the net increase in current liabilities. At the same time, deferred income taxes rose by $855,000, which amounts to an offset to current income taxes, since the impact has been moved into the future

Exhibit 2–3

SCM CORPORATION
MODIFIED STATEMENT OF CASH FLOWS, 1965

Year Ended June 30

(thousands of dollars)

Item	Amount	Source¶
Operating Cash Inflows:		
Net sales	$149,657	O.S.
+ Other income	54	O.S.
+ Increase in current liabilities*	1,191	B.S.
+ Increase in deferred income taxes ..	855	B.S.
+ Decrease in other assets†	260	B.S.
Total Operating Cash Inflows	$152,017	
Operating Cash Outflows:		
Cost of sales‡	$ 97,439	O.S.
+ Selling and general expense	41,425	O.S.
+ Income taxes	2,891	O.S.
+ Increase in accounts receivable	3,119	B.S.
+ Increase in inventories	277	B.S.
Total Operating Cash Outflows ...	$145,151	
Net Cash Inflows from Operations	$ 6,866	
Financial Outlays:		
Interest	$ 1,664	O.S.
+ Retirement of long-term debt	1,208	B.S.
Total Financial Outlays	$ 2,872	
Financial Receipts:		
Net additions to common stock§	$ 1,611	B.S.
+ Bank loans	1,500	B.S.
+ Retirement reserve	1	B.S.
Total Financial Receipts.........	$ 3,112	
Discretionary Outlays:		
Capital expenditures	$ 3,855	B.S.
+ Stock dividends	1,703	O.S.
+ Cash dividends	660	O.S.
Total Discretionary Outlays	$ 6,218	
Cash Position:		
Excess of inflows over outflows	$ 888	
+ Beginning cash balance	1,250	B.S.
Ending Cash Balance	$ 2,138	B.S.

* Excludes loans payable and current portion of long-term debt.
† Consists of other current assets, other assets, and investments.
‡ Excludes depreciation of $2477.
§ Net of changes in common stock, capital surplus and preferred stock, since not enough data are available to analyze the details of the conversion, stock dividends, and option transactions.
¶ Under the *Source* column, O.S. refers to the operating statement and B.S. to the balance sheet.

because of differences between book accounting and tax accounting. Most likely the corporation is using accelerated depreciation methods for tax purposes, while using slower write-offs for its books from which operating statements are prepared. Through this action the corporation is saving cash outlays for current taxes, but recognizes its liability for future higher taxes when fast write-offs expire in its tax accounting.

Net cash inflows from operations of $6.9 million were available for financial and discretionary outlays. Financial outlays included interest and the retirement of notes payable. Discretionary outlays in turn were comprised of capital expenditures, cash dividends and stock dividends. The latter are not really a cash item and can be offset against the increase in common stock, if desired. Financial receipts, apart from the net additions to common stock which are largely noncash items, provided direct cash inflows in the form of additional bank loans.

Because we have observed funds flow principles throughout, the result of the analysis must be a reconciliation of all the cash movements down to the ending cash balance as reflected on the balance sheet. Therefore, the ending cash balance must equal the beginning cash balance *plus* the difference between net operating inflows and financial and discretionary outlays *plus* financial receipts. These relationships hold whether the analysis deals with past or future events.

For SCM Corporation, net cash flows from operations were sufficient by a wide margin to cover interest payments, as well as other financial outlays. Capital expenditures were also comfortably covered, and only about one half of the additional borrowing was required to keep the cash balance of the previous year. The financial analyst will be particularly interested in the company's ability to cover its financial obligations from current operating cash flows, as this reflects upon the credit worthiness of the company.

The subdivisions on the modified statement of cash flows are not static. To *discretionary outlays* might well be added (1) contributions to employees' retirement plans; (2) research and development expense; (3) advertising programs; and many other major outlays which can be varied to some extent upon the judgment of management. Variations in these categories can significantly alter the cash flow pattern, although tax deductibility modifies the impact of changes. If taxable income is positive, a reduction of one dollar in such outlays adds only 52 cents to available cash (assuming a tax rate of 48 percent). The other 48 cents becomes part of the tax bill. If taxable income is negative, a reduction of one dollar adds the full amount to available cash, even though provisions in the tax law on loss adjustments through carry-forward and income averaging may eventually wipe out that advantage. Similarly, the addition of interest charges to the income picture is modified through tax deductibility.

Exhibit 2–3 is largely illustrative in that it deals with a single annual period. Comparative statements covering several years are needed if the analyst is to (1) draw conclusions as to the manner in which the items which make up the cash flows statement adjust to changing sales and production patterns, and (2) judge the normal level of operating cash flows and the range of their variation.

While the cash flows framework provides a useful *focus*, it is little more than a starting point. To proceed further, it is necessary to probe beneath the summary statistics. At the level of operating inflows, the changing sales mix and price-volume relationships are especially important, for total dollar sales—a crucial variable—may conceal changes which affect other items as well. In the case of SCM Corporation, for example, a 20 percent increase in total sales over 1964 was the net result of higher sales of military products and electronic devices relative to the original product line of the corporation, typewriters and related items, a trend which has taken place over several years. A logical effect of this trend is a shift in the relative importance of certain operating cash outflows, such as research and development expense.

Unfortunately for the analyst, balance sheets and operating statements fail to sort components in the desired manner. Inferences can be drawn in overall terms by correlating cost of sales, selling and general expense, and the like with sales. Without more refined data, however, it is difficult to evaluate the reliability of observed patterns in the aggregate.

In the scheme of Exhibit 2–3, financial outlays precede discretionary outlays. The assumption is that financial outlays are fixed, contractual payments for the most part and that cash dividends and capital expenditures must bear the brunt of volatile cash flows from operations in the short run. Cash dividends and capital expenditures nevertheless consume cash, and they sometimes adjust slowly to changing conditions. Later chapters will take up some of these questions in more detail.

SELECTED REFERENCES

ANTHONY, ROBERT N. *Management Accounting.* 3rd ed. Homewood, Ill.: Richard D. Irwin, Inc., 1964, chap. 16.

GRAHAM, B.; DODD, D. L.; AND COTTLE, S. *Security Analysis, Principles and Technique.* 4th ed. New York, N.Y.: McGraw-Hill Book Company, 1962, chap. 13.

GUTHMANN, H. G., AND DOUGALL, H. E. *Corporate Financial Policy.* 4th ed. Englewood Cliffs, N.J.: Prentice-Hall, Inc., 1962, chap. 6.

HORNGREN, CHARLES T. *Cost Accounting, A Managerial Emphasis.* Englewood Cliffs, N.J.: Prentice-Hall, Inc., 1962, chap. 3.

STETTLER, HOWARD F. "Break-Even Analysis: Its Uses and Misuses," *The Accounting Review,* 37 (July, 1962), pp. 460–63.

PROBLEMS

1. The XYZ Corporation has fixed costs of $250,000. Variable costs per unit of product are $2, while the selling price is $4.50. Determine the volume break-even point. Illustrate operating leverage by determining the increase in profits resulting from a 10 percent increase in volume from 125,000 units, and from 150,000 units. Draw a suitable chart.

Observe separately the change in operating leverage resulting from a 40 cents drop in price; a 10 percent reduction in variable costs; an increase of $50,000 in fixed costs. Refigure volume break-even points, and percentage changes in profits resulting from the volume increases given above, and comment on the results.

2. From the following balance sheets and income statements, prepare a Modified Statement of Cash Flows for the ABC Company as indicated in Exhibit 2–3 of this chapter. Comment on the results.

ABC COMPANY

Balance Sheets, December 31
(millions of dollars)

	1965	1966	Change
Cash	$ 2,510	$ 3,167	+$ 657
Marketable securities	475	625	+ 150
Accounts receivable	8,635	9,420	+ 785
Notes receivable	100	—	− 100
Inventories	15,210	13,520	− 1,690
Total Current Assets	$26,930	$26,732	−$ 198
Plant and equipment	$54,312	$63,478	+$9,166
Less: Accumulated depreciation	22,560	26,913	+ 4,353
Total Fixed Assets	$31,752	$36,565	+$4,813
Prepaid items	25	20	− 5
Total Assets	$58,707	$63,317	+$4,610
Accounts payable	$ 3,312	$ 4,498	+$1,186
Notes payable	1,500	1,000	− 500
Accrued expenses	45	18	− 27
Accrued federal income tax	2,174	2,827	+ 653
Current portion of long-term debt	3,000	3,000	—
Total Current Liabilities	$10,031	$11,343	+$1,312
Long-term debt	$15,000	$12,000	−$3,000
Preferred stock	10,000	12,500	+ 2,500
Common stock	5,000	5,000	—
Earned surplus	18,676	22,474	+ 3,798
Total Liabilities and Net Worth	$58,707	$63,317	+$4,610

ABC COMPANY

Income Statement
For the Year Ended December 31, 1966
(millions of dollars)

Sales (net)	$88,432
Cost of goods sold*	53,976
Gross margin	$34,456
Selling and administrative expense	22,394
Operating profit	$12,062
Interest expense	650
Other income	(312)
Profit before taxes	$11,724
Provision for federal income tax	6,176
Net income after tax	$ 5,548
Dividends paid	1,750
Addition to earned surplus	$ 3,798

* Includes depreciation for the period of $4625.

Chapter 3

RATIOS AS TOOLS
OF ANALYSIS

MOVING ON FROM an examination of the shifts of funds in and about the business, we now turn to a number of comparative indicators and measures to help us appraise the financial condition, efficiency, and profitability of a business. We recall that the basic purpose of funds flow analysis was an appraisal of the soundness of the decisions for shifting funds; now the analyst becomes interested in the results of the business operations as reflected in the relationships among balance sheet and operating statement items.

When the analyst concerns himself with the financial facts of a business, he asks questions about its ability to meet current obligations, the true worth of its various assets, the extent and character of its liabilities, its resourcefulness and ability to earn a fair return on its investment, its ability to withstand possible setbacks from external or internal sources, its ability to raise new funds when needed, and so on. The analyst's viewpoint and approach will differ somewhat depending on his purposes. A business executive intimately familiar with his company's operations will have to take few formal steps to appraise its financial condition and operating efficiency. The outside analyst, who is reviewing a business for purposes of extending credit, investing funds, or management consulting will wish to make certain tests and apply certain standards to be able to rank, classify, and judge the merits of a company by comparing it to other companies of similar nature or to relevant averages.

It is often helpful, therefore, to relate financial data to each other in order to obtain ratios, or index numbers, which express a *significant* comparison more useful than the raw figures themselves. For example, to compare the amount of the current assets on the balance sheet to the amount of current liabilities is more meaningful than simply to look at each amount without reference to the other, since current assets are frequently considered the major reservoir of funds for meeting current obligations, especially when the future of the firm is in jeopardy. On the other hand, it would be nonsensical to compare "other assets" with "accounts payable" and hope to obtain a significant relationship. One basic caution must be remembered here:

Ratio analysis of financial statements must be preceded by careful thought as to the kinds of insights the analyst wishes to obtain. Ratios are not ends in themselves, rather, on a selective basis they *may help* answer significant questions.

Before going into a discussion of the major ratios commonly used, it is very important to call attention to the many limitations inherent in ratio analysis. The first and most obvious drawback lies in the differences found among the accounting methods used by various companies, which seriously impair the comparability of many situations, even in the same industry. Methods of recording and valuing assets, write-offs, costs, expenses, and so on, vary with the customs, policies, and character of the company investigated. For example, the various methods for establishing inventory values leave great leeway to management, just as the extent of depreciation claims can fluctuate widely. In short, the balance sheet accounts do not necessarily correspond to the value of the firm, either as a going concern or in liquidation, and liability accounts may be incomplete or understated (for example, nonrecording of lease obligations). Thus no one business is exactly comparable to any other.

More importantly, however, financial statements are based upon past performance and past events, and we must project our evaluation from this basis. Needless to say, for any such evaluation, be it for credit extension or internal control, the significance lies in what can be *expected to happen*. Past events are guides only to the extent they can *reasonably* be considered as clues to the future. Their use must be tempered by the best possible knowledge about the outlook for the business.

Where, then, lies the usefulness of ratio analysis? Within relatively rough limits, ratio analysis will provide guides and clues especially in spotting trends toward better or poorer performance, and in finding significant deviations from any average or relatively applicable standard. It is in the *interpretation* of such trends and deviations that the analyst will use his skills and experience (and intuition) to the fullest extent.

Keeping the limitations and possible uses of ratios in mind, we can now turn to the major ratios and discuss each briefly. An indication will be given of the kinds of answers each ratio can provide and its significant applications will be pointed out. The accompanying 1965 data for Crown Zellerbach Corporation have been used to illustrate the ratios.

CROWN ZELLERBACH CORPORATION

CONDENSED OPERATING STATEMENTS*
Years Ending December 31, 1964 and 1965
(millions of dollars)

	1965	1964
Sales (net)	$709.4	$662.2
Cost of goods sold†	$541.9	$496.7
Selling and administrative cost	66.7	62.3
Taxes, other than on income	21.2	20.4
Operating costs	$629.8	$579.4
Operating profit	$ 79.6	$ 82.8
Other income	5.9	13.2‡
Total income	$ 85.5	$ 96.0
Other expenses	8.8	5.0
Income before U.S. and foreign income taxes	$ 76.7	$ 91.0
Provision for income taxes	29.3	34.3
Net income	$ 47.4	$ 56.7
Cash dividends	31.7	30.1
Income retained in business§	$ 15.7	$ 26.6

* Adapted from 1965 annual report.
† Includes depreciation and amortization of $35 million in 1965 and $30.9 million in 1964.
‡ Includes special item—$10.1 million gain on sale of St. Helens paper mill.
§ To earned surplus.

CROWN ZELLERBACH CORPORATION

CONDENSED BALANCE SHEETS AND CHANGES*
December 31, 1964 and 1965
(millions of dollars)

Assets	1965	1964	Changes
Cash	$ 27.9	$ 26.0	+$ 1.9
Short-term investments	15.2	.5	+ 14.7
Accounts receivable (net)	83.2	75.8	+ 7.4
Inventories	118.0	108.2	+ 9.8
Prepaid expenses	11.1	11.0	+ 0.1
Total Current Assets	$255.4	$221.5	+$ 33.9
Properties: Timberlands,† buildings, machinery and equipment	$818.7	$725.5	+$ 93.3
Less accumulated depreciation	298.7	275.3	+ 23.4
Net Proprerties	$520.0	$450.2	+$ 69.8
Investments in affiliated companies	$ 15.0	$ 7.7	+$ 7.3
Other investments and receivables	14.6	14.4	+ 0.2
Deferred charges	1.7	1.4	+ 0.3
Total Assets	$806.7	$695.2	+$111.5

Liabilities			
Trade accounts payable	$ 65.5	$ 64.2	+$ 1.3
Accrued U.S. and Canadian taxes	10.3	23.1	− 12.8
Dividends payable	7.6	7.6	0
Long-term debt due in one year	5.1	5.0	+ 0.1
Total Current Liabilities	$ 88.5	$ 99.9	−$ 11.4
Long-term debt	171.3	76.9	+ 94.4
Deferred income taxes	49.1	40.9	+ 8.2
Reserve for self-insurance‡	8.9	6.4	+ 2.5
Minority interests—Canadian subsidiaries	7.9	5.9	+ 2.0
Cumulative preferred stock	24.7	25.3	− 0.6
Common stock	76.5	76.4	+ 0.1
Other surplus	96.2	95.6	+ 0.6
Income retained in business	283.6	267.9	+ 15.7
Total Liabilities and Net Worth	$806.7	$695.2	+$111.5

* Adapted from 1965 annual report.
† Included net of depletion allowances.
‡ So-called surplus reserves are not counted as part of the capitalization or net worth of the company. As a general rule only surplus items not specifically set aside for a definite purpose are so counted, which includes most "contingency" reserves.

A. RATIOS MEASURING A COMPANY'S LIQUIDITY AND INDEBTEDNESS

1. *The Current Ratio*

$$\frac{\text{Current assets}}{\text{Current liabilities}} = \frac{\$255.4}{88.5} = 2.89{:}1$$

The current ratio is one of the most commonly used indexes of financial strength, although it is a rather crude measure. The basic question underlying this ratio is the ability of the business to meet its current obligations with a margin of safety to allow for a possible shrinkage of value in its various current assets, such as inventories and receivables. This test, applied at a single point in time, implies a liquidation approach rather than a judgment on the going concern, for it does not explicitly take into account the *revolving* nature of current assets and current liabilities.

The general impression regarding this measure is that the higher the ratio the better.[1] From the point of view of the creditor this may be true, but from the standpoint of prudent management there may be serious doubts about the wisdom of an excessive buildup especially of redundant cash lying idle, or worse, a buildup of inventories out of proportion to the needs of the business. Another distorting factor is the seasonal character of some businesses which can be reflected to a great extent in a fluctuating current ratio. In the interpretation of this ratio thought should therefore be given to the components (for example, cash, accounts receivable, inventories, accounts payable, and so forth) forming the ratio, the character of the business and the industry, as well as future expectations.

A generally popular rule of thumb for the current ratio is considered to be a 2:1 relationship. Used without caution and discrimination, however, such a vague overall standard is rather dangerous. A 2:1 current ratio, or even a 10:1 current ratio does not of itself guarantee reserve strength to meet current obligations, or the ability to turn current assets (especially inventories) into cash as needed (liquidity). Much depends on the quality and character of the current assets. Furthermore, the type of

---

[1] In fact, there are many instances where financial managers try to improve the current ratio of periodic balance sheets by paying off with cash as many of their current obligations as possible on the day prior to the balance sheet date. If the company has a current ratio of better than 1:1, this process will raise the current ratio, since the same amount will be deducted from both sides of the ratio. The process will worsen the picture if the ratio is less than 1:1.

industry involved plays a major role in the need for more or less current financial strength and liquidity. For instance, a public utility with a preponderance of fixed assets and a steady cash flow faces needs for current payment much different from those of a wholesaler whose primary investment is in inventory and receivables subject to changes in value. A manufacturer has financial problems different from those of a dime store, because of differences in the character of investments and operations. The attached exercises taken from widely different industries will serve to illustrate some of these characteristics. Exhibit 3–2, among other ratios to be covered later, contains a series of "typical" current ratios, which must be treated with great caution since they are averages. Exhibit 3–3 compares Crown Zellerbach Corporation ratios with those of other major paper and forest products manufacturers.

A figure related to the current ratio is the item "net current assets" or "working capital." This is simply the difference between current assets and current liabilities. The analyst (especially the credit analyst) looks upon this figure, and its movements over several periods, as an indicator of reserve strength to weather adversities. Bank loans are often tied to a minimum requirement for working capital.

2. The Liquidity Ratio or "Acid Test"

$$\frac{\text{Cash, marketable securities, receivables}}{\text{Current liabilities}} = \frac{\$27.9 + \$15.2 + \$83.2}{\$88.5} = \underline{\underline{1.43:1}}$$

This ratio arises from the same basic desire to measure a business' ability to meet its current obligations through the use of its current assets as does the current ratio. It is, however, a far more severe test since it is an attempt to eliminate some of the disadvantages of the current ratio by concentrating on strictly *liquid* assets whose value is fairly certain. By excluding inventories from consideration, the question asked in fact becomes: "If the business were to stop selling today, what are its chances for paying off its current obligations with the readily convertible funds on hand?" The acid test thus again backs

away from the assumption of a going concern, by not considering future funds flows of the business.

A rule of thumb of 1:1 is commonly applied here with a little
more justification, since a preselection of presumably liquid
assets has been made. A result far below 1:1 can be a warning
signal, but a blind application of this rule should be avoided.

3. Debt Ratios

There are several ratios we can use to express the balance
between all borrowed funds on one hand and ownership funds
on the other which together constitute the resources of a business. Again the purpose of the analysis is to appraise this relationship with regard to the company's ability to weather times
of stress and to meet both its short-term and long-term obligations. The ratios supply some insight into the relative size of the
"cushion" of ownership funds creditors can rely upon to absorb
possible losses from operations, decreases in asset values, and
poor estimates of future funds flows. A very large cushion is not
always the best policy for a firm to pursue, since the firm's operations and industry may have such favorable risk characteristics that it would be prudent to make use of low-cost debt to
maximize profits. Three ratios most commonly used are:

$$a) \; \frac{\text{Total debt}}{\text{Total assets}} = \frac{\$88.5 + \$171.3 + \$49.1}{\$806.7} = \underline{\underline{38.29 \text{ percent}}}$$

This ratio compares both short-term and long-term liabilities
to total assets, and thereby shows what proportion of funds has
been contributed by all the company's creditors.

$$b) \; \frac{\text{Long-term debt}}{\text{Capitalization}} =$$

$$\frac{\$171.3}{\$171.3 + \$24.7 + \$76.5 + \$96.2 + \$283.6} = \underline{\underline{26.27 \text{ percent}}}$$

A more selective measure of the proportion of debt in the
capital structure of the company, which does not take into account current liabilities, is represented by the ratio above. This
very common ratio is used as an expression of a company's

long-term financial policy on the balance of funds sources. Both measures reflect the relative reliance on equity (owner-ship) funds, and the relative risk from the point of view of the creditors.

$$c) \frac{\text{Net worth (equity)}}{\text{Total debt}} = \frac{\$24.7 + \$76.5 + \$96.2 + \$283.6}{\$88.5 + \$171.3 + \$49.1} = 155.72 \text{ percent}$$

or:

$$\frac{\text{Total debt}}{\text{Net worth (equity)}} = \frac{\$88.5 + \$171.3 + \$49.1}{\$24.7 + \$76.5 + \$96.2 + \$283.6} = 64.22 \text{ percent}$$

These measures again express selective relationships to help appraise the relative position of creditors and owners.

B. RATIOS APPRAISING FUNDS MANAGEMENT ("TURNOVER" RELATIONSHIPS)

1. *Accounts Receivable*

The value of receivables, if no detailed credit information on their age is available, can be roughly appraised by relating the accounts to the sales from which they arose. The result is expressed in terms of "days' sales represented by receivables" or, more commonly, as the "collection period." This measure can be compared to the credit terms granted to customers in the industry in question, and a major deviation from this norm toward slower collections will be a warning signal, especially if there is a trend over a number of periods. The promptness with which accounts are collected is an indicator of the managerial effectiveness of the credit department, as well as a reflection of the quality of the accounts receivable. Extremely close adherence to credit terms could, on the other hand, mean that the credit policies of the company are unduly strict, and profits from sales to somewhat slower customers are being lost. The income can be computed as follows:

a) Obtain the average daily sales:

$$\frac{\text{Sales}}{\text{Days}} = \frac{\$709.4}{360} = \$1.97/\text{day}$$

b) Obtain days' sales represented by receivables:

$$\frac{\text{Receivables}}{\text{Sales per day}} = \frac{\$83.2}{\$1.97} = 42.2 \text{ days}$$

A quicker way of obtaining the same result is to calculate the percentage of receivables to sales for the period, and to apply this percentage to the number of days in the period. The end result will be the same. On the slide rule, the measure can be obtained through one setting, by placing sales over receivables and moving the hairline to the number of days on the slide.

As pointed out before, the collection period is a rough measure of the overall quality of the accounts receivable and of the credit policies of a business, but is subject to distortion, especially if sales fluctuate widely in a given period. Also, a business selling both for cash and on account presents a problem, since a separation of credit sales must be made. For a more exact picture, a detailed "aging" of accounts receivable can be prepared, through a classification of accounts into groups by dates of sale, in monthly or other relevant time intervals (depending on the credit terms) to see which portion is current and which is overdue. A ratio analysis of overdue accounts in proportion to outstanding accounts from selected or all periods can then be made. This information is not always available to the outsider, however.

2. *Accounts Payable*

From the point of view of the creditor of a business, as well as the financial analyst, it is often desirable to apply a test to accounts payable similar to the one for accounts receivable. The basis of this measure is a comparison of the accounts payable balance with the purchases for the period. Again, a detailed aging of the accounts would yield the most exact picture of the way in which the business handles its obligations to trade creditors, that is, how promptly its bills are paid. In the absence of such data, the rougher measure must suffice. The calculation of day's purchases is made exactly as in the previous example, by dividing the number of days for the period into the purchases made during the period. The result is divided into accounts payable to obtain "days' purchases represented by payables." This figure can then be compared to the credit terms extended by the suppliers of the business to see if any abuses of these terms are made, and trends may be significant.

This ratio is seldom available to outsiders, however, since the amount of purchases is not commonly made public. In the case of a manufacturing firm, purchases may be approximated by taking the material cost from the operating statement and adjusting for the change in the raw materials content of inventories. Lacking such detail, some analysts take cost of goods sold and adjust for the change in inventories. The latter measure is a very crude approximation, since usually cost of goods sold contains many cash charges, such as labor, repairs, and so forth. It can be used without difficulty in the case of a merchandising firm, however. Another difficulty lies in the fact that accounts payable often include debts incurred for purposes other than raw material purchases and such debts may vary greatly from time to time. Consequently, the ratio, if obtained, is usually less reliable than the accounts receivable measure.

3. *Inventories*

The inventory account is of interest to the analyst both in terms of the value of the material or merchandise involved and its size in relation to other funds needs and the sales volume it supports. An exact appraisal of the true value of the inventories is usually not possible short of a detailed count and verification. The financial analyst can make some judgments via a ratio analysis, however, by relating the inventory account to the current assets, or total assets, and more commonly to cost of sales (cost of goods sold) and the volume of sales generated during the period.

There are three main ways of presenting the relationship of inventory to other relevant figures:

$$a) \ \frac{\text{Cost of sales (cost of goods sold)}}{\text{Average inventory}\dagger} = \frac{\$541.9^*}{1/2 \ (\$118.0 + \$108.2)} = \underline{\underline{4.79 \ \text{times}}}$$

This relationship expresses the frequency with which the average level of inventory investment was "recouped" or "turned over" through operations. Presumably, the higher the turnover, the better the performance by the firm, for it has managed to operate with a relatively small average commitment of funds. This in turn may indicate that the inventory must be relatively "current" and useful, and contains little unusable stock. On the other hand, a high turnover could mean inventory shortages and incomplete satisfaction of customer desires. The final judgment will depend upon the industry, company, the method of valuing inventories, and any observable trends.

$$b) \ \frac{\text{Sales}}{\text{Ending inventory}} = \frac{\$709.4}{\$118.0} = \underline{\underline{6.01 \ \text{times}}}$$

This ratio is a cruder standard for the same purpose as (a). Its most important shortcoming lies in the use of the ending inventory figure, which may not be representative of the level of inventory throughout the year. Furthermore, the investment in inventory corresponds in terms of value to the cost of goods sold, whereas sales contain the markup for other costs and profit over and above the recorded cost of the goods as carried in inventory. Thus, the relationship is not entirely that of comparable figures. Finally, comparability between companies may be impaired through differences in the gross margin taken on sales, which is more adequately represented by cost of goods sold.

$$c) \ \frac{\text{Inventory (ending or average)}}{\text{Sales}} = \frac{\$118.0}{\$709.4} = \underline{\underline{16.63 \ \text{percent}}}$$

The third ratio, as the reverse of the prior ratio, interprets the relationship between inventory and sales mainly for internal forecast purposes and intraindustry comparison. The ratio represents the level of inventory investment required to support a

---

* Includes depreciation of $35 million.
† One half of sum of beginning and ending inventories.

given level of sales, and thus is useful both in judging the size of the current capital commitment as well as the possible investment need for future sales.

4. Fixed Assets

The turnover concepts just presented are often applied by analysts to total assets, net worth, and to gauge the level of investment in plant and equipment required to support a given level of sales. They are especially used to obtain a measure for comparing companies within an industry and then to make judgments upon the efficiency with which the companies are utilizing their assets to create sales. Again, these are relatively crude measures and are hampered especially by the question of real asset values, which may be quite different from the book values recorded. Furthermore, the measures are an attempt to express a relationship between investment and sales volume, which is by far not as important or even relevant as the relationship between investment and profit, to which the next section is devoted.

C. RATIOS REFERRING TO PROFITABILITY

When speaking of profitability, the analyst has in mind the return of value over and above the values put into a business endeavor, as was already demonstrated in the first chapter of this book. This return, or profit, is generated through the sales or service efforts carried on by the company, and the extent or relative size of profit can be measured and compared by two major groups of ratios:

1. Profitability as Related to Investment

The relationship between the size of the annual profits and the investment committed to attaining this profit is one of the most basic fundamentals of business enterprise. Many arguments have been raised about the various methods of calculating this relationship, since accounting methods, asset valuation, expense policies, and so on, all affect the components of the relationship. Several ratios are commonly used:

$$a) \frac{\text{Earnings before interest and taxes (EBIT)}}{\text{Total assets}} = \frac{\$85.5}{\$806.7} = \underline{\underline{10.60 \text{ percent}}}$$

This ratio measures the earnings of the business on all of its assets, before taxes and compensation of the various contributors of these assets (creditors and stockholders). Some analysts adjust this measure by using *average* assets held during the year, while others prefer beginning balances or ending balances.

A variation is found in the following formula:

$$b) \frac{\text{Net profit}}{\text{Total assets}} = \frac{\$47.4}{\$806.7} = \underline{\underline{5.88 \text{ percent}}}$$

This measure relates the profits left after taxes and *after* compensation of part of the contributors of the company's assets (the creditors who are paid interest) to the total assets shown. For the latter reason the ratio is often considered not to be a completely adequate measure of profitability for all purposes. The outside analyst appraising the earnings power of the assets may not use the measure while the stockholder interested in the earnings belonging to him relative to the company assets may find the measure relevant.

A third and very common measure relates net profit to the net worth (net assets) of a business:

$$c) \frac{\text{Net profits}}{\text{Net worth}} = \frac{\$47.4}{\$24.7 + \$456.3} = \underline{\underline{9.86 \text{ percent}}}$$

This is a way of measuring the return to the owners of the business after all taxes and interest have been paid. In this sense it is a fair measure (with limitations) for appraising the earning power of the ownership investment, which is especially crucial to the financial analyst interested in investing equity funds. Frequently, the net worth figure is adjusted to reflect the *average* amount during the year (result: 9.96 percent). Also, the credit analyst will often wish to adjust the formula to reflect only the "tangible net worth," by subtracting from the owner's investment all intangible assets such as goodwill, patents, organization expense, and so forth. His reasoning is based on the desire to appraise in the most conservative way the values of the various assets. Again, the accounting and operating policies of a firm influence the reliability of this measure.

2. Profitability as Related to Sales ("Profit Margin")

The analyst is also concerned about the relationship of profits to the sales volume attained. This ratio helps him appraise the efficiency of the operations, although such considerations as pricing and volume fluctuations may limit the reliability of this measure. Also, as pointed out before, the more crucial test of business efficiency and profitability lies in the return on investment ratio, since it is possible that a high profit percentage on sales could still mean a very low profit percentage on investment if the sales volume is relatively low. Conversely, a low profit margin coupled with a rapid turnover of net worth (high sales volume) could result in a large profit percentage on net worth.

$$a) \frac{\text{Earnings before interest and taxes}}{\text{Sales}} = \frac{\$85.5}{\$709.4} = \underline{12.05 \text{ percent}}$$

$$b) \frac{\text{Net profit}}{\text{Sales}} = \frac{\$47.4}{\$709.4} = \underline{6.68 \text{ percent}}$$

Both ratios shown are used by analysts and are general indicators of relative efficiency, especially in intra-industry comparisons. (Exhibit 3–3 shows data for five major forest products companies.)

Many more ratios can be developed from the operating statements to obtain indicators of the way individual expenses have been controlled by the business. Among these are:

$$c) \frac{\text{Cost of sales}}{\text{Sales}} = \frac{\$541.9}{\$709.4} = \underline{76.39 \text{ percent}}$$

$$d) \text{ Gross margin: } \frac{\text{Sales}-\text{Cost of sales}}{\text{Sales}} = \frac{\$709.4 - \$541.9}{\$709.4} = \underline{23.61 \text{ percent}}$$

Ratios (c) and (d) reflect the markup of the cost of merchandise or products and may also indicate high-cost operations, price pressures, volume fluctuations, and so on. Examination of other ratios and data will be helpful to shed additional light upon the situation.

e) Relationship to sales of individual expense items selected at the discretion of the analyst.

These ratios are useful to check on the relative efficiency of operations, especially in period-to-period analysis, budgetary control, and so forth. In fact, one of the best starts to appraising the operations of a company can be made by tracing changes in gross margin, operating expenses, profit before taxes, and similar items, all expressed as percentages of net sales.

Relationships between Ratios

As became apparent, especially in the last part of the previous section, there are not only common risks of misinterpretation in the family of ratios, but also many close interrelationships which help the analyst confirm or alter his tentative conclusions.

For instance, one can arrive at the profit percentage on assets (or other investment figure) via the profit percentage on sales and the turnover of assets in sales:

$$\text{Profit percentage on sales} = \frac{\text{Net profit}}{\text{Sales}}$$

$$\text{Asset turnover} = \frac{\text{Sales}}{\text{Assets}}$$

$$\text{Profit percentage on assets} = \frac{\text{Net profit}}{\text{Sales}} \times \frac{\text{Sales}}{\text{Assets}} = \frac{\text{Net profit}}{\text{Assets}}$$

Here we observe that a grouping of ratios intimately connected with each other will give a fuller answer than any one of the three alone.

Another example of the need for grouping of ratios is the investigation of the current position of a business. To derive the current ratio only is not as meaningful as adding to the picture an investigation of the components of the ratio. Thus, a turnover of inventories will bespeak the quality of the inventory, while analysis of receivables and payables will help assess the current situation. Finally, a test of the growth or decline of net working capital may indicate significant funds movements.

As demonstrated by the system in Exhibit 3–1, certain major ratios are interrelated meaningfully. The changes and trends in each of the components affect the family of ratios as a whole:

Exhibit 3–1

INTERRELATIONSHIPS OF COMMON RATIOS[*]

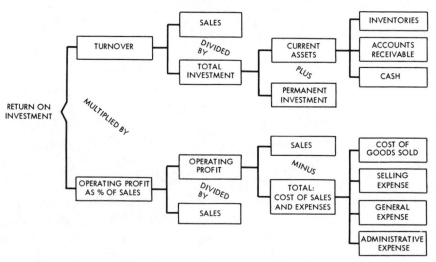

[*] For a more detailed explanation of this system, see: C. A. Kline, Jr. and Howard C. Hessler, "The DuPont Chart System for Appraising Operating Performance," *Readings in Cost Accounting, Budgeting, and Control*, William E. Thomas (ed.) (rev. ed.; Cincinnati: South-Western Publishing Co., 1960), p. 799. Reproduced by permission.

Because of these interrelationships it is possible to design a system for management control to monitor the effect of changes in the performance of a company as expressed in the various components of the ratios. The illustration in Exhibit 3–1 is taken from the well-known DuPont Chart System of control, which utilizes the ratio dependencies to provide a most sensitive series of charts and indicators calling management's attention to favorable as well as adverse trends of divisional and corporate performance. The student is invited to trace through the effect on return on investment of a change in any of the components of the chart. Once a company has developed standards of perform-

Exhibit 3–2

MAJOR COMPARATIVE RATIOS—SELECTED INDUSTRIES*

(Five-Year Average 1950–1955)

	Current Ratio	Net Profit to Net Sales	Net Profit to Tangible Net Worth	Collection Period	Fixed Assets to Tangible Net Worth	Total Debt to Tangible Net Worth
A) Manufacturing						
Cotton goods, converters, nonfactored	3.16	1.47%	7.35%	49 days	1.5%	131.3%
Drugs	3.36	6.53	11.82	41	38.7	54.8
Electrical parts and supplies	2.54	4.35	12.80	36	36.4	74.1
Fruit and vegetable canners	2.11	2.33	6.81	18	53.6	90.6
Furniture	3.20	2.88	8.38	37	31.7	54.5
Lumber	3.18	4.88	8.09	31	36.9	48.8
Machinery (industrial)	2.74	4.01	10.54	43	34.3	70.2
Meat-packers	2.16	0.67	6.05	11	55.7	72.2
Paints, varnishes, and lacquers	3.51	2.54	6.66	34	32.6	51.7
Paper	2.62	5.75	10.11	27	65.3	50.7
Petroleum (integrated)	2.14	8.04	12.18	31	83.9	45.8
Printers (job)	2.48	2.90	7.94	36	48.8	52.2
Radio parts and supplies	1.90	3.64	13.79	36	38.6	96.5
Shoes	2.68	2.25	7.72	39	16.9	65.5
Soft drinks	1.89	3.64	8.66	16	66.8	53.9
Steel, struct. fabricators	2.80	3.75	12.43	41	34.5	71.3
B) Wholesaling						
Auto parts and accessories	3.24	2.03	7.02	33	14.2	62.1
Confectionery	3.45	1.20	7.31	21	13.9	39.0
Drug and drug sundries	2.60	1.80	9.51	30	10.5	65.4
Dry goods	3.40	1.02	3.79	45	4.5	63.1
Electrical parts and supplies	2.46	1.77	8.85	40	11.6	79.2
Men's furnishings	3.53	2.86	8.68	45	4.8	56.3
Gasoline, oil	2.10	1.56	7.58	31	39.1	82.8
Groceries	2.70	0.76	6.61	16	13.8	89.7
Hardware	2.12	2.12	6.69	32	13.9	64.2
Lumber	2.92	1.14	7.36	33	9.3	79.9
Paints, varnishes	3.02	1.98	6.28	37	18.2	61.7
Paper	2.74	1.45	7.66	32	13.0	77.8
Shoes	3.00	1.27	6.17	50	4.1	63.9
Wines, liquors	1.95	0.87	6.02	35	15.3	98.6
C) Retailing						
Clothing—men's, boys'	3.66	2.96	6.67	—†	11.8	73.6
Department stores	3.55	2.24	6.20	—†	25.3	59.2
Furniture	3.57	2.11	5.60	—†	10.5	65.5
Furniture—installment	3.97	2.84	5.21	148	12.3	67.5
Lumber and building materials	3.50	2.12	6.53	50	21.4	63.5
Shoes	3.15	2.09	6.28	—†	12.8	74.4
Women's specialty shops	2.72	2.41	7.09	—†	20.0	73.5

* Based on Roy A. Foulke, *Twenty-five Years of the 14 Important Ratios* (Dun & Bradstreet, Inc., 1957), pp. 60–78. (These are averages of at least 25 enterprises in each category.)
† Information not sufficient to determine breakdown between cash and credit sales.

Exhibit 3–3

CROWN ZELLERBACH CORPORATION
AND FOUR MAJOR FOREST PRODUCTS COMPANIES
SELECTED RATIOS FOR 1964 AND 1965
(dollar figures in thousands)

		Crown Zeller-bach Corp.	Inter-national Paper Co.	Weyer-haeuser Co.	Georgia-Pacific Corp.	St. Regis Paper Co.
Net sales ...	—1965	$709.4	$1303.7	$721.4	$575.0	$635.2
	1964	$662.2	$1245.8	$663.3	$481.0	$616.6
Total assets .	—1965	$806.7	$1120.0	$808.2	$844.3	$629.7
	1964	$695.2	$1080.4	$708.1	$643.0	$598.4
Net working capital ...	—1965	$166.9	$ 260.7	$130.7	$144.9	$153.8
	1964	$121.6	$ 261.8	$128.4	$115.5	$144.5
Current ratio	—1965	2.89:1	3.05:1	2.09:1	2.72:1	3.22:1
	1964	2.22:1	3.11:1	2.24:1	2.66:1	3.37:1
Acid test	—1965	1.43:1	1.64:1	1.25:1	1.24:1	1.74:1
	1964	1.02:1	1.75:1	1.36:1	1.18:1	1.74:1
Total debt to total assets .	—1965	38.29%	13.40%	21.25%	57.41%	31.15%
	1964	31.94%	13.15%	16.55%	58.15%	30.75%
Long-term debt to capital structure ..	—1965	26.27%	0	7.76%	49.85%	21.68%
	1964	14.19%	0	2.16%	52.05%	22.70%
Days' receivables	—1965	42.2 days	43.2 days	38.9 days	47.7 days	45.4 days
	1964	38.0 days	42.4 days	37.6 days	40.0 days	41.5 days
Ending inventory turnover (sales) ...	—1965	6.01x	7.41x	7.23x	4.75x	6.82x
	1964	6.13x	7.43x	7.31x	4.96x	6.61x
Net fixed assets turnover (sales) ...	—1965	1.38x	2.30x	1.38x	1.51x	2.01x
	1964	1.48x	2.32x	1.48x	1.97x	2.25x
Net profit to total assets	—1965	5.88%	7.91%	10.31%	5.52%	5.70%
	1964	6.70%	7.53%	9.54%	5.63%	4.50%
Net profit to net worth	—1965	9.86%	9.11%	13.15%	12.37%	8.27%
	1964	10.02%	8.67%	11.45%	13.38%	6.50%
Net profit to net sales .	—1965	6.68%	6.69%	11.55%	8.01%	5.65%
	1964	7.02%	6.53%	10.18%	7.53%	4.36%
Operating profit to net sales	—1965	11.63%	11.46%	13.15%	14.29%	7.51%
	1964	12.71%	10.70%	11.93%	14.24%	5.41%

ance regarding the various ratios, it is fairly easy to gauge performance changes with such a system.

As part of such an appraisal—formal or informal—the results of funds flow analysis may be used to supplement the findings from ratio analysis, and vice versa.

Other Comments

A number of references have been made throughout the previous sections to the caution which must be exercised in the use of the tools of analysis described. Here is a summary of useful hints to keep in mind:

a) Select only data which are relevant to the analysis. The *purpose* of the investigation itself yields clues to the nature of the ratios which will be helpful.

b) Extend your analysis over several past periods as well as for the current period, to be able to observe any noticeable trends.

c) Concentrate on all major variations from any applicable standard, such as industry data, especially if there is a consistent trend over a period of time, and attempt to analyze their causes by cross-checking with other ratios and raw data.

SELECTED REFERENCES

Bogen, J. I. (ed.). *Financial Handbook*. Rev. ed. New York: The Ronald Press Co., 1957, Sec. 5, pp. 242–55.

Cohen, Jerome B., and Robbins, Sidney M. *The Financial Manager, Basic Aspects of Financial Administration*. New York: Harper & Row, Publishers, 1966.

Dun & Bradstreet, Inc. *14 Important Ratios in 72 Lines of Business* (Years 1957–1961). New York, 1962.

Foulke, Roy A. *The Genesis of the 14 Important Ratios*. New York: Dun & Bradstreet, Inc., 1955.

Guthmann, H. G. *Analysis of Financial Statements*. 4th ed. Englewood Cliffs, N.J.: Prentice-Hall, Inc., 1953.

Howard, Bion B., and Upton, Miller. *Introduction to Business Finance*. New York: McGraw-Hill Book Co., 1953, chap. 6.

Hunt, Pearson; Williams, Charles M.; and Donaldson, Gordon. *Basic Business Finance*. 3rd ed. Homewood, Ill.: Richard D. Irwin, Inc., 1964.

Moore, Carl L., and Jaedicke, Robert K. *Managerial Accounting*. Cincinnati, Ohio: South-Western Publishing Company, 1963, chap. 6.

PROBLEMS AND EXERCISES

1. Work out the following exercises:

a) A company with a current ratio of 2.5:1 has current liabilities of $130,000. Indicate whether the individual transactions described below increase or decrease the current ratio, or the amount of working capital, and by how much in each case. Treat each item separately.

Purchase of $10,000 worth of merchandise on account.

Company collects on $5000 of accounts receivable.

Repayment of currently due note payable with cash from bank account $15,000.

Acquisition of $40,000 machine, paid for with $10,000 cash and balance due in 18 months (lump sum).

Sale of machinery for $10,000. Accumulated depreciation was $50,000; original cost was $80,000.

Company pays dividends, $10,000 in cash, $10,000 in stock.

Company borrows $30,000 for one year. Proceeds are used to increase bank account by $10,000 to pay off accounts due supplier ($15,000), and to acquire the right to patents worth $5000.

Company writes down inventories by $7000, and organization expense by $5000.

Wages are paid to the extent of $15,000. Of this amount, $3000 had been shown on the balance sheet as accrued (due).

Company sells $25,000 worth (cost) of merchandise from stock to customers who will pay in 30 days. Company has a gross margin of 40 percent.

b) From the following data compute the collection period for Company A, using both methods described in the note, and the amount of accounts receivable for Company B. Credit terms for both companies are n/30 days.

	Company A	Company B
Sales for the year:	$142,000	$793,000
Accounts receivable	11,500	—
Collection period	—	48 days

c) Compute the days' accounts payable outstanding for Company C in two ways (the company buys on terms of 2/10, n/30):

	Company C
Sales for 90 days	$892,500
Cost of sales	525,000
Purchases during 90 days	374,000
Ending inventory	437,000
Accounts payable	94,500

d) Compute the inventory turnover according to the methods discussed in the note:

	Company D
Net sales	$1,325,000
Beginning inventory	132,000
Ending inventory	318,000
Cost of sales	896,000

e) Compute the rate of return on total assets from the following data for Companies E and F:

	Company E	Company F
Net sales for year	$25,375,000	—
Total assets	—	$4,250,000
Net profit on sales	4%	19%
Turnover of total assets	6 times	—
Gross margin	38%	$468,000 (25%)

2. Prepare a ratio analysis of the financial statements of the following three companies (a manufacturer, a public utility, and a retail firm), through the eyes of a credit analyst who is investigating the granting of a sizable loan to each. Compare the results of your analysis to the historical company ratio information and industry data provided and observe major trends and deviations. What are some of the factors which may tend to limit the usefulness of the ratios? Observe the differences between the three types of companies. What are the main factors behind these differences?

TEXAS INSTRUMENTS, INCORPORATED

BALANCE SHEETS
December 31, 1964 and 1965
(thousands of dollars)

	1965	1964
Cash and U.S. government securities	$ 59,594	$ 41,385
Receivables (net)	73,221	46,308
Inventories	64,751	44,818
Prepaid expenses	3,162	1,904
Payments received on government contracts	(14,661)	(10,915)
Total Current Assets	$186,067	$123,500
Property, plant and equipment	141,707	107,635
Accumulated depreciation	59,806	50,626
Net property account	$ 81,901	$ 57,009
Other assets	2,857	348
Total Assets	$270,825	$180,857

Accounts payable	$ 31,443	$ 21,710
Accrued income tax	22,010	18,384
Accrued pensions and profit sharing	19,360	13,558
Other accruals and liabilities	15,605	10,962
Current portion of long-term debt	—	1,012
Total Current Liabilities	$ 88,418	$ 65,626
Debentures (4.80%, due 1990)	46,580	—
Other long-term debt	2,128	3,938
Deferred incentive compensation	1,082	—
Common stock ($1 par)	5,058	5,024
Paid-in surplus	13,669	12,539
Accumulated retained earnings	113,890	93,730
Total Liabilities and Net Worth	$270,825	$180,857

OPERATING STATEMENTS

Years 1964 and 1965

(thousands of dollars)

	1965	*1964*
Net sales	$436,369	$327,579
Cost of goods and services	308,023	230,388
Gross profit	$128,346	$ 97,191
Selling, general and administrative expenses	$ 62,515	$ 49,005
Employee profit sharing and retirement	19,365	13,478
	$ 81,880	$ 62,483
Operating profit	$ 46,466	$ 34,708
Other income	873	693
	$ 47,339	$ 35,401
Interest paid	1,066	544
	$ 46,273	$ 34,857
Provision for income taxes	21,434	16,816
Net profit	$ 24,839	$ 18,041

	1965	*1964*
(Depreciation and amortization:	$19,257	$14,105)
(Common dividends:	5,046	5,264)
(Miscellaneous surplus credits:	367	—)

MAJOR RATIOS

	Fill in	*Past Ratios*					
	1965	*1964*	*1963*	*1962*	*1961*	*1960*	*1959*
Current ratio		1.9	2.1	2.4	2.3	2.1	1.7
Acid test		1.3	1.5	1.7	1.7	1.7	1.7
Total debt to total assets		38.4%	36.7%	33.4%	35.5%	38.9%	46.6%
Long-term debt as percent of capitalization		3.7%	5.5%	7.8%	10.1%	13.1%	17.5%
Total debt to net worth		62.6%	58.0%	50.4%	57.4%	66.6%	92.4%
Days' receivables		50.9	59.4	54.6	50.5	42.7	54.2
Ending inventory turnover (sales)		7.3x	6.9x	7.9x	10.4x	9.8x	8.3x

	Fill in			Past Ratios			
	1965	1964	1963	1962	1961	1960	1959
Ending inventory turnover (cost of sales)		5.1x	4.9x	5.9x	7.5x	6.7x	5.5x
Net property turnover ...		5.7x	5.7x	5.6x	5.2x	5.1x	4.7x
Total assets turnover		1.8x	1.8x	1.8x	1.8x	2.0x	1.8x
Net profit to total assets ..		10.0%	7.9%	6.4%	7.4%	13.0%	13.3%
Net profit to net worth ...		16.2%	12.4%	9.6%	11.5%	21.4%	24.9%
Net profit to net sales		5.5%	4.4%	3.6%	4.0%	6.7%	7.3%
Gross profit		29.6%	28.3%	25.8%	27.8%	31.3%	33.5%

INDUSTRY COMPARISONS

A) RAYTHEON COMPANY

	1965	1964	1963	1962	1961	1960	1959
Current ratio	2.0	2.1	2.1	1.8	1.8	1.5	1.5
Acid test	0.9	0.8	0.9	0.8	0.9	0.7	1.0
Total debt to total assets .	54.1%	53.8%	53.7%	57.4%	60.5%	59.3%	61.2%
Long-term debt as percent of capitalization	24.9%	26.7%	27.4%	28.0%	30.7%	10.1%	12.4%
Days' receivables	64.0	48.7	52.8	47.3	54.6	45.1	78.9
Days' payables°	20.4	15.1	16.4	15.5	20.0	13.4	14.6
Ending inventory turnover (sales)	4.2x	4.0x	4.9x	5.6x	6.0x	5.3x	9.4x
Ending inventory turnover (cost of sales)	3.6x	3.4x	4.3x	4.9x	5.3x	4.6x	8.0x
Net property turnover ...	10.9x	11.6x	12.8x	12.9x	12.6x	15.4x	18.9x
Total assets turnover	1.8x	1.9x	2.1x	2.3x	2.2x	2.4x	2.4x
Net profit to total assets .	4.2%	3.5%	2.7%	3.7%	2.7%	3.6%	5.1%
Net profit to net worth ..	8.8%	7.6%	5.8%	8.8%	6.9%	8.8%	13.1%
Net profit to net sales ...	1.8%	2.1%	1.1%	2.1%	1.2%	1.5%	2.1%
Gross profit	15.0%	14.4%	12.5%	13.0%	12.3%	12.5%	14.8%

B) SPERRY RAND CORPORATION

	1965	1964	1963	1962	1961	1960	1959
Current ratio	2.3	2.5	2.7	1.9	1.9	2.1	2.4
Acid test	1.0	1.1	1.0	0.8	0.8	1.0	1.2
Total debt to total assets .	57.7%	56.6%	60.1%	60.2%	58.3%	57.5%	55.4%
Long-term debt as percent of capitalization	39.7%	41.0%	45.9%	38.2%	36.6%	37.4%	38.7%
Days' receivables	59.0	51.8	55.2	60.0	63.4	61.2	68.7
Days' payables°	72.9	52.6	59.1	60.2	56.4	56.1	55.5
Ending inventory turnover (sales)	3.7x	4.2x	3.5x	3.5x	3.7x	4.0x	3.8x
Ending inventory turnover (cost of sales)	2.6x	3.1x	2.6x	2.5x	2.7x	3.0x	2.8x
Net property turnover ...	4.3x	4.0x	4.4x	4.7x	4.1x	4.6x	4.1x
Total assets turnover	1.4x	1.4x	1.4x	1.4x	1.3x	1.4x	1.3x
Net profit to total assets .	2.4%	3.0%	1.5%	2.8%	3.1%	4.4%	3.6%
Net profit to net worth ..	5.7%	6.9%	3.9%	7.1%	7.5%	10.3%	8.0%
Net profit to net sales ...	1.8%	2.1%	1.1%	2.1%	2.4%	3.2%	2.8%
Gross profit	29.9%	26.6%	25.3%	27.2%	26.3%	24.6%	25.5%

° Figures distorted because of summarized data.

BOSTON EDISON COMPANY

BALANCE SHEETS
December 31, 1964 and 1965
(thousands of dollars)

	1965	1964
Utility plant	$587,764	$556,643
Accumulated depreciation	181,963	171,746
Net utility plant	$405,801	$384,897
Other property and investments	5,668	5,025
Total Plant and Investments	$411,469	$389,922
Cash and treasury bills	$ 5,108	$ 4,383
Receivables (net)	19,537	18,100
Materials and supplies	9,692	9,077
Prepayments	1,653	1,282
Other current items	171	110
Total Current Assets	$ 36,161	$ 32,952
Other assets	1,958	2,387
Total Assets	$449,588	$425,261
Common stock	$ 74,677	$ 74,677
Preferred stock	43,000	43,000
Premium on capital stock	54,665	54,665
Retained earnings	49,683	45,120
Total Net Worth	$222,025	$217,462
Long-term debt	$170,141	$145,671
Notes payable	$ 14,250	$ 22,000
Accounts payable	6,358	4,789
Accrued taxes	3,242	6,102
Accrued dividends, interest, etc.,	6,456	5,632
Total Current Liabilities	$ 30,306	$ 38,523
Deferred credits	3,722	2,263
Deferred taxes and construction costs	23,394	21,342
Total Liabilities and Net Worth	$449,588	$425,261

OPERATING STATEMENTS

Years 1964 and 1965
(thousands of dollars)

	1965	1964
Operating revenue	$156,576	$147,494
Operating expenses	$ 67,163	63,098
Maintenance	9,724	9,252
Depreciation	15,633	14,834
Deferred federal income tax*	2,172	1,909
Deferred investment tax credit†	1,333	602
Federal income tax	10,615	12,592
General taxes	25,771	22,902
Total Operating Revenue Deduction	$132,411	$125,189

Net operating revenue	$ 24,165	$ 22,305
Other income	174	314
Gross Income	$ 24,339	$ 22,619
Interest on long-term debt	$ 4,980	$ 4,842
Other interest and deductions	(115)	(761)
Net Profit	$ 19,474	$ 18,538
Preferred dividends	$ 1,960	$ 1,960
Common dividends	12,247	11,351
Total Dividends	$ 14,207	$ 13,311
Retained earnings	$ 5,267	$ 5,227

° Resulting from accelerated depreciation for tax purposes.
† Resulting from the spreading of the investment tax credit over the life of the facilities acquired.

MAJOR RATIOS

	Fill in 1965	Past Ratios					
		1964	1963	1962	1961	1960	1959
Current ratio		0.9	1.7	1.9	1.4	1.8	2.8
Acid test		0.6	1.2	1.4	1.0	1.3	2.2
Total debt to total assets		47.9%	46.7%	46.8%	48.2%	47.8%	47.5%
Long-term debt as percent of capitalization		40.1%	40.7%	41.7%	42.3%	42.9%	43.9%
Long-term debt as percent of net plant		37.8%	40.5%	41.9%	42.3%	43.9%	46.2%
Total debt to net worth		0.9	0.9	0.9	0.9	0.9	0.9
Gross plant per dollar of revenue°		$3.8	$3.7	$3.6	$3.7	$3.8	$3.9
Accumulated depreciation to gross plant		30.9%	30.8%	29.9%	28.5%	27.6%	27.0%
Total assets turnover		0.35x	0.36x	0.35x	0.34x	0.33x	0.31x
Net profit to total assets		4.4%	4.4%	4.0%	3.8%	3.7%	3.5%
Net profit to net plant		4.8%	4.8%	4.5%	4.3%	4.2%	4.0%
Net profit to net worth		8.5%	8.3%	7.6%	7.4%	7.4%	6.6%
Net profit to gross operating revenue		12.5%	12.3%	11.4%	11.2%	11.4%	11.2%
Operating ratio†		74.6%	73.2%	74.7%	73.9%	73.8%	74.1%
Depreciation to gross operating revenue		10.1%	10.2%	10.3%	10.1%	10.2%	10.5%
Maintenance to gross operating revenue		6.3%	6.1%	6.4%	6.0%	7.3%	6.8%

° "Turnover" figure used in public utilities.
† Total of operating expenses, maintenance, depreciation and taxes other than taxes on income, related to gross operating revenue.

INDUSTRY INFORMATION°

	1964	1963	1962	1961	1960	1959
Current ratio	0.97	0.94	1.01	0.96	0.99	0.99
Total debt to total assets	57.2%	57.8%	57.9%	58.1%	58.0%	57.9%
Long-term debt as percent of capitalization	51.8%	52.1%	52.4%	52.8%	52.8%	52.8%

Long-term debt as percent of						
net plant	50.5%	50.7%	51.5%	51.8%	52.0%	52.3%
Total debt to net worth	1.4	1.3	1.3	1.4	1.3	1.4
Plant per dollar of revenue	$4.17	$4.18	$4.17	$4.22	$4.22	$4.21
Accumulated depreciation to						
gross plant	20.8%	21.5%	20.8%	20.1%	19.6%	19.1%
Total assets turnover	0.26x	0.28x	0.27x	0.26x	0.25x	0.25x
Net profit to total assets	4.5%	4.2%	4.2%	4.0%	4.0%	3.9%
Net profit to net plant	4.9%	4.7%	4.6%	4.4%	4.4%	4.4%
Net profit to net worth	10.9%	10.1%	9.9%	9.5%	9.5%	9.4%
Net profit to gross operating						
revenue	16.0%	15.4%	15.2%	14.9%	15.0%	14.9%
Depreciation to gross electric						
operating revenue	11.3%	11.2%	11.0%	10.9%	10.7%	10.4%
Operating ratio	77.3%	76.9%	77.2%	78.0%	78.2%	78.5%

° Adapted from Moody's "A Nationwide Survey of Public Utility Progress," *Moody's Public Utility Manual 1965*, pp. a22–a23. (Privately owned Class A & B Electric Utilities.)

MONTGOMERY WARD & COMPANY, INCORPORATED

Balance Sheets
February 2, 1966 and February 3, 1965
(thousands of dollars)

	2/2/66	2/3/65
Cash	$ 30,502	$ 33,716
Receivables (net)	231,505	145,442
Inventories	400,206	349,867
Prepaid costs and supplies	42,022	43,602
Total Current Assets	$ 704,235	$572,627
Net equity in subsidiaries	121,096	100,534
Other assets	2,299	–
Land, buildings, fixtures and leasehold improvements	335,021	296,510
Less: Accumulated depreciation	100,396	87,721
Net property	$ 234,625	$208,789
Total Assets	$1,062,255	$881,950
Notes payable	$ 64,000	$ 73,865
Accounts payable	101,945	89,455
Accruals	58,902	53,931
Federal income taxes due	17,775	7,369
Total Current Liabilities	$ 242,622	$224,620
Deferred federal income tax°	12,900	11,080
Debentures (4⅞%, due 1990)	150,000	–
Capital stock	211,190	211,115
Earned surplus	445,543	435,135
Total Liabilities and Net Worth	$1,062,255	$881,950

° Resulting from accelerated depreciation for tax purposes.

OPERATING STATEMENTS

Fiscal Years 1964 and 1965

(thousands of dollars)

	1965	1964
Net sales	$1,748,360	$1,697,391
Cost of goods sold*	1,266,507	1,238,530
Gross margin	$ 481,853	$ 458,861
Operating, selling and administrative expense	447,290	429,661
Operating profit	$ 34,563	$ 29,200
Interest earned	775	951
Interest expense	(5,833)	–
Income before taxes	$ 29,505	$ 30,151
Federal and state taxes	12,103	12,546
Net earnings of owned subsidiaries	(6,561)	(5,804)
Deferred income taxes	–	1,544
Net Income	$ 23,963	$ 21,865

	1965	1964
* Includes depreciation:	$17,551	$16,019
Cash dividends paid:	$13,555	$13,550

MAJOR RATIOS

	Fill in 1965	Past Ratios					
		1964	1963	1962	1961	1960	1959
Current ratio		2.6	3.8	4.9	5.5	6.0	5.1
Acid test		0.8	1.3	2.2	2.3	3.1	2.9
Total debt to total assets		26.8%	19.7%	16.4%	14.4%	13.5%	17.1%
Long-term debt as percent of capitalization		0	0	0	0	0	0
Days' receivables*		30.8	21.4	16.1	52.8	70.0	105.0
Days' payables		25.9	28.4	19.1	20.5	20.3	18.7
Ending inventory turnover (sales)		4.8x	4.6x	4.5x	4.1x	4.3x	4.3x
Ending inventory turnover (cost of sales)		3.5x	3.4x	3.3x	3.0x	3.2x	3.1x
Net property turnover		8.1x	8.4x	11.1x	10.9x	11.2x	11.7x
Total assets turnover		1.9x	1.9x	1.9x	1.8x	1.7x	1.6x
Net profit to total assets		2.5%	2.6%	2.7%	2.1%	2.0%	3.9%
Net profit to net worth		3.4%	3.3%	3.2%	2.5%	2.4%	4.8%
Net profit to net sales		1.3%	1.4%	1.4%	1.2%	1.2%	2.5%
Gross margin		27.0%	26.9%	26.4%	25.3%	26.2%	27.8%

* No separation of cash and credit sales; figure also distorted by credit subsidiary operations.

Industry Comparisons

A) SEARS, ROEBUCK & COMPANY

	1965	1964	1963	1962	1961	1960	1959
Current ratio	2.2	2.5	3.1	4.6	5.4	4.3	3.9
Acid test	1.3	1.9	2.2	3.1	3.5	2.7	2.4
Total debt to total assets .	55.6%	52.8%	49.4%	39.2%	35.2%	33.1%	35.6%
Long-term debt as percent of capitalization ..	16.8%	18.3%	20.4%	17.1%	18.1%	19.2%	20.2%
Days' receivables*	153.1	146.1	137.8	97.6	70.4	7.8	68.3
Days' payables†	16.6	15.4	13.4	11.7	18.4	12.0	10.8
Ending inventory turn-over (sales)	6.7x	6.8x	6.7x	7.0x	7.1x	6.8x	6.7x
Ending inventory turn-over (cost of sales) ...	4.1x	4.2x	4.1x	4.4x	4.5x	4.4x	4.3x
Net property turnover ...	11.8x	11.2x	10.4x	10.2x	10.1x	12.0x	12.8x
Total assets turnover ...	1.3x	1.3x	1.4x	1.6x	1.7x	1.9x	1.9x
Net profit to total assets ..	6.6%	7.1%	7.1%	8.4%	9.0%	8.7%	9.2%
Net profit to net worth ..	14.8%	15.1%	14.1%	13.7%	13.9%	13.0%	14.4%
Net profit to net sales ...	5.1%	5.3%	5.1%	5.1%	5.2%	4.6%	4.9%
Gross margin	38.6%	38.4%	38.0%	37.2%	36.3%	35.4%	35.6%

*No separation of cash and credit sales; figure also distorted by credit subsidiary operations.
†Cost of sales includes buying and occupancy expenses.

B) SPIEGEL, INCORPORATED

	1965*	1964	1963	1962	1961	1960	1959
Current ratio	N.A.	2.3	2.5	2.9	3.0	2.7	3.4
Acid test	N.A.	2.1	2.3	2.6	2.7	2.4	3.0
Total debt to total assets .	N.A.	80.4%	78.6%	79.2%	78.8%	81.6%	73.0%
Long-term debt as percent of capitalization	N.A.	57.7%	59.9%	60.8%	61.4%	56.8%	54.8%
Days' receivables†	N.A.	436	391	375	344	368	251
Days' payables	N.A.	25.6	22.7	20.3	24.5	22.8	29.6
Ending inventory turnover (sales)	N.A.	12.1x	13.0x	12.0x	13.5x	10.8x	12.5x
Ending inventory turnover (cost of sales)	N.A.	6.5x	7.1x	6.7x	7.6x	6.1x	7.2x
Net property turnover ...	N.A.	11.6x	33.1x	29.4x	28.0x	30.0x	31.6x
Total assets turnover	N.A.	0.7x	0.7x	0.8x	0.8x	0.9x	1.0x
Net profit to total assets ..	N.A.	2.0%	2.0%	2.0%	2.0%	4.1%	5.3%
Net profit to net worth ..	N.A.	10.4%	10.4%	9.5%	9.4%	18.3%	19.7%
Net profit to net sales ...	N.A.	3.0%	2.7%	2.6%	2.5%	4.4%	5.1%
Gross margin	N.A.	46.1%	45.5%	44.7%	44.1%	43.4%	42.2%

* Company was merged into Beneficial Finance Co., Oct. 25, 1965; N.A. means not available.
† No separation of cash and credit sales; figures unreliable.

Chapter 4

BASIC FINANCIAL
FORECASTING

IN THE PRECEDING chapters a discussion of funds flows and ratio analysis was presented with the aim of appraising past performance of a business enterprise. It was pointed out that past actions and results were basically only guides to analysis and that expected future performance and its fulfillment were the real criteria for success, credit worthiness, and investment merit.

In view of these considerations, an important task of the manager or analyst is that of financial forecasting, which in simplest terms is but a systematic projection of the expected actions of management in the form of schedules, budgets, and financial statements. In this process, past physical statistics, financial ratios, relationships and funds flows, as well as expected economic conditions, policy decisions, and future activities are combined and arranged in a working plan for the desired period. The usefulness of such planning is best seen when one considers the several areas where it is helpful. Forecasting becomes the basis of coordinated thinking about the future and reduces emergency decisions and surprises. It can be used to set standards of performance to measure and control the separate and collective decisions in the various parts of the company. It can be used to anticipate upcoming financial needs, or the financial effects of new or changing policies. It also forms a good basis for discussing funds needs with prospective creditors.

This chapter is a brief introduction to the basic framework of financial forecasting with emphasis on the commoner tools used. Much sophistication has been achieved in the forecasting of economic activity with the help of modern statistical techniques and data processing installation, but such refinements are be-

yond the scope of this book. At the end the student is directed
to various references for further study, if desired. The accompanying exercises will help him test his understanding of the
material.

I. *Pro Forma Operating Statements and Balance Sheets*

The most familiar expression of forecasted business activity
is a set of "pro forma" (hypothetical, anticipatory) statements
consisting of an operating (income) statement for the period
under study, and a balance sheet as of the end of the period.
For the preparation of such a set of statements much of the
reasoning and analytical groundwork introduced in the preceding chapters is helpful. No rigid set of rules exists for construct-
ing pro forma statements, since considerable common sense and
judgment are necessary to balance practical considerations such
as the degree of accuracy required against effort and time involved in the process. The format of the statements may vary
from "back-of-the-envelope" figures on key accounts to elaborate and detailed reports, depending on the needs of the manager or analyst. Also, in some cases, valid and precise figures on
future activities are available, while frequently the best data
obtainable are based on intuitive assumptions. Lacking more
specific information, it is often necessary merely to assume that
a past relationship, expressed as a ratio, can validly be extended
into the immediate future. In other cases, sophisticated statistical approaches to obtaining estimates of future performance
are warranted as a basis for detailed pro forma statements. For
purposes of illustration, a generalized approach is used below to
introduce pro forma statement preparation.

a) The *pro forma operating statement* is built around an estimate of the expected sales for the forecast period. The basis for
this estimate may vary from rule-of-thumb methods to profes-
sional economic estimates, market research, and detailed analyses of the competitive situation. Whatever the origin, the financial manager must give due consideration to the reasonableness
of the figures he puts on the operating statement. In many instances, if a long period is involved, a breakdown of the ex-

pected sales by months and weeks may be useful in forecasting, among other items, inventory and receivables levels as will be shown later.

Next, the manager tackles the cost of goods sold (cost of sales) section of the statement. Here he may use a simple analysis of past operating data, obtain a reasonably accurate percentage of sales to reflect current operating efficiency, cost expectations, and price trends. Thus he may use a figure such as 65 percent, or 75 percent, or any magnitude which may arise from an analysis of the past and future expectations.

A more detailed approach would be to consider independently what each component of the cost of goods sold section might be in relation to the sales total. In the case of a merchandising firm this question is answered relatively quickly by an examination of the prices and markups of the various goods handled. In an industrial firm, production cost accounting renders the analysis more complex. The basic objective here is that of taking the cost of expected production operations in the period (based on operating schedules and budgets) in terms of materials used, labor cost, and overhead cost, and determining how much of this production, if any, was used to build up inventories of finished goods, or whether less was produced than sold, which would mean a reduction in inventories of finished goods. In other words, if operating plans call for a buildup or reduction in finished goods inventories, the costs charged to the sales of the period must be less or more than the costs of production incurred in the period. Some achieve this allocation by adjusting all production costs by the difference between the beginning inventory of finished goods and the planned or estimated ending inventory of finished goods.[1] In this process, a schedule of unit production can be helpful, together with estimates of unit costs. Others simply determine expected unit costs and multiply these by the number of units expected to be sold, to obtain the cost of sales.

Complicating factors arise in the methods of inventory cost-

---

[1] Increases representing inventory buildups are subtracted, while decreases, representing inventory declines, are added.

ing, price level changes, and the proportion of fixed costs in the cost picture of a company. The last can become important if great changes in operating volume are expected, since product unit costs would be affected by the unchanged fixed costs.

In practice, detailed schedules and supporting data of operations, material use, labor cost, and overhead allocation, as well as inventory analysis, are of great help in estimating cost of goods sold. If such data are not readily available, as is usually true for the outsider, more sweeping estimates must suffice.

The other cost items in the operating statement pose somewhat less of a challenge. Selling cost are generally charged to the period in which they are incurred. Consequently, an estimate of future selling activity, and costs taken from promotional plans, manpower schedules, advertising commitments, etc., can be placed on the operating statement. Often the past ratio of selling expense to sales is a sufficiently reliable guide. Similarly, general and administrative expenses can be taken as percentages of sales from past experience, or as absolute dollar estimates from detailed budgets prepared separately. In both cases, however, the relationship of fixed and variable portions of these expenses should be remembered if one chooses to take a simple percentage-of-sales figure. Large changes in operating volume may lead to less than proportional changes in these expenses.

Other income and expenses, such as interest, rent, and so forth, can be estimated from the expected size of investments or obligations. The income tax bill can be estimated on the basis of the tax regulations, or a simple 50 percent rate may be sufficiently accurate for corporations. Dividend payments or other dispositions of earnings can usually be predetermined fairly well.

This brings us to the completion of the pro forma operating statement (see example), based on many assumptions, extrapolations, hopes, and expectations, but representing a reasonable estimate of expected revenues, costs, expenses and profits, taxes, and other magnitudes of financial interest.

b) The construction of the *pro forma balance sheet* is partially based upon the information represented in the operating statement, as well as the schedules and budgets, if any, sup-

ABC COMPANY

EXAMPLE OF PRO FORMA OPERATING STATEMENT
For the Quarter Ended September 30, 1966

Sales .... $175,000—Based on sales budget of $40,000 in July, $65,000
in August and $70,000 in September

Cost of sales: °
    Materials .... $ 70,000—Based on experience: 40% of sales
    Labor .... 35,000—Based on experience: 20% of sales
    Overhead .... 32,500—Based on experience: 23.6% of cost of goods sold

    $137,500

Gross profit .... $ 37,500

Selling expense ...... $ 16,000—Based on budget for three months
General and
    administrative ..... 15,000—Based on experience: $6250 fixed cost, plus vari-
    $ 31,000   able expense of 5% of sales

Operating profit 6,500
Interest expense ...... 500—Based on outstanding obligations, at 5%
Profit before taxes .... $ 6,000
Income taxes .... 1,800—Based on tax rate of 30% (under $25,000 net profit)

Net profit .... $ 4,200
Dividends .... 2,000—Based on dividend policy

    Net Profit to
    Earned Surplus $ 2,200   Net profit to be retained—see pro forma balance
                                     sheet

° Cost of sales could also be derived from estimated materials use, labor cost, and overhead costs for the *period*, adjusting this total by the change between beginning and ending inventories of finished goods and work in process.

porting the latter. It is in essence a forecast of expected funds flows, and each account of the balance sheet is independently examined and forecasted accordingly.

Beginning with the cash balance, the financial manager or analyst can assume a minimum level desired at the end of the period, or he can set any amount he wishes to have on hand. This flexibility in forecasting the amount of cash is characteristic of much of the process of drawing up pro forma statements, which are reflections of *future* policies. We shall return to the cash account later on, since it will be shown that a balance must be struck eventually between the forecasted uses and the forecasted sources of funds.

Next on the list is the accounts receivable balance. In the attempt to reflect the amount owed to the company by customers at the end of the forecast period, the financial manager can make use of the schedule of sales (sales budget) he used for his pro forma operating statement, or he can fall back on a ratio analysis of past performance. With valid assumptions, each method should yield a workable approximation of future accounts receivable. In the former method the financial manager can trace through estimated credit sales and estimated collections of these accounts, starting with the accounts outstanding at the beginning of the period. He will arrive at a balance of accounts receivable based on his detailed expectations of collections subtracted from credit sales on a day-to-day, week-to-week, or month-to-month basis. For this purpose it is helpful to have a *detailed* sales forecast. In the latter method, he can simply assume that at the end of the period a certain number of days' receivables will be outstanding, based on expected credit policies and collection success.

The use of this method without caution carries the risk of obscuring great fluctuations in sales. This may cause an under- or overstatement of accounts receivable. Both approaches, of course, are based on an assumption about the future quality of customers' accounts.

Inventories similarly can be estimated on the basis of turnover ratios or other relationships on one hand, or through careful estimates of purchase, production, and selling schedules on the other. The selection of the proper *ratio* or relationship will depend on an interpretation of past operating data together with an examination of future policies. The use of *schedules* in principle involves an analysis of the additions to the beginning inventory balances, such as purchases of materials or merchandise and production of goods, and reductions of these inventories through use and sale of the materials and goods. A more exact picture can usually be determined through the latter process, but the additional work and data required should be considered in relation to the need for this additional refinement. If severe ups and downs of activity are expected during the period, the more detailed method may become necessary. Incorrect inventory forecasts can lead to serious shortages of goods or financial strain.

Fixed assets, and changes in these accounts, are usually determined without much difficulty, since outlays for plant and equipment are generally planned ahead for some time, while depreciation schedules are relatively fixed and predictable.

Other assets, such as prepaid expenses, patents, goodwill, and so forth, can usually be predicted fairly easily for the forecast period, but often it is simply assumed that no changes will occur, barring specific information to the contrary.

On the liability side, accounts payable can be estimated by tracing through purchases and payments for the period, or by estimating the days' purchases to be outstanding at the end of the period. If no specific information on either approach is available, then the outside analyst is forced to select another reasonable historical relationship, such as accounts payable to cost of goods sold or materials cost, and apply it to future estimates.

Expected notes payable balances can easily be predicted since repayment schedules are known. Also, plans for specific borrowings can quickly be incorporated into the pro forma balance sheet. As will be seen later, however, this account is often used as the balancing figure ("plug") to equalize assets and liabilities, especially if the purpose of the pro forma forecast is to ascertain the expected need for borrowing funds on the basis of short-term notes.

Accrued liabilities, if analyzed by components, can be estimated in detail by determining the pattern of wage payments (e.g., monthly, weekly, or daily payrolls) tax payments, and interest obligations. These patterns can then be related to the data of the pro forma balance sheet and accruals determined. To avoid this detailed work the assumption of "no change" can also be made, unless the balances at the beginning of the period are grossly out of line with normal operations.

Long-term obligations, preferred stock, and common stock balances can be predicted with ease, since changes in these accounts depend on long-range plans to raise or repay capital. Capital surplus (paid-in surplus) is likewise determinable without great difficulty.

Earned surplus, in the simplest case, is predicted by adjusting the old balance for any profit or loss indicated in the pro forma operating statement, and for expected dividend payments, write-offs, or other adjustments to be made during the period.

Once all components of the pro forma balance sheet have been obtained, they are put in the form of a balance sheet and added accordingly (see accompanying example).

ABC CORPORATION

EXAMPLE OF PRO FORMA BALANCE SHEET
As of September 30, 1966

	Actual—June 30, 1966	Pro Forma—September 30, 1966
Cash	$ 11,000	$ 10,000—Minimum balance
Accounts receivable	42,500	70,000—30 days' sales (latest month)
Inventories	51,000	63,500—Annual turnover 8.66x
Total Current Assets	$104,500	$143,500
Fixed Assets	$ 94,500	$ 98,000—Planned acquisition of $3500 in August added
Accumulated depreciation	38,000	41,000—$1000 per month
Net fixed assets	$ 56,500	$ 57,000
Other assets	2,500	2,500—Assume same level
Total Assets	$163,500	$203,000
Accounts payable	$ 36,000	$ 39,000—Based on 40 days' purchases*
Notes payable	14,000	31,500—"*Plug*"*figure* (additional funds need $17,500)
Accrued liabilities	12,500	14,300—Increase in tax liability (see operating statement on p. 00)
Total Current Liabilities	$ 62,500	$ 84,800
Long-term debt	10,000	20,000—Expect to borrow $10,000 more in September
Common stock	50,000	55,000—Will raise $5000 from sale of stock in September
Earned surplus	41,000	43,200—Profit retained for period (see operating statement on p. 00; $2200)
Total Assets and Liabilities	$163,500	$203,000

* Purchases in August were $27,000, in September $30,000.

More likely than not the totals of assets and liabilities will not agree on the first attempt to construct a pro forma balance sheet. The reason is simply that each item was derived independently and according to the policies and conditions expected in the future. Funds flows were assumed without regard to debits or credits, or to balancing sources and uses. The balancing element now can be the cash account, or, if a desired balance has been established there, the notes payable (or any other liability account) to see *what effect the expectations of management had on the funds availability or needs of the enterprise.* The picture is thus completed by putting in a "plug figure" which will equalize the assets and liabilities. This figure can be positive or negative, depending on the funds flows assumed. A positive cash balance or a negative notes payable balance will represent an excess of funds over the forecast needs, while a negative cash balance or a positive notes payable balance will signal the need for obtaining additional funds. Appropriate adjustments must be made, of course, to reflect the plans of management.

The pro forma operating statement and balance sheet now represent the estimated complete picture of operations and financial condition at the end of the forecast period. The main use of these statements lies in appraising the funds needs or generation of the enterprise as of a *specific point in time,* its financial strength or weakness, the effect of growth or retrenchment, and the effect of changing policies over time. They usually are of a form and character familiar to the management, and directly comparable to statements on past performance. They also present the future relationships of assets, liabilities, revenues, costs, and profits, and thereby can be interpreted, for example, in the light of known credit requirements such as minimum working capital, a certain current ratio, debt versus equity restrictions, and other relationships.

Pro forma statements also share some of the drawbacks of analytical processes. Unless the forecast period is very short, or unless the financial manager prepares a series of weekly or monthly statements spanning the period, there is a risk that the pro forma statements, as rather sweeping summaries of individual transactions and fluctuations in the volume of operations, may obscure sizable funds needs or financial crises which can lie *between* the balance sheet dates. In this sense the pro forma analysis requires decisions regarding the choice of periods and dates for analysis, similar to those in funds flow and ratio analysis, as was pointed out in previous chapters. The following part of this chapter presents an approach to obtain data of a more continuous nature.

II. Cash Budgets

Instead of trying to determine profits and account changes over a given period, this method, somewhat more limited in scope, concerns itself with forecasting on a day-to-day, week-to-week, or month-to-month basis all *cash* receipts and payments. From these, cash surpluses or shortages are determined for each subperiod desired, and added to or subtracted from the cash balance on hand at the beginning of the forecast period. A cumulative running total of these additions and subtractions shows when the minimum cash balance (if stipulated by policy) has been reached, when the need for borrowing begins, how much is needed, and when the repayment of the loan can be made. Repayment is indicated, of course, only if the generation of cash during the forecast period is sufficient to pay off a temporary loan. Otherwise, the cash budget may have to be extended, or the raising of permanent capital may fill the gap.

In short, the cash budget is a schedule over time of cash inflows and outflows, not unlike a personal budget, and it represents the attempt to pinpoint cash surpluses and shortages so that the financial manager can always be certain to have sufficient money in the bank to cover the maturing obligations of the firm; similarly, he will know when he can invest any surpluses at a profit.

The basis for the cash budget again is formed by the various estimates or schedules of sales, purchases, production, sales activity, and so forth. Careful distinctions must be drawn, however, between the incidence of a credit sale, for instance, and the time of its collection. While the pro forma income statement recognizes sales when *made* (the accrual method of accounting), *not when collected*, the cash budget recognizes only *receipts*, regardless from which particular sales period they may stem, just as it only recognizes *payments*, regardless of the particular point of time at which the liability for the expenditure arose. Also, in the framework of the cash budget an expense does not necessarily represent a disbursement and therefore may not be shown, as in the case of depreciation. In short, the financial manager wants to determine, with the help of the cash budget, *when* he can expect to have a certain cash balance on hand and *when* he is expected to make disbursements from the bank account in order to meet current payment needs.

The various budgets and forecast schedules must, therefore, be rearranged to show the incidence of the cash flows as differentiated from the broader concept of funds flows. For this purpose, an analysis of collection period, credit terms, accrual periods, and so on, is necessary to be able to make the proper assumptions about the expected cash flow. For instance, if a 30-day collection period can be assumed, it is easiest to put on a monthly cash budget the receipts from credit sales of the prior month; for example, August sales would be September receipts. If a 15-day collection period is assumed, half of August credit sales would be collected in August while the other half would be received in September. This, of course, assumes a uniform volume of sales during the month. If more detailed assumptions can be drawn from the data, patterns such as "50 percent collection in month of sale, 30 percent in the following month, and 20 percent in third month" can be established.

Similar reasoning applies to purchases, where payments are often staggered with 10-, 15-, or 20-day lags, or in any other pattern reasonably observable. Cash purchases (and sales) would, of course, be recorded in the month of occurrence. The basic reasoning is simply that of putting into the proper time period the reasonably certain incidence of payment or receipt. All other receipts and disbursements are placed into the budget at the time cash changes hands. The accompanying example serves as an illustration.

ABC CORPORATION

EXAMPLE OF CASH BUDGET
For the Quarter Ended September 30, 1966

	May	June	July	August	September	Total for Quarter
Raw Data:						
Sales (credit) .	$45,000	$42,500	$ 40,000	$ 65,000	$ 70,000	$ 175,000
Purchases (on account) ..	27,000	27,000	24,000	27,000	30,000	81,000
Receipts:						
Collections (previous month's sales, i.e., assumed 30-day collection period)			$ 42,500	$ 40,000	$ 65,000	$ 147,500
Proceeds from sale of common stock			—	—	5,000	5,000
Proceeds from additional long-term debt issued			—	—	10,000	10,000
Total Receipts			$ 42,500	$ 40,000	$ 80,000	$ 162,500
Disbursements:						
Payment for purchases (staggered by 1⅓ months, i.e., payments made after 40 days)			$ 27,000°	$ 25,000	$ 26,000	$ 78,000
Outlays for labor (as per monthly operating plan)			10,500	11,500	12,500	34,500
Overhead (cash outlays per month)			10,000	10,500	11,000	31,500
Selling expenses (outlays per sales department budget)			5,000	5,000	6,000	16,000
General and administrative expense (outlays as per administrative budget)			5,000	5,000	5,000	15,000
Interest payments (due in September)			—	—	500	500
Payments for purchase of machinery (scheduled for August)			—	3,500	—	3,500
Dividends paid (scheduled for September)			—	—	2,000	2,000
Total Disbursements			$ 57,500	$ 60,500	$ 63,000	$ 181,000
Net receipts (disbursements)			$(15,000)	$(20,500)	$ 17,000	$ (18,500)
Cumulative net effect on cash			(15,000)	(35,500)	(18,500)	(18,500)
Beginning cash balance			$ 11,000	$ (4,000)	$(24,500)	$ 11,000
Net receipts (disbursements)			(15,000)	(20,500)	17,000	(18,500)
Ending cash balance			$ (4,000)	$(24,500)	$ (7,500)	$ (7,500)
Minimum cash balance			10,000	10,000	10,000	10,000
Funds Need; Additional Borrowing			$ 14,000	$ 34,500	$ 17,500	$ 17,500

To show the total borrowing of the company, the loan outstanding at the beginning of the period† should be added in:

Funds need; additional borrowing			$ 14,000	$ 34,500	$ 17,500	$ 17,500
Original loan			14,000	14,000	14,000	14,000
Total Borrowing Required			$ 28,000	$ 48,500	$ 31,500	$ 31,500

° Payment for last 10 days of May and first 20 days of June. Purchases during the last 10 days of June and all of July (a total of 40 days) are as yet unpaid at the end of July.
† See balance sheets, p. 90.

Reconciliation of Cash Budget with Pro Forma Statements

a) Funds Need:

The additional funds need is the same in both cases: $17,500, as is the total funds need: $31,500. Notice how the cash budget reveals an intermediate maximum additional funds need of $34,500, and a total funds need of $48,500 in August, which is concealed by the pro forma statements.

b) Cost of Sales and Inventories:*

Beginning inventory (balance sheet, June 30)	$ 51,000
Add:	
Materials purchases (raw data, cash budget)	81,000
Labor (cash budget)	34,500
Overhead (cash budget)	31,500
Depreciation (per pro forma balance sheet)	3,000
	$201,000
Less: Cost of sales (per pro forma operating statement) ...	137,500
Ending inventory (pro forma balance sheet, September 30)	$ 63,500

* Operating plan in cash budget must conform with inventory buildup or reduction, and cash outlays for labor and overhead must equal expenses; otherwise the reconciliation must make allowance for accruals.

c) Selling expense, general and administrative, interest, taxes, dividends and purchase of fixed assets are reflected equally in both places, again under the assumption that cash outlays equaled expenses. If this is not true, adjustments for accruals must be made.

Cash budgets and pro forma statements are intimately related, as they are both based upon the same basic information. In a sense, the cash budget is subsidiary to the pro forma statements, since the former deals only with on account, *cash*. It is possible to convert the information on the cash budget into pro forma statements and vice versa, if the assumptions are known and if information about noncash items such as depreciation can reasonably be determined. It is necessary, however, to have the balance sheet at the beginning of the period to make use of the various accounts in determining the ending balances.

Basically, forecasting in both frameworks is a summarization and simplification of the thousands of individual transactions expected to take place during the forecast period. Thereby it is vitally important to select the proper time intervals for which to plan, since fluctuations in activities and fluctuations in funds needs are of great importance to the financial manager. The need for careful selection of the time period and subperiods is intensified if a business is relatively short of funds, to avoid being embarrassed by an unforeseen peak borrowing need.

Some words of caution must be expressed at this point. All of the forecasting methods described here are based upon estimates, upon the best knowledge of what can be expected in the future. Consequently, whatever the use to be made of these forecasts, for internal performance evaluation, external credit investigation, or investment analysis, the results should not be considered as inviolable or fixed. A composite of estimates can at best be an approximation of what will really happen, because the uncertainty of the future cannot be reduced below a certain level. Sometimes a range of expected performance is profitably used to forecast the best and the worst possible outcome.

In view of the uncertainty of future events, it is also useful in many cases to rework forecasts with changes in certain *key* figures, such as inventory levels, accounts receivable balances, or sales volume. In the interest of economy of effort, much of the framework of the original forecast can be preserved in this process. As the analyst's skill improves, he can easily trace through with little additional work the effect of varying assumptions about key figures.

Also, the commonly encountered phenomenon of "conservatism" in estimates often defeats the purpose of forecasting as the best possible estimate of the future. Biased data under the guise of a "conservative outlook" can result in dangerous over- or understatements of forecast figures. This is especially troublesome when, as is common, the extent of the bias is not spelled out explicitly and is only vaguely assumed in the minds of the reviewers and users of the data. Insistence upon honest estimates and recognition that forecasts are not "sacred" or unchangeable do much to overcome this essentially administrative problem.

The preference of one type of forecast over the other, or even the simultaneous use of both methods, will depend on the purpose, the data provided, and the time and effort available. In whichever specific form it is made, the attempt systematically to make the best possible estimates and plans, *subject to revision*, is a legitimate and necessary function of management, which is especially well regarded by the prospective creditors or investors of the firm.

SELECTED REFERENCES

AMERICAN MANAGEMENT ASSOCIATION. Financial Management Series No. 87. *Budgetary Control and Financial Forecasting.* New York, 1958.

GUTHMANN, H. G., AND DOUGALL, H. E. *Corporate Financial Policy.* 4th ed. Englewood Cliffs, N.J.: Prentice-Hall, Inc., 1962, chaps. 5 and 6.

HOWARD, BION B., AND UPTON, MILLER. *Introduction to Business Finance.* New York: McGraw-Hill Book Co., 1953, Part III.

HUNT, PEARSON; WILLIAMS, CHARLES M.; AND DONALDSON, GORDON. *Basic Business Finance.* 3rd ed. Homewood, Ill.: Richard D. Irwin, Inc., 1964.

JOHNSON, ROBERT W. *Financial Management.* 2d ed. Boston, Mass.: Allyn & Bacon, Inc., 1962, chaps. 4 and 5.

PROBLEMS AND EXERCISES

I. *Forecasting the Impact of Policies*

1. The ABC Manufacturing Company has the following balance sheet as of September 30, 1966 (thousands of dollars):

Cash	$ 105
Marketable securities	35
Accounts receivable (net)	328
Inventories	490
Total Current Assets	$ 958
Fixed assets	$1,392
Accumulated depreciation	433
Net fixed assets	$ 959
Other assets	37
Total Assets	$1,954
Accounts payable	$ 175
Notes payable	150
Accrued expenses	166
Accrued taxes	49
Total Current Liabilities	$ 540
Mortgage payable	100
Preferred stock	300
Common stock	600
Earned surplus	414
Total Liabilities and Net Worth	$1,954

Sales for the past year were $6,350,000, cost of goods sold $5,430,000, purchases $3,672,000, depreciation $125,000, taxes $81,000, and net profit $83,000. The company desires a minimum cash balance of $40,000.

a) Assume that the company is contemplating a change in credit policy over the next year, so that by the end of the period it will have a collection period of 40 days. Sales, profits, and so on are expected to remain at the same level and, as in the past year, without seasonal swings. Balance sheet items not affected by the above data will be unchanged. What is the impact of the new credit policy on the balance sheet in terms of the current position? What sources of funds might be marshaled? Will the company have to borrow? What will be the effect if the collections slow to 60 days?

b) With the same assumptions as in (*a*) (but *no change* in credit policy), evaluate a shift in the suppliers' policy of extending credit to ABC, so that accounts outstanding at the end of the period will be 10 days' purchases. Note the impact on the balance sheet and on funds requirements.

c) Separately evaluate the start of a dividend policy of paying out 50 percent of earnings, and together with this the purchase of $133,000 of fixed assets.

d) If the company's ending inventory turnover were to change to six times cost of goods sold due to a policy of putting dealers' stocks on a consignment basis, what would be the financial effects? Assume *no* other changes in policy, such as given in (*a*), (*b*), or (*c*).

II. *Pro Forma Statements*

1. On September 1, 1966, the treasurer of Percy-Bowles, Inc. was in the process of forecasting the operations of his manufacturing firm for the next 12 months. The sales department had notified him of an expected sales volume of $3,950,000 for the coming fiscal year. He had before him the operating statement of the year just ended, and he examined it for guides to forecasting future operations (see below). A percentage analysis of this operating statement revealed a gross margin of 35 percent and a net profit of 10 percent of sales. The expected increase in volume was hoped to bring a favorable change in some of the components of the operating statement while other items would be affected differently.

a) Direct labor would constitute 24 percent of sales. While wage rates were expected to go up, efficiencies of larger scale production would more than offset this rise.

b) Materials cost was expected to continue unchanged in proportion to sales.

c) Depreciation would not be changed in the dollar amount, as no asset acquisitions or retirements of any consideable size were planned.

d) Overhead costs would rise by about 9 percent of the additional sales volume, the increase representing the variable portion of these costs.

e) Selling expense was to be stepped up by $100,000.

f) General and administrative expense would rise in proportion to sales.

g) Taxes, as in the past, were estimated at 50 percent of profits.

PERCY-BOWLES, INC.

OPERATING STATEMENT

For the Fiscal Year Ended August 31, 1966

(thousands of dollars)

Net Sales		$3,240	100%
Less: Cost of goods sold:			
Direct labor	$810		25%
Materials	486		15
Depreciation	130		4
Overhead	680	2,106	21 65
Gross profit		$1,134	35%
Selling expense	$292		9%
General and administrative expense	194	486	6 15
Profit before taxes		$ 648	20%
Federal income taxes		324	10
Net profit		$ 324	10%

Prepare a pro forma operating statement for the fiscal year ended August 31, 1967. What are the new percentage relationships?

2. In July, 1966, the food wholesale firm of Hepplefinger & Company was expecting another problematic year of operations. For purposes of planning the firm's funds needs and to obtain a picture of the future financial condition, the secretary-treaturer was asked to prepare a pro forma balance sheet as of June 30, 1967.

Below appears the balance sheet as of June 30, 1966. Hepplefinger & Company had a policy of maintaining a cash balance of at least $40,000. Acquisitions planned for the year were building improvements of $10,000, and the purchase of a delivery truck, $4,000. Net sales for the ensuing year were forecast at $2,650,000 with a gross margin of 8 percent. Purchases of merchandise were expected to total $2,475,000. The collection period was expected to be 14 days, and accounts payable outstanding would be 25 days. Profits for the period were budgeted at .4 percent of sales before taxes, and .2 percent after taxes. Dividends of $2500 would be paid during the year. Mortgage payments were $1500 per year, while the bank loan fluctuated with inventory as needed. Depreciation was expected to be $8300 for the coming year.

Prepare a pro forma balance sheet for Hepplefinger & Company as of June 30, 1967. Any accounts not specifically mentioned or provided for should be assumed as unchanged. Comment on your findings.

HEPPLEFINGER & COMPANY

BALANCE SHEET

June 30, 1966

Cash	$ 54,600
Accounts receivable	87,200
Inventories	221,900
Total Current Assets	$363,700
Land, buildings, equipment, trucks	$111,400
Accumulated depreciation	73,700
Net fixed assets	$ 37,700
Other assets	5,100
Total Assets	$406,500
Accounts payable	$150,900
Note payable—bank (secured by inventory)	120,000
Accrued expenses and taxes	11,300
Total Current Liabilities	$282,200
Mortgage payable—real estate	24,000
Capital stock	75,000
Earned surplus	25,300
Total Liabilities and Net Worth	$406,500

3. Ideas, Inc. was a new electronics manufacturing and research firm just founded by a group of graduates of well-known eastern schools of engineering and business administration. The founders contributed $55,000 in exchange for common stock, while $45,000 came from outsiders, also in exchange for common stock. The new firm expected to rent manufacturing space for $3000 per month. Overhead was estimated at $25,000 per month, plus $2000 depreciation on equipment worth $60,000 which was purchased with part of the initial funds. Firm orders for $500,000 worth of products were on hand with more expected. Sales would be $100,000 per month and a manufacturing capacity of $110,000 worth of goods per month (at sales prices) was expected to be attained shortly after operations began. Labor costs were estimated to amount to $20,000 per month, while materials and supplies would be purchased at the rate of $40,000 per month. The sales and administrative expenses were expected to run about $18,000 per month for the first several months. Collections would average about 40 days, while purchases were to be made mostly on terms of net 30 days. Inventories on hand were expected to average about $20,000 in raw materials and $60,000 in goods in process and finished goods. Patents, organization expense, and prepaid items would amount to about $5000; accrued wages would represent about one week's operations; while the income tax accrual (at 50 percent of profits) would be carried as incurred. The cash balance needed for operations was $15,000. The management was interested in the additional financial needs of the company after six months' operations. For this purpose, prepare both a pro forma operating statement and pro forma balance sheet. How much additional money is needed, and when do you believe the need will arise?

III. *Cash Budgets*

1. The general manager of Sooper Dooper Market, Inc. was planning his cash requirements for the coming six months beginning with October, 1966. He knew that there would be a number of outlays beyond the normal course of the business, and he wished to ascertain at which times he might have to look for additional funds, if any, and how large these needs might be. The following information was at his disposal (neglect income taxes for this example):

a) Sales: According to past experience, the manager expected sales of $250,000 in October, January, and March, $260,000 in December, $240,000 in November, and $230,000 in February. All of these sales would be cash sales.

b) The company sold a small lot it owned to local interests. Payments of $5000 each were to be received in January, February, and March.

c) Merchandise: Terms on groceries, meat, and produce averaged net 15 days, which meant that the manager would pay one half of his current purchases in a given month, as well as one half of the purchases of the previous month. The cost of merchandise averaged 78 percent of sales, and purchases were scheduled in proportion to expected sales. (Purchases in September were $196,000.)

d) Salaries and wages had been running at a constant 10 percent of sales and were paid in the month in which they occurred.

e) Rent of $4000 was paid every month.

f) Operating expenses had averaged 8 percent of sales and were paid when incurred.

g) Two payments of $5000 each on a note given to the local bank were to be made in October and January.

h) New store equipment costing $60,000 was acquired in September. Four monthly installments were to be paid in October, November, December, and January.

i) The officers of the company had advanced $12,000 of their own funds to the business. It was expected to reimburse the officers in two equal installments in February and March.

Prepare a cash budget for Sooper Dooper Market, Inc. Show the difference in receipts and disbursements for each month, and the cumulative difference. Also, show the effect of the six months' operations on the cash balance of the company, which is $50,000 on September 30. It is company policy not to let the cash balance drop below $25,000. How much in additional funds is needed, and when?

2. The New Frontier Manufacturing Company had experienced a period of very rapid sales growth, accompanied, however, by a relatively greater buildup of finished goods inventories which had resulted from management's anticipation of this growth and its desire to be able to meet all customer demands promptly. The president was concerned about the strain placed upon the company's finances by this growth and wished to institute a period of level production, in a determined effort to reduce the size of the company's inventories, together with greater pressure upon the company's customers to pay within the n/30 terms granted by the company. Outstanding accounts in August, 1966, represented 60 days of sales. The president asked the treasurer to prepare a cash budget for the next six months to ascertain the timing and amount of funds to be obtained under the new policies. The treasurer collected the following information for this purpose:

a) Sales: The sales manager estimated the sales for the next six months as follows: September, $1,450,000; October, $1,525,000; November, $1,625,000; December, $1,750,000; January, $1,825,000; February, $1,900,000. (Sales in July were $1,275,000 and $1,350,000 in August.) The credit manager expected to bring the collection period from 60 days on August 31 to 45 days on September 30, and to 30 days by October 31. Thereafter, he expected to keep the collections current.

b) The level production plan would involve the following monthly expenditures:

> Purchases of raw materials: $430,000 (terms n/45; July purchases were $500,000 and August purchases were $450,000).
> Wages and salaries: $145,000 (paid in the month of occurrence).
> Supplies, utilities, maintenance, overhead $280,000 (paid in the month of occurrence).

c) Selling and administrative expenses would be as follows: 15 percent of sales in September and October, 14 percent of sales in November and December, and 13 percent of sales in January and February, all paid within the month of occurrence.

d) Interest and dividends payable in January were $500,000, installments of federal income tax due were $250,000 on September 15, and $250,000 on December 15 (25 percent of estimated 1966 tax liability in each case).

e) Payments on notes payable were scheduled at $500,000 each in October and January.

Prepare the cash budget requested by the president. Also, what would be the amount of the funds generated or required (and their timing) if the collection period remained at 60 days? Explain the factors behind this difference.

3. The Havital Department Store was approaching the busy Christmas season and its attendant financial requirements. Two thirds of the store's sales were for cash, the remainder on charge accounts which averaged a collection period of 90 days.[1] Half of purchases were made on an n/45 day basis, 40 percent were on terms of 2/10, n/30 and 10 percent were for cash. The company's policy was to meet these terms. Accounts payable at the end of September were as follows:

Due from October 1 through October 10
  (2% discount to be taken) .... $ 50,000
Due during October (no discount) 165,000
Due by November 15 (no discount)   90,000
                                      $305,000

A cash budget was to be prepared to judge the possible financial needs of the company. The following information was available on estimated data (assume an even flow of sales and purchases during each month):

a) Sales:

October $570,000	January $480,000
November 510,000	February 420,000
December 750,000	March 540,000

b) Purchases:

October $450,000	January $250,000
November 400,000	February 390,000
December 230,000	March 350,000

c) Wages and salaries: average 18% of sales.
d) Cash operating expenses (advertising, supplies, etc.): 15% of sales.
e) Cash dividend due December 31, 1966: $25,000.
f) Federal income tax installment due December 15: $15,000.
g) Repayment of mortgage on property: $5000/month.
h) Beginning cash balance: $75,000 (October 1).
    Minimum cash balance: $50,000 (company policy).

Prepare the requested cash budget, showing by months the requirements for seasonal funds, if any.

IV. *Combination Problem*

1. From the cash budget worked out for New Frontier Manufacturing Company in section III, item 2, prepare a pro forma income statement

---

[1] Receivables outstanding at the end of September were aged as follows:

Due in October $170,000
Due in November 155,000
Due in December 180,000
                 $505,000 (assume no bad debt losses)

for the two months ended October 31, and a pro forma balance sheet as of October 31. The following supplementary information will be helpful:

NEW FRONTIER MANUFACTURING COMPANY

BALANCE SHEET
August 31, 1966

Cash	$ 525
Accounts receivable	2,625
Raw materials	1,920
Finished goods	4,260
Total Current Assets	$ 9,330
Fixed assets	$ 8,240
Accumulated depreciation	3,490
Net fixed assets	$ 4,750
Other assets	1,280
Total Assets	15,360
Accounts payable	$ 700
Notes payable	3,030
Accrued liabilities	1,490
Accrued taxes	250
Total Current Liabilities	$ 5,470
Long-term debt	3,500
Preferred stock	1,000
Common stock	3,500
Earned surplus	1,890
Total Liabilities and Net Worth	$15,360

a) Depreciation was scheduled at $35,000 per month.

b) Past experience showed that cost of goods sold had averaged 70 percent of sales. (Do not detail cost of goods sold on the pro forma operating statement.)

c) Materials usage during September and October was expected to be $550,000 per month.

d) Income taxes are assumed to be 50 percent.

e) Assume no changes in other assets and accrued liabilities, as well as in long-term debt and net worth.

Chapter 5

COST OF CAPITAL AND NEW FINANCING

THIS CHAPTER describes major cost of capital considerations, and relates them to other parts of the book, where they are applicable. The main emphasis is on the impact of changing a corporate capital structure through additional financing, since the techniques of analysis in this incremental framework are relatively straightforward. Later in the chapter, some discussion of the overall cost of capital of an existing capital structure will be broadly sketched.

Basic techniques of measuring and analyzing the choice between obtaining different types of capital, that is, debt, preferred stock, and common stock will be presented. In keeping with the character of the book as a collection of basic techniques, much of the background of theoretical knowledge and discussion must be omitted. Suffice it to say that the concept of cost of capital has been given increasing attention in recent years, especially as it affects the proper economic choices among investment opportunities (Chapter 6 presents major aspects of investment analysis); but there has also been considerable discussion on the proper measurement of the cost of capital itself, and how the circumstances around such an analysis affect the methods chosen. There is, of course, no such thing as *the* cost of capital applicable to all problems, since the concept is part of the dynamic and ever-changing financial and operational environment of the corporate enterprise. The interested student is referred to the references listed at the end of the chapter.

The Point of View

For purposes of this chapter, the point of view taken is that of the management of the corporation, responsible to its stockholders for a fair return on their investment. As pointed out in Chapter 1, management must make long-run plans and current operating decisions to balance the flow of funds and to supply corporate resources in the most advantageous manner within the specified risk exposure tolerated and the operating goals and policies established. The mixture of funds available allows for varying degrees of risk exposure, since the proportion of debt and equity (see Chapter 3) to a large extent determines the ability of a company to fulfill its obligations in periods of high and low earnings. This problem, of course, is tied to the concept of operating and financial leverage, explained in Chapter 2. Much thought and care must, therefore, go into the determination of the "right mix" of debt and equity in a company's capital structure—enough low-cost debt to boost the owners' return by applying debt funds to projects earning more than the cost of borrowing the funds required to finance them, and not too much debt to endanger the stockholders' return and even the company's solvency in low earnings periods. The latter point relates to the fact that fixed debt obligations must be met regardless of the circumstances.

Throughout the existence of a corporation the management thus makes financing decisions which result in changes in the funds sources used, and quite often in changes of the capital structure itself. These range from minor modifications to possible recapitalization. Each increment of change involves an increment of cost, as well as casting an effect on the cost of the total capital structure. For the time being let us concentrate on the increments of funds involved when a corporation incurs additional debt, or raises funds through issuing additional preferred or common stock. Techniques for measuring the cost of the many alternatives open to management discussed here are an important part of the decision process involved in making final commitments in the choices available.

The Cost of Debt

Debt in the course of business takes many forms, which range from trade obligations (accounts payable) to long-term mortgage

loans or debenture (bond) issues, and include simple notes payable to banks or individuals, tax payments owed to various governmental agencies, wages due, payments due on installment
purchases, and even lease obligations. The many types of debt,
and literally dozens of others not mentioned, can be analyzed
relatively easily as to the explicit cost involved for the company
incurring any one of them. Normally, debt arrangements carry
specific interest provisions payable either during the debt
period, at the end of it, or deducted from principal in advance
(called discounting). The explicit cost of debt thus can be reck-
oned as the cost to the corporation of this interest commitment.

Before we take up specific debt types and the analysis of their
cost, it should be remembered that interest is tax deductible for
corporations and that, therefore, the cost to a corporation (at
least to those with sufficient profits to pay taxes or able to apply
tax-averaging provisions) will be the fraction of the annual interest payment multiplied with a factor of "one minus the applicable tax rate." For example, if a corporation pays 6 percent
per annum on the principal of a note payable, and its effective
tax rate for incremental revenue or cost is 48 percent, the net
annual effective interest cost of this note will be:

$$1.0 - 0.48 = 0.52$$
$$0.52 \times 6 \text{ percent} = \underline{\underline{3.12}} \text{ percent (after taxes)}$$

The effect of the tax deductibility provision is to *reduce* the
cost of debt to corporations (and to individuals under many
circumstances) to a net amount after applying the prevailing tax
rate. This represents a contrast to other forms of capital, as will
be shown in later sections.

a) Operating Debt

First a few comments about operating debt, that is, short-term
or revolving obligations incurred in the ordinary everyday operations of most businesses. Some of these debt funds are in fact
provided free of any explicit cost, under trade terms generally
accepted in the type of industry in which the company operates.
Foremost in this category are accounts payable, which are in-

curred under terms such as 2/10, n/30, or 3/15, n/45, or n/45, and many variations thereof. Up to 10 or 15 days, therefore, or even as long as 45 days the company being billed for goods or services received can hold off payment and make use of the values received on credit without cost. In most cases, if payment is made within a specified period, such as 2/10, or 3/15, which means 2 percent discount if paid in 10 days, or 3 percent discount if paid within 15 days from the date of the invoice, the company can in fact reduce the cost of goods or services by the amount specified. This inducement is given to help the vendor collect his funds faster and thus to reduce the funds tied up in accounts receivable. If the discount period is missed, however, the net amount is due the vendor by the end of the credit period specified. If the debtor company makes use of this option, a very definite cost is incurred for this prolonging of the time it can make use of the funds. The cost is an *opportunity cost* incurred in the form of cash discounts lost. For instance, if the credit terms are 2/10, n/30, the cost of using the funds involved for an extra 20 days amounts to 2 percent in cash discounts lost, or an annual rate of

$$\frac{360 \text{ days}}{20 \text{ days}} \times 2 \text{ percent} = \underline{\underline{36 \text{ percent}}} \text{ (before taxes)}$$

In this case, however, the corporation does not have to report as income the cash discount it would have earned otherwise, and the explicit net cost must be reduced by the taxes saved. If taxes can be assumed at 48 percent of income, the net cost for 20 days' use of the creditor's funds amounts to

$$1.0 - 0.48 = 0.52$$
$$0.52 \times 2 \text{ percent} = \underline{\underline{1.04 \text{ percent}}} \text{ (after taxes)}$$

On an annual basis, this cost works out to a still fairly sizable figure, as compared to the "prime interest rate" (between 4 percent and 6 percent) generally charged large corporations of impeccable credit rating:

$$\frac{360 \text{ days}}{20 \text{ days}} \times 1.04 \text{ percent} = \underline{\underline{18.72 \text{ percent}}} \text{ (after taxes)}$$

Some companies, especially small and rapidly growing enterprises, make it a practice to use accounts payable as a source of credit, often unilaterally exceeding the outside limits of credit terms by sizable periods. The explicit cost of accounts payable credit drops, of course, the longer the funds are kept, since normally no interest charges are levied by the trade creditor. In extreme cases, unpaid accounts may even be converted to notes payable, with or without interest, upon the request of the trade creditor who wishes to establish a somewhat stronger claim. From the standpoint of credit worthiness and company reputation, it is clearly a poor practice to go beyond the credit period stipulated, since other prospective creditors will take such tardy performance into account when evaluating further credit extension. This is a part of the implicit cost of credit and other forms of capital, which will be discussed later.

Another form of operating debt is the short-term note or an installment contract in which interest is charged ahead of time, or is added to the amount of principal stated in the contract. For example, a $1000 note which carries 6 percent interest will provide the debtor with only $940, if the time period is one year and the note is discounted, that is, the interest is deducted in advance. The effective cost before taxes is thus higher than the stated interest, since the company is paying $60 for the privilege of borrowing $940 for one year:

$$\frac{\$60}{\$940} = 6.39 \text{ percent (before taxes)}$$

The tax adjustment to this figure is made in the identical fashion as shown before. In the case of an installment contract for, say, $1000 payable in four quarterly installments, with interest of 5 percent on the original balance, the effective cost of interest is much higher than stated, since over the term of the contract decreasing amounts of principal are outstanding and used by the borrowing company. A quick method of calculating the approximate effective cost is to argue that over the term of the contract the principal amount drops from $1000 to zero, with the average amount outstanding being roughly 1/2 of the principal, or $500. The contractual interest was 5 percent of $1000, or $50, which became part of each of the four payments. When this interest is applied to the average amount of capital in the hands of the borrowing company, the following doubling of the cost is the result:

$$\frac{\$50}{\$500} = \underline{\underline{10 \text{ percent}}} \text{ (before taxes)}$$

Tax adjustments again are the same as before. If the contract runs over more than one year, care must be taken to annualize the interest cost, that is, to relate the result to the period in question to arrive at a truly annual cost, which is the usual period of comparison.

The approximate results achieved with the calculation just presented can be refined by present value (time-discounting) techniques described in Chapter 6, which is a useful approach where precision is required and where the timing of the funds flows extends over considerable time periods in various patterns. In fact, banks and other lending institutions use tables based on present value techniques to calculate charges and payments connected with contracts of this sort. It should be added, however, that the simple averaging technique is applicable in many circumstances, including personal finance, to obtain a fair approximation of the "true" (effective) or explicit cost of contracts of this type.

The preceding discussion has shown ways to ascertain the cost of common operational debt obligations, whose explicit cost may range from zero to quite substantial rates of interest. The explicit cost documented here is not the only aspect of such debt or debt in general, however. As already mentioned, repayment schedules have to be met, and while repayment of principal has no cost aspect in an explicit sense, it nevertheless forces the financial manager to forecast and plan cash receipts and disbursements with care. Chapter 3 has shown techniques to this effect. Another aspect of the burden of debt, and one that will become more important in the ensuing discussion, is the *implicit* impact of various forms of debt obligation on the credit worthiness of a company for future capital needs. In other words, the balance between debt and equity may become precarious and forestall further borrowing for some time, until the company has "worked itself from under" its debt obligations. Having "closed off the top," as debt-heavy operations are often characterized, can be a costly endeavor, both in terms of the risk of not meeting obligations as they fall due, and in having to turn to much costlier sources of credit or equity funds as additional needs arise. More detail will be given later.

b) Debt in the Capital Structure

So far we have concentrated on operating debt and discussed essentially short-term obligations and their cost. More important in the long run, however, is the cost and proportion of debt in the more permanent form—as part of the long-term capital structure of the corporation. Here planning decisions involving cost and the amount of debt must be made relative to investments in expanded or diversified activities, and commitments made in this area are by their nature bound to have a much more lasting impact than short-term working capital decisions. At times, long-run decisions involve refinancing or even recapitalization, with significant and far-reaching changes in a company's capital structure. We shall, therefore, turn our attention to the role of debt in the capital structure, at first limiting the discussion to incremental amounts of debt added to an existing structure.

Since the basic objective and obligation of management normally is to provide adequate earnings to the stockholders, and to maintain or even enhance their investment, we shall continue to take this point of view in analyzing a hypothetical company, the ABC Corporation, whose balance sheet (abbreviated) looks as follows:

ABC CORPORATION

BALANCE SHEET

(millions of dollars)

Assets		Liabilities and Net Worth	
Current assets	$15	Current liabilities	$ 7
Fixed assets (net)	29	Common stock	10
Other assets	1	Retained earnings	18
Total	$45	Total	$45

The corporation has 1 million shares of common stock outstanding, with a par value of $10 per share. Most recently, ABC Corporation has earned $11 million before taxes on sales of $115 million. Income taxes paid amounted to 5.3 million. To appraise the current position of the ABC stockholders in this picture, we first calculate the earnings per share of common stock (eps), using a format which will be useful throughout this chapter. This format also lists the obligations of the corporation in order of their normal priority. The start is made by stating the earnings before interest and taxes (EBIT)—we are ignoring short-term interest obligations because of their temporary nature and their position as part of the normal operating picture, and these charges are assumed to have been deducted properly in arriving at the EBIT figure quoted. The data will be arranged as follows:

ABC CORPORATION

EARNINGS PER SHARE CALCULATION
(thousands of dollars, except per share)

Earnings before interest and taxes (EBIT)	$11,000
Less interest charges on long-term debt	0
Earnings before income taxes	$11,000
Federal income taxes at 48%	5,280
Earnings after income taxes	$ 5,720
Less preferred dividends	0
Earnings available for common stock	$ 5,720
Common shares outstanding (number)	1 million
Earnings per share (eps)	$ 5.72
Less common dividends per share	2.50
Retained earnings per share	$ 3.22
Retained earnings in total	$ 3,220

The preceding analysis has made provision, as part of the general framework adopted, for interest on long-term debt and preferred dividends, both of which do not appear at this stage, since the hypothetical ABC Corporation has neither long-term debt nor preferred stock outstanding. The result of the calculations shows that with the prior claims removed by assumption, and federal income taxes paid, the residual of earning available to common stockholders provides them with a claim of $5.72

per share, which is legally theirs and of which a dividend of $2.50 per share has been voted as a cash distribution by the board of directors. It should be noted that the value of dividends to individual stockholders varies considerably, depending among other things on the income and tax bracket of the individual involved. For purposes of this discussion we must think of the management obligation to the group of stockholders as a whole. The determination has been made by the board that a $2.50 cash dividend meets with the corporate policy the stockholders have come to accept. We assume that this dividend payout (between 40 percent and 50 percent of earnings) has been carried out for many years and that earnings have steadily grown by about 6 percent over the years. Let us further assume that the stock is widely held and traded, and that it commands a price of about $60 to $65 in the current stock market, roughly 11 times current earnings. This is the picture which at the moment is presented to the current stockholders.

The introduction of debt to this capital structure and the earnings position of the company will demonstrate the concepts discussed earlier in this chapter, and will also point the way toward the investment considerations in Chapter 6. Let us assume that the corporation is planning to borrow $10 million in order to exploit a new product it has developed. There is the possibility of issuing bonds which are not secured by specific assets of the company, but are issued upon the general corporate credit standing. The "debenture" bonds will carry an interest rate of 6 percent, will become due 20 years from the date of issue, and will carry a sinking fund provision of $400,000 per year, beginning with the fifth year. The final balance outstanding at the end of 20 years will become payable as a "balloon" payment of $4 million. After the new product has been introduced, the company hopes for increased earnings of at least $1,500,000 before taxes, and expects little risk of obsolescence or competitive inroads for the next 10 to 15 years.

Let us now trace the impact of debt added to the current corporate picture, both in terms of the effect on the stockholders' position expressed in earnings and dividends, and in terms of the explicit cost of the newly created debt. The general framework used earlier will again be employed, and the calculation will be made for two situations: first, the immediate impact of issuing debt without the offsetting benefits of the investment, and second, the picture presented once the investment has become operative and the additional earnings from the new product have come about.

The results of the calculations (see below) show that the effect of adding debt to the capital structure is an immediate reduction of the earnings to the common stockholders, an "immediate dilution" caused by the interest cost entering the earnings pattern of ABC Corporation. Earnings after interest and taxes dropped in total by $312,000, which is, of course, 52 percent (1.0 minus 0.48) of the pretax interest cost of $600,000. Earnings per share dropped about 31 cents, a reduction of 5.4 percent from the prior level, purely because of the additional interest burden which on a per share basis amounts to about 31 cents: $312,000 divided by 1 million shares.

ABC CORPORATION

EARNINGS PER SHARE WITH NEW BOND ISSUE
(thousands of dollars, except where per share)

	Current	With New Product
Earnings before interest and taxes (EBIT)	$11,000	$12,500
Less interest charges on long-term debt	600	600
Earnings before income taxes	$10,400	$11,900
Federal income taxes at 48%	4,992	5,712
Earnings after income taxes	$ 5,408	$ 6,188
Less preferred dividends	0	0
Earnings available for common stock	$ 5,408	$ 6,188
Common shares outstanding (number)	1 million	1 million
Earnings per share (eps)	$ 5.41	$ 6.19
Less common dividends per share	2.50	2.50
Retained earnings per share	$ 2.91	$ 3.69
Retained earnings in total	$ 2,908	$ 3,688
Original eps	$ 5.72	$ 5.72
Change in eps	$ −0.31	$ +0.47
Percent change in eps	−5.4%	+8.2%

The explicit cost of capital of this increment in funds is thus 52 percent of 6 percent, or 3.12 percent per annum, given the tax rate of 48 percent. Another way of figuring this cost is, of course, the relationship of after-tax interest cost per annum to the amount provided, which in this case is $312,000 for $10 million, or 3.12 percent. Finally, we can also argue that the explicit cost is the specific change in earnings to the stockholders, as pointed out before. If earnings are not disturbed by any other factor, as we have assumed, the drop represents the explicit cost, or, if earnings were sufficient on the new investment just to offset the drop through interest costs, leaving earnings unchanged, the investment would have earned precisely the explicit cost of the capital provided for the purpose. This reasoning leads us to investigate the second column of calculations, which show the effect of the new product operations.

We observe that as soon as the new product has been successfully brought out, the additional earnings generated more than offset the explicit cost of the debentures. The after-tax earnings in the second column jump to $6,188,000, a net increase over the original situation of $468,000. As a consequence, earnings per share climbed 46.8 cents above the original level, an increase of about 8 percent. The successful investment of the funds provided by the debentures has more than offset their explicit cost, and thereby boosted common earnings per share by about 8 percent. In the economic sense, incremental earnings exceed incremental cost, and the investment—given our earnings assumption is going to be proven true—has made possible a true increment of value. In fact, would it not have been sufficient for the investment to earn, after taxes, only $312,000, since it leaves the stockholders as well off as before? By earning more, financial leverage (Chapter 2) has taken over and given the equity owners a "free ride"—or has it?

At first glance, the statements just made seem reasonable, but there are a number of serious questions which must be asked. First of all, no mention has been made of the sinking fund obligations which will begin five years hence, and which call for a cash outlay of $400,000 per year. Even though this amount is not tax deductible and must be paid out of the cash flows generated by the company, are we justified in ascribing no "cost" to this obligation? In fact, this debt burden amounts to 40 cents per share per year which is no longer available for dividends or other corporate purposes because it is committed to repayment of principal. If the investment just earns the interest cost on the debt, how could we repay the principal? Chapter 6 deals with this concept and how to calculate proper measures. Another question is again related to the investment purpose: What if the earnings of the investment turned out much worse than expected? Should this risk have a bearing on the "cost" considerations? What risk is incurred here—especially since interest of $600,000 per year must be paid during the first five years, and the sinking fund is added to the slowly decreasing interest in the remainder of the period? Is this obligation pattern of any consequence to future or current creditors, stockholders, and other interested parties? Finally, should the explicit after-tax cost of 3.12 percent per annum be used as a criterion to judge the return or yield of the investment, or is a broader, more overall cost of capital applicable here? Will there always be an opportunity to borrow at this cost, and will it not be necessary to raise funds in some form other than debt next time? Could the investment project stand up under such conditions? In other words, is it possible to look at capital costs in small increments, depending on the type of capital raised?

These significant questions lead into the whole framework of capital budgeting and the many areas of economic reasoning and theory involved. Clearly, the debt burden implicitly costs the company some of its flexibility. The risk of changes in earnings and the contractual obligation for fixed debt service payments is real, and must be carefully appraised. Some of the ratios in Chapter 3 are helpful, and clues as to the reasonableness of "earnings coverage" of the obligations can be gained from them. The judgment of the investment must be made in broader terms, and the incremental debt cost is not sufficient, as will be seen later. In short, we have seen only the beginning of the analysis of such a decision, and are limited by the scope of this book to consider all aspects. The need to interrelate the cost and effects of different types of capital to the total structure and to considerations of operational and investment strategy has been established here, and we shall return to this broader subject after having discussed the other two main types of funds in the capital structure, preferred stock and common stock.

The Cost of Preferred Stock

The next analysis deals with the cost of adding preferred stock to a capital structure. This type of equity holds a middle ground between debt on the one hand, and common stock on the other. Subordinated to the various creditors of the corporation, the preferred stockholder has a prior claim to corporate earnings up to the amount of the preferred dividend. In the case of liquidation, his claims are satisfied before the common stockholders receive any compensation toward their claims from the residual. Because of the near-equity position of the preferred stock, the preferred dividend is not considered a tax-deductible corporate expense by the Internal Revenue Service, and such dividends therefore represent an outflow of *after-tax* funds from the corporation. For instance, a 7 percent preferred stock, par value $100 per share, costs the issuing corporation $7 in after-tax earnings, so that for each dollar of dividends to be provided, the corporation must earn $1.92 before taxes. Where our 6 percent bond had an after-tax cost of 3.12 percent, the 7 percent preferred has an after-tax cost of 7 percent. Thus, the stated dividend rate on a preferred stock is directly comparable to the *tax-adjusted* interest rate on a bond. We have been assuming all along, of course, that in our examples the bonds or preferreds were issued at such prices as to yield the corporation proceeds exactly equal to the par or face value—in other words, the corporation receives $100 for a share of $100 preferred after expenses of issuing the shares. Where there is a difference, as often happens because of market conditions, it is necessary first to calculate an *effective* interest or dividend rate based on the amount of capital effectively received, and then to proceed with the tax adjustments to arrive at comparable figures.

To illustrate further the effect of introducing preferred stock to a corporate capital structure, we return to the example of the ABC Corporation. This time the $10 million in capital to be added is raised via 7 percent preferred stock (100,000 shares) at $100 per share net proceeds to the corporation after legal and issuing expenses.

The results of the calculations (see below) reflect a sizable drop in the earnings under the initial conditions—a much more serious effect than in the case of the 6 percent bonds, and a small increase in earnings after the investment became operative, again much different from the bond alternative. The stated 7 percent dividend rate is the cause, since it is slightly higher than the bond interest, and crucially so since it is not tax deductible. This time the annual cost is shown as a deduction from after-tax earnings, and the immediate dilution amounts to 70 cents per share, or 12.2 percent. The eventual increase with the new earnings is only 8 cents per share or 1.4 percent. A total of $700,000 of after-tax funds is committed, which leaves very little room for a net gain from the earnings generated by the investment—$1,500,000 before taxes and $780,000 after taxes.

ABC CORPORATION

EARNINGS PER SHARE WITH NEW PREFERRED ISSUE
(thousands of dollars, except per share)

	Current	With New Product
Earnings before interest and taxes (EBIT)	$11,000	$12,500
Less interest charges on long-term debt	0	0
Earnings before income taxes	$11,000	$12,500
Federal income taxes at 48%	5,280	6,000
Earnings after income taxes	$ 5,720	$ 6,500
Less preferred dividends	700	700
Earnings available for common stock	$ 5,020	$ 5,800
Common shares outstanding (number)	1 million	1 million
Earnings per share (eps)	$ 5.02	$ 5.80
Less common dividends per share	2.50	2.50
Retained earnings per share	$ 2.52	$ 3.30
Retained earnings in total	$ 2,520	$ 3,300
Original eps	$ 5.72	$ 5.72
Change in eps	$ −0.70	$ +0.08
Percent change in eps	−12.2%	+1.4%

Again we observe financial leverage at work, although the higher fixed cost imposed allows only an 8 cents per share increase, only a little more than a 1 percent rise or boost in common earnings over prior levels. Had the investment earned precisely $\frac{\$700}{0.52} = \$1,346,154$ before taxes, no change in earnings per share would have resulted—the cost offsetting the earnings to break even. Note that this sizable break-even earnings figure compares with $600,000 required for the bonds.

Similar questions as in the first case arise. What about the repayment of principal? Even though preferred stock is generally a very long-term proposition, provisions for a "call" of the stock may have been made, or a sinking fund may be established eventually to retire the stock. Even though these are not necessarily contractual obligations, these potential actions can cause future funds drains. Also, there is the question of the risk of not earning the preferred dividend, and similarly blocking common dividends thereby. This risk must be analyzed in terms of the likely range of earnings to be encountered, and the factors of uncertainty in the corporate picture. As far as the explicit cost of the preferred was concerned, it was established as the effective dividend rate divided by the factor of "one minus the tax rate," but what about the effect of the preferred on future financing? Again, is it fair to assess the investment proposal against this specific cost? What if next time only common stock could be used to finance the next investment because we have reduced our flexibility by imposing the layer of claims on our capital structure? Let us now turn to the analysis of the cost and effect of common stock to complete the picture of the three alternatives.

The Cost of Common Stock

When we stated earlier that management is responsible to maintain or improve the position of the common stockholder, the implication was that what a company represented to its stockholders is a three-fold benefit. First, it provides earnings which are accumulated for various purposes; second, it may pay dividends in part to pass on these earnings to the stockholder; and third, it provides appreciation of the value of the shares of stock in the market, in response to growing earnings and/or dividends or both, all of which hopefully do not fluctuate too much around a normal growth trend. Any action, especially in the form of long-term commitments, which jeopardizes or materially changes the stockholder's expectations about a particular company should be deemed harmful or at least worthy of serious reappraisal. (Chapter 7 takes up questions relating the value of securities to the circumstances surrounding them.)

How are these considerations related to calculating a cost of capital in a particular circumstance? There is no directly measurable aspect in this problem, as there was in the case of interest cost for bonds and dividend cost for preferred. Common dividends are declared at the discretion of the corporate board of directors, and while many companies strive for a stable and consistent dividend policy (e.g., American Telephone and Telegraph Company), others pay very erratic dividends or none at all. In fact, many small "growth situations" of the space age scientific bent would not even consider paying a dividend, since stockholders of this type of company prefer to see earnings reinvested in the company to achieve maximum acceleration of growth and hopefully a corresponding rise of the value of the stock in the market. Yet, one cannot argue that issuing stock without considering paying a dividend means that this stock has no cost to the issuing company and the existing stockholders!

In the previous examples we calculated earnings per share and discussed the effect of the cost of incremental capital in terms of the immediate dilution of earnings. Let us use the same approach for stock and then discuss the implications. ABC Corporation, we assume, will issue $10 million worth of new common stock, at an assumed net price of $50 per share to the corporation after underwriters' fees and legal expenses. The discount from the current market price of $60 should ensure the success of the issue. Under these conditions, a total of 200,000 shares have to be issued, an increase of 20 percent in the number of shares outstanding. The calculation of the earnings picture is shown on the next page:

ABC CORPORATION

Earnings per Share with New Common Stock Issue
(thousands of dollars, except per share)

	Current	With New Product
Earnings before interest and taxes (EBIT)	$11,000	$12,500
Less interest charges on long-term debt	0	0
Earnings before income taxes	$11,000	$12,500
Federal income taxes at 48%	5,280	6,000
Earnings after income taxes	$ 5,720	$ 6,500
Less preferred dividends	0	0
Earnings available for common stock	$ 5,720	$ 6,500
Common shares outstanding (number)	1.2 million	1.2 million
Earnings per share (eps)	$ 4.77	$ 5.42
Less common dividends per share	2.50	2.50
Retained earnings per share	$ 2.27	$ 2.92
Retained earnings in total	$ 2,720	$ 3,500
Original eps	$ 5.72	$ 5.72
Change in eps	$ −0.95	$ −0.30
Percent change in eps	−16.6%	−5.3%

We observe that the initial dilution under current conditions is a full 95 cents per share, a drop of 16.6 percent which is the most severe among the three examples analyzed. Common stock, when viewed in this light, must surely be the costliest type of capital, since it causes the greatest dilution in the stockholders' position. Moreover, an annual funds drain of at least $500,000 in after-tax earnings is imposed in the form of dividends, assuming that the corporation will continue its policy of paying regular cash dividends. This funds drain amounts to a pre-tax earnings requirement of

$$\$2.50 \times 200{,}000 \text{ shares} = \$500{,}000 \text{ (after taxes)}$$

$$\frac{\$500{,}000}{0.52} = \$961{,}538 \text{ (before taxes)}$$

This requirement of almost $1 million can be compared to $600,000 for the bonds and $1,346,154 for the preferred.

Not only is there the immediate dilution effect, but a continuing dilution, since in contrast to the other two types of capital, which had fixed interest and dividend provisions, the new shares created share on an equal footing with the old in any increase (and decrease) of corporate earnings. Growth in earnings per share will thus tend to be retarded, because of the additional 20 percent of new shares outstanding.

When we turn to the second column to study the effect of the increased earnings from the new product, it is quite apparent that there remains a net dilution of earnings per share of 30 cents, or 5.3 percent. The earnings from the new investment were not sufficient to offset the earnings claims of the new stockholders and at the same time maintain the old level of per share earnings. The explicit cost of the stock thus is greater than the earnings from the capital raised, under our framework of analysis. The explicit cost of the common stock can be expressed by relating the earnings required to maintain the old eps level to the amount of capital provided by the stock. This is done most easily on a per share basis, where the earnings required for each new share are precisely $5.72 (the old level), and the proceeds to the company are $50. The result of the calculation can be shown as follows:

$$\frac{\$5.72}{\$50.00} = \underline{\underline{11.44 \text{ percent (after taxes)}}}$$

It should be noted that this must be compared with 3.12 percent for the bonds and 7 percent for the preferred. The same result can be achieved by making the analysis on a total basis. The $10 million provided is represented by 200,000 shares, for each of which earnings of $5.72 must be provided to leave the old stockholders' earnings position unchanged. Thus, a total of $1,144,000 in earnings after taxes ($2,200,000 before taxes) must be achieved by the investment of this capital to maintain the break-even situation. This works out to 11.44 percent after taxes, and a full 22 percent before taxes. One look at the investment proposition we have assumed here shows that projected earnings are not sufficient to provide this offsetting effect. Had the earnings from the new product been higher than $2.2 million before taxes, the investment would boost the earnings per share of both old and new stockholders.

This discussion of explicit cost has not touched upon the third expectation of stockholders, that for growth in market value of their shares. This growth is related, but not exclusively, to the performance of corporate earnings over the long run, and the static picture shown so far is not flexible enough to deal with this aspect. We also recall that in the previous examples some questions were raised as to possible fluctuations in earnings and their effect upon the fixed obligations incurred by the corporation with the type of capital chosen. Since it is too laborious to calculate earnings per share and other data for a great number of earnings levels and assumptions, we can exploit the linear relationships between the factors analyzed and use a graphic approach to compare the alternate sources of financing and to gauge the relative impact of fluctuations in EBIT as part of the measurement of cost and relative desirability.

Graphic Analysis of Earnings Fluctuations

First it will be useful to recap the data developed to this point, for the original situation as well as for the three alternatives of financing the new product. The eps data will be recorded as points on a chart, often called "EBIT chart," which has earnings per share in dollars on the vertical axis, and EBIT in millions of dollars on the horizontal axis. The straight lines can be drawn once two points have been determined for each, and it is common to develop for this purpose the intersection of each line with the horizontal axis, where eps are zero. These points can easily be found by working our framework of analysis backward, that is, starting with the eps of zero and building up to the EBIT which just provides for this condition. This calculation, for each of the alternatives and the original situation, is shown below the recap of the previous eps analyses.

These two sets of calculations provide us with sufficient data to draw the linear functions of eps and EBIT for the various situations, as shown in the graphic presentation on page 125. There it can be quickly observed visually that the conclusions drawn from the previously analyzed two EBIT levels hold true over the fairly wide range presented. There is one difference, however, and that is the behavior of eps under the common stock alternative, which has a slope different from all others and in fact intersects the debt and preferred eps lines. The latter two alternatives are represented by parallel lines, which are also parallel to the line for the original situation. This phenomenon is easily explained in that the parallel shift to the right represents the superimposition of fixed interest or dividend charges on earnings available to the common stockholders, whose number of shares does not change over the whole range of EBIT studied. The addition of common stock, on the other hand, represents a proportional dilution of earnings for the common stockholders at all levels, and the imposition of 20 percent additional shares causes earnings per share for everyone to rise less rapidly with EBIT. This accounts for the lesser slope of the common stock line.

The significance of the intersections should now become clear: It is not possible to speak of "a cost of capital" for incremental common stock without referring to the "normal" earnings level the existing stockholders have come to expect—if we accept the framework of analysis used here. There are overall EBIT levels in the lower ranges where the imposition of additional common stock can have a lesser effect upon eps than one

ABC CORPORATION

RECAP OF EPS ANALYSES
(thousands of dollars, except per share)

	Original	Debt	Preferred	Common
EBIT	$11,000	$12,500	$12,500	$12,500
Less interest	0	600	0	0
Earnings before tax	$11,000	$11,900	$12,500	$12,500
Taxes at 48%	5,280	5,712	6,000	6,000
Earnings after tax	$ 5,720	$ 6,188	$ 6,500	$ 6,500
Preferred dividends	0	0	700	0
Earnings to common	$ 5,720	$ 6,188	$ 5,800	$ 6,500
Common shares	1 million	1 million	1 million	1.2 million
eps	$ 5.72	$ 6.19	$ 5.80	$ 5.42
Common dividends	2.50	2.50	2.50	2.50
Retained earnings	$ 3.22	$ 3.69	$ 3.30	$ 2.92
Total retained	$ 3,220	$ 3,688	$ 3,300	$ 3,500
Original dilution	0	−5.4%	−12.2%	−16.6%
Final eps change	0	+8.2%	+1.4%	−5.3%
Explicit cost	0	3.12%	7.0%	11.44%

ABC CORPORATION

ZERO EPS CALCULATION
(thousands of dollars)

	Original	Debt	Preferred	Common
eps	0	0	0	0
Common shares	1 million	1 million	1 million	1.2 million
Earnings to common	0	0	0	0
Preferred dividends	0	0	$ 700	0
Earnings after tax	0	0	700	0
Taxes at 48%	0	0	646	0
Earnings before taxes	0	0	$1346	0
Interest	0	$600	0	0
EBIT	0	$600	$1346	0

ABC CORPORATION

RANGE OF EBIT AND EPS CHART

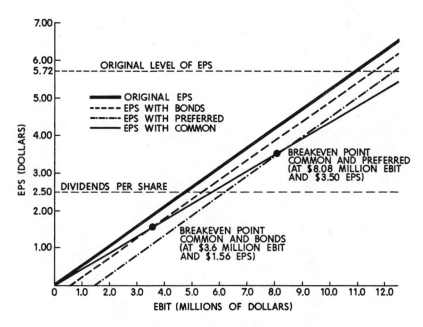

or the other alternatives, or both. This has a bearing upon the analysis of the choice to be made, since it is possible to tell the effect on eps if EBIT should fluctuate rapidly in the future. If future EBIT levels are expected to move fairly well within the range bounded by the two break-even points, common stock looks more attractive from the standpoint of depressing eps than preferred stock, for instance. If EBIT can be expected to move fairly well to the right of the second break-even point, the issuance of common stock appears to be the least desirable alternative from the eps standpoint. All these considerations are made, of course, without changing the assumptions about the terms under which the three forms of capital can be issued. If those terms, such as the issue price of common stock, can be expected to change, a new chart must of course be drawn up.

We can quite easily determine the intersections between the eps lines, which represent the break-even points among the alternatives. For this purpose we simply express the conditions of any pair of lines in the form of equations, in which eps is considered equal and we solve the equations for EBIT. To illustrate, let the following conditions stand:

E = EBIT level for break-even among alternatives
i = annual interest on bonds, in dollars (before taxes)
t = tax rate applicable
p = annual preferred dividends, in dollars
n = number of common shares outstanding

The equation for any particular line can be found by substituting known facts in the following expression:

$$\text{eps} = \frac{(E - i)(1 - t) - p}{n}$$

We can now find the EBIT break-even level for bonds and common stock. For this purpose, we write the two expressions and consider them as equal:

$$\overset{(Bonds)}{\frac{(E - 600,000)\,0.52 - 0}{1,000,000}} = \overset{(Common)}{\frac{(E - 0)\,0.52 - 0}{1,200,000}}$$

Solving for E we obtain the following result:

$$0.52\,E - 312,000 = \frac{0.52\,E}{1.2} \;;$$
$$0.624\,E - 374,400 = 0.52\,E$$
$$E = \$3,600,000$$

This result can easily be verified on the chart shown on page 000. When the same approach is applied to the preferred stock and common stock alternatives, the following result emerges:

$$\begin{array}{cc} (Preferred) & (Common) \\ \dfrac{(E-0)\,0.52 - 700,000}{1,000,000} = & \dfrac{(E-0)\,0.52 - 0}{1,200,000} \end{array}$$

$$0.52\,E - 700,000 = \frac{0.52\,E}{1.2}$$

$$0.624\,E - 840,000 = 0.52\,E$$

$$E = \underline{\$8,076,920}$$

Again, the chart can be used for verification of this result.

Apart from the use of the EBIT chart for the representation of EBIT fluctuations and the attendant impact on eps, it is also possible to show the impact of the dividend requirement for common stock on the three alternatives. The horizontal line at eps $2.50 in the chart on page 125 represents the current annual dividend, and where this line intersects the alternative eps lines we can read off the minimum level of EBIT required in each case to supply this dividend. Similarly, it is possible to reflect on the chart the burden of sinking funds or other regular repayment provisions, by carrying the calculations one step further and arriving at so-called uncommitted earnings per share (ueps) for each alternative. This is done simply by subtracting the after-tax cost of such repayments on a per share basis from those alternatives where they apply, and drawing lines for these uncommitted eps, which will fall to the right of the straight eps lines.

By now the usefulness of this framework for the analysis of the various alternatives should be clear, and the student is invited to think through the implications of the variety of tests that can be applied. As another example, it is possible to check the EBIT level under each alternative which would endanger the $2.50 per share dividend assuming a variety of payout ratios, such as 50 percent. In this case, a line could be drawn at the $5.00 eps level extending horizontally, and the intersections would represent the minimal EBIT levels to support a $2.50 dividend under the 50 percent payout assumption. The decision maker would have to assess the likelihood of the EBIT reaching this level and the risk this represents to the stockholders. Again it must be emphasized, however, that the chart works only under the fixed assumptions about proceeds received and interest and preferred dividend rates. If these can reasonably be assumed to change, the positions of the eps lines on the graph must be changed.

An additional word about the significance of changes in the issuing conditions: As the "spread" between the alternatives increases, that is, as the differences among the explicit cost of the alternatives increase, the distance between the parallel lines will increase. This is simply a reflection of the increasingly depressant effect on eps of the imposition of fixed obligations. A similar effect is achieved by increasing the relative size of the increment capital issue. The slope of the lines is governed by the degree of "leverage" in the existing capital structure. In other words, if there had already been debt or preferred stock in the original capital structure, the original eps would have risen and fallen much more sharply, and with them the eps of the fixed cost alternatives. The slope of the eps line for the common stock alternative is, of course, governed by the relative number of shares issued, which in turn is related to the explicit cost of common stock as we have defined it—normal eps compared to the issue proceeds.

The Choice among the Alternatives

So far we have essentially limited the incremental analysis of the several alternatives to determining the explicit cost of each, and making some comparisons in the process. At this point it will be helpful to summarize the total framework in which the decision maker must consider the choice among the three alternatives. During the discussion of explicit cost it became clear that cost is only one factor in this choice, that there are implicit "costs" involved, and that the problem must be seen in the perspective of time and under changing conditions. There are at least four major areas of consideration involved, and the discussion of incremental analysis would not be complete without the highlights of each of these.

The first area is, of course, the question of the *explicit cost* of the alternatives, which we have discussed in detail. This aspect increases in importance with the spread between the alternatives, and the risk of earnings fluctuations which could cause default. Clearly, the decision maker will wish to minimize the cost he has to pay for funds, in the interest of enhancing the stockholders' earnings.

The second area is the question of *flexibility*, which has been mentioned before. As an increment of capital is added, the choice among alternatives may be limited on the next round, because the current choice may have imposed fixed obligations, restrictive covenants, and other constraints. The importance of this problem must be seen in the light of future capital needs, and the deliberations must include long-range plans and corporate policies with regard to expansion and diversification. Also present in this area of flexibility is the problem of the funds flows required to service each alternative. Again, long-range planning is required to forecast the impact of these requirements on the corporate treasury.

The third element in the decision is *timing*, in relation to the movements of prices in the securities markets. There is a direct relationship to relative explicit cost, since price and cost are inseparable. Thus, the timing aspect will influence the spread between the alternatives, but more than that, will at times preclude or favor particular alternatives. For instance, in times of depressed stock prices, bonds may prove to be the most suitable alternative both from a cost and a demand standpoint. Since the proceeds from an issue depend on the success of the placement—public or private—of the securities involved, the conditions at the time can seriously affect the choice.

Finally, there is the element of *control*, that is, the relative dilution of ownership and control of the enterprise suffered by the existing stockholders. This issue is most important in the case of the common stock alternative, since the only direct dilution can come from issuing additional shares. In an indirect sense the control of existing stockholders may be endangered by restrictive provisions and covenants necessary to obtain bond financing, or by the prior and preferrred rights of preferred stockholders. The degree of dilution of ownership will be much more important in closely held corporations, as it may affect the immediate direction certain majority stockholders exercise over the company. The dilution of earnings and the possible retardation of earnings growth connected with a dilution of ownership is, of course, a more generally applicable phenomenon.

It is clear from this brief résumé of considerations that the decision among alternative sources of incremental capital is not one that can be simply made on cost alone, even though cost is a most important first consideration. There are no hard and fast rules as to precisely how such decisions can be made, since they depend so much on circumstances and points of view of the decision makers. The techniques presented earlier can assist in specifically calculating quantifiable results, which then must be entered in the decision process.

Cost of Capital in Composites

At the beginning of this chapter, we stated that the main emphasis would be on incremental reasoning in connection with determining cost of capital under particular circumstances. We have done this and wound up with an overall framework of analysis. In order to have a better perspective of cost of capital, it is necessary to cover briefly the most difficult area in this economic analysis—the problem of an overall composite cost of capital in an existing capital structure for the purpose of judging the desirability of existing and new investment projects. Here a variety of problems converge: The reliability and meaning of recorded values (see Chapter 7) carried on the balance sheet, the reliability and meaning of earnings in the measurement process, and the reliability and meaning of market values for stocks involved, to name just the most important ones. To keep the discussion manageable within the framework of this book, we shall assume from the start that a weighted cost of capital is the proper concept to use, and that common equity consists of the total of stated stock values and retained earnings. Furthermore, we shall not deal with the problem of cash flows from depreciation and their cost, since some aspects of this are covered in Chapter 6. The interested student is referred to the bibliography at the end of this chapter for further reading on these aspects as well as on the ones briefly covered here.

From the outset we shall state that any source of funds to a corporation has a cost attached to it, either explicit or implicit, at times in the form of an opportunity cost. The composite of funds open to corporate management contains many types, the relative importance of which usually is determined by corporate policy, but whose amounts may fluctuate from time to time as conditions change. As we observed earlier, no one particular funds source can be used as a cost standard to gauge the desirability of investments, rather, over the long run it is the mixture of funds sources that will determine the economic cutoff point for investment propositions. One common attempt at arriving at such a measure, namely, the minimum allowable return from an investment in the interest of the stockholders is the weighted cost of the capital structure. We return to our ABC Corporation, which we assume has undergone a few changes over the years, and now has a capital structure which in the view of its management represents closely the long-run relationships they would like to see perpetuated. An abbreviated balance sheet is shown below:

ABC CORPORATION

BALANCE SHEET
(thousands of dollars)

Assets		Liabilities and Net Worth	
Current assets	$27,500	Current liabilities	$ 9,500
Fixed assets (net)	35,000	Bonds (6%)	12,000
Other assets	1,500	Preferred stock ($7)	6,000
	$64,000	Common stock	10,000
		Retained earnings	26,500
			$64,000

We further assume that the market price of the common stock currently fluctuates between $70 and $75, that most recent eps were $6.25, and that overall company prospects are quite satisfactory, with normal growth in earnings per share forecasted by financial analysts. Management is faced with the problem of having to decide among a variety of capital investments, both of a replacement and minor expansion nature, and wishes to set a minimum "floor" in the form of a weighted cost of capital below which the yield of investments to be made should not fall.

The first step will be to determine the proportions of capital types in the long-term capital structure, the second will be to attach a relevant explicit cost to each, and finally the combined cost has to be determined. In the first step we take each of the long-term forms of capital and make a judgment as to which relative value they represent. The obvious initial reaction will be to take the book value of each as recorded on the balance sheet, but upon some reflection doubts will arise as to the wisdom of this action in every case. For instance, the bonds of the corporation, if traded publicly, may currently be quoted above or below par and thus represent quite a different value from what is shown on the balance sheet. Similarly, preferred stock may be traded at market values different from what is recorded on the books. The most critical difference of this sort is likely to exist in the case of common stock, whose value in the market rarely corresponds with the recorded owner's equity—stated value plus retained earnings and any unspecified surplus reserves. We observe that in the case of ABC Corporation there is such a differential, namely, while the 1 million shares on the books of the corporation are represented by a book value of $36.50 per share, the current market is trading these shares between $70 and $75—just twice the stated value.

Those arguing for taking the book value of each type of capital will say that the assets recorded on the other side of the balance sheet are represented on the same terms (original "cost"), and that this would preserve consistency of approach. The other side of the argument, however, must be that the increase in the market value of the stock in fact represents an increase in the value of the corporation's assets as reflected in the market judgment about the earnings power of these assets in the framework of the company. If this is so, the balance sheet is no longer representative of economic facts, and must be adjusted to reflect the realities of valuation with which the common stockholder is faced. (See Chapter 7 for a discussion of valuation concepts.) Counterarguments will bring up the point that the vagaries of the marketplace are not a reliable judgment of value, as witnessed, for instance, by the great slide in the stock market in 1966, when within a few months the stock market averages dropped by one-fourth from the highs achieved at midyear.

Without going into the many fine points which can be discussed here, it should by now be clear that a satisfactory answer to the first step will lie neither in the precise book value proportions (although many financial analysts will start from here) nor in current market value proportions, but somewhere between these values. In some instances, neither measure may provide any satisfaction, and a judgmental valuation must be established. In keeping with the basic nature of the book, we shall present the two approaches mentioned while cautioning that many considerations call for utmost care in the application of the results.

The book value approach will result in the following proportions of capital sources:

Bonds	$12,000	22.02%
Preferred	6,000	11.01
Common stock	36,500	66.97
Totals	$54,500	100.00%

The market value approach will look as follows, if we assume that common stock has a fair market value of $72.50 per share, and that preferred stock is traded at $110 per share, and bonds at par:

Bonds	$12,000	13.18%
Preferred	6,600	7.24
Common stock	72,500	79.58
Totals	$91,100	100.00%

The second step is to determine the cost of the individual components. The simplest of these is the cost of the bonds, whose explicit cost based on the interest charges is 3.12 percent after taxes. The next item, preferred stock, can differ whether we take the book value or the market value into our calculations. In the first instance, the after-tax cost is simply the $7.00 dividend rate, or 7 percent, while in the other we must adjust for the premium at which the stock is trading in the market by relating the $7 dividend to the $110 market price per share. This works out to an effective cost of $7 ÷ $110 = 6.36 percent. Finally, the explicit cost of the common stock was earlier established as the normal earnings per share related to the normal market value. In the case of ABC Corporation, this works out to $6.25 eps related to a normal market price of $72.50, or 8.62 percent. We shall apply this cost both to the book value and market value approaches.

The completed calculations will now appear as follows:

	Book Value Approach			Market Value Approach		
	Cost	Weight	Composite	Cost	Weight	Composite
Bonds	3.12%	0.220	0.6864	3.12%	0.132	0.4118
Preferred	7.00	0.110	0.7700	6.36	0.072	0.0460
Common stock	8.62	0.670	5.7754	8.62	0.796	6.8615
Totals		1.000	7.2318%		1.000	7.3193%

It is apparent that the results under the two approaches do not differ materially, yet, it is also clear that under different circumstances there could be sizable differences in the two cost of capital figures. Such differences can be due to varying spreads among the types of capital provided, the relative proportions of capital in the capital structure, and in the case of common stock the size, stability and nature of earnings and their valuation in the marketplace. The student is invited to make calculations on his own to observe the differences under varying assumptions. One example would be to calculate the results for the ABC Corporation in the earlier sections of this chapter, by assuming acceptance of the different incremental capital propositions.

This brief discussion of cost of capital under some stipulated conditions has served to demonstrate the complexity of the problem, and the need to analyze carefully the many economic issues involved. The concept of cost of capital cannot be separated from the particular application intended—otherwise the results are meaningless. Yet, as applications and points of view differ, so do the results of the calculations, and assumptions even within a specified framework for analysis can become tenuous. One way to help minimize the problem of uncertainty about the results is to reason out the range within which variables can be reasonably expected to fluctuate, and then to establish the limits or extremes for the results as the basis for deliberation. This is not new, in fact this approach is sound under most problem-solving conditions, and cost of capital considerations are no exception.

SELECTED REFERENCES

DONALDSON, GORDON. *Corporate Debt Capacity: A Study of Corporate Debt Policy and the Determination of Corporate Debt Capacity.* Boston, Mass.: Division of Research, Harvard Business School, 1961.

HUNT, PEARSON; WILLIAMS, CHARLES M.; AND DONALDSON, GORDON. *Basic Business Finance.* 3rd ed. Homewood, Ill.: Richard D. Irwin, Inc., 1964.

COHEN, JEROME B., AND ROBBINS, SIDNEY M. *The Financial Manager: Basic Aspects of Financial Administration.* New York: Harper & Row, Publishers, 1966.

JACOBY, NEIL H., AND WESTON, J. FRED. "Factors Influencing Managerial Decisions in Determining Forms of Business Financing: An Exploratory Study." *Conference on Research in Business Finance.* National Bureau of Economic Research, 1952, pp. 145–85.

LINTNER, JOHN. "The Cost of Capital and Optimal Financing of Corporate Growth." *Journal of Finance* 18 (May, 1963), pp. 292–310.

MAYER, ROBERT W. "Analysis of Internal Risk in the Industrial Firm," *Financial Analysts Journal* 15, No. 5 (November 1959), pp. 91–95.

SOLOMON, EZRA. *The Management of Corporate Capital.* New York: Free Press, 1959. (Selected articles.)

————. "Leverage and the Cost of Capital." *Journal of Finance* 18 (May, 1963), pp. 273–79.

PROBLEMS AND EXERCISES

I. *Earnings Calculations*

a) The ABC Corporation is considering the issue of 50,000 shares of common stock, in addition to the 300,000 shares already outstanding.

The proceeds are to be used for an expansion program which will boost expected operating profit by 20 percent. The company's pro forma operating statement which includes the additional profit is forecast as follows:

ABC CORPORATION
PRO FORMA OPERATING STATEMENT

For the Year Ended December 31, 1967
(thousands of dollars)

Net sales	$69,000
Cost of sales*	42,300
Gross profit	$26,700
Selling and administrative expense	9,250
Operating profit	$17,450
Interest	450
Profit before taxes	$17,000
Federal income tax (50%)	8,500
Net profit	$ 8,500

* Includes depreciation of $2250.

In the company's capital structure are bonds of $10 million, with an annual sinking fund provision of $900,000.

Calculate the eps, ueps, and cash flow per share with and without the expected additional profit. Also calculate the immediate dilution and the net dilution in eps.

b) In the data assumed above, substitute an issue of 50,000 shares of 6 percent preferred stock for the common. Calculate the eps and ueps for the preferred alternative, and determine the immediate dilution and the net dilution.

c) Instead of the preferred stock in (b), substitute an issue of $5 million of 5 percent debentures with no sinking fund. Make the same calculations.

II. Cost of Capital, Break-Even Analysis, Leverage, etc.

a) The earnings per share of XYZ Company are currently $8.50 on 100,000 shares outstanding. Interest paid on outstanding long-term obligations is $250,000 per annum, and preferred dividends amount to $150,000. Depreciation is charged at the rate of $125,000 per annum, while taxes average 50 percent of profits. The company plans to raise an additional $3 million in capital, either through issuing 24,000 shares of common at $125 net, or through issuing 30,000 shares of 5 percent preferred stock. What is the explicit cost of capital of either alternative? What is the explicit cost of capital in problem I (c)? What generalizations can you make about the explicit cost of capital? Show calculations (long form).

b) Determine the eps equivalency point between the two alternatives listed in (a). (Common stock and preferred stock.)

c) Demonstrate the effect of leverage with the preferred stock alternative listed in (*a*), by assuming EBIT levels of $1 million, $1.5 million, $2.25 million and $3,375 million, and by observing the eps increases resulting from the EBIT increases. Comment.

d) Assume a common dividend of $6 per share. Determine the eps/dps break-even point for the common stock alternative under (*a*). (By calculation.)

III. *Comprehensive Problem*

The LSB Company was faced with a choice of three alternative ways of financing a diversification program which would help assure greater stability in sales and profits. The $25 million needed could be raised as follows: First, 500,000 shares at $50 (net to the company) could be issued. Second, 250,000 shares of 6 percent preferred stock could be sold, while the third alternative was an issue of 4.5 percent sinking fund ($1 million per year) debentures. The company had debt outstanding on which an annual sinking fund payment of $1 million was made and annual interest of $1.2 million was paid. Also, dividends on preferred stock outstanding were $1.2 millions per year, and common shares numbered 1 million.

EBIT levels of the company had fluctuated between $12 million and $30 million. The earnings expected from the additional funds were estimated at $4 million (EBIT). The most recent annual EBIT had been $22 million. Common dividends currently paid were $2 per share. (Relationships are exaggerated for better contrast; assume proceeds to the company after expenses equal the par value of the securities issued in the second and third alternatives.)

From this information calculate and also graphically illustrate the following:

1. Eps; ueps; (draw chart),
2. Immediate dilution; net dilution; explicit cost of capital,
3. Break-even point between eps,
4. Dividend coverage; zero eps.

Chapter 6

TECHNIQUES OF
INVESTMENT ANALYSIS IN
CAPITAL BUDGETING

THE PURPOSE OF this chapter is to discuss, with due regard to the conceptual and administrative setting, some of the major techniques of investment analysis which are part of the broad process of capital budgeting. There are innumerable refinements, areas of learned dispute, and unresolved issues connected with the techniques and concepts of capital budgeting which are clearly beyond the scope of this book. Instead, we have attempted to explain the basic character of the techniques of investment analysis and to give the student a foundation upon which further specialized knowledge could be built up. References at the end of this chapter point to opportunities for additional study and information.

The Nature of Capital Budgeting

As was pointed out in Chapter 1, one of management's basic duties is to regulate the flow of funds in such a way that the objectives of an enterprise (normally represented by the desires of the stockholders) are fulfilled. There should result a properly balanced grouping of investments on the one hand, and a properly balanced capital structure on the other. This structural combination is established through innumerable operating and investment decisions made in the course of time. Hopefully these will yield the desired earnings and growth pattern within the constraints of competitive, technological, and managerial risk. Uncertainty surrounds this framework because of the various risks encountered, and because of the fact that investment decisions as well as financing decisions are made for the *future*, whereby past experience can only be a guide.

The process of allocating funds to their proper uses on the one hand and the choice of proper sources of these funds on the other can be pictured in the following diagram:

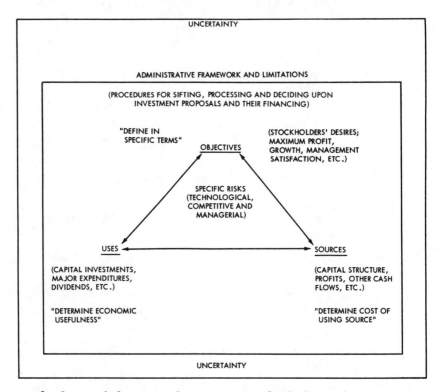

The base of the triangle represents the balance between uses and sources of funds, while the top of the triangle represents the objectives of the enterprise, however these may be defined. Whenever management makes a decision to invest funds to build a new plant, to increase the level of working capital, or for any other purpose, it must consider both the sources of those funds and their propriety, and the nature of the objectives of the enterprise. Similarly, if management wishes to raise funds in one way or another, the uses of the funds and the objectives of the enterprise must be considered. This closely knit relationship between the three corners of the triangle is indicated by the double arrows connecting each corner with the others. The whole process is carried out in the specific administrative framework of the organization which must enhance the flow of ideas and the making of proper decisions under conditions of uncertainty. In the center of the triangle, as a major issue to be considered, are the specific risks encountered in the funds allocation scheme. No part of this triangular reasoning can be handled effectively without consideration of risk factors, since the uncertain nature of the decisions calls for rational analysis and deliberative judgment. Were it possible to reduce all elements entering into the funds allocation decisions to fully reliable quantities, the process of determining optimum decisions would merely be a matter of mathematical calculation. Without such perfect knowledge, however, approximations and "educated guesses" must be substituted, which makes the whole process more difficult and subject to human error. Furthermore, the availability of funds from various sources and the need for skilled manpower to handle the analysis and institution of investment projects are real constraints.

An additional factor complicating this picture is the dynamic nature of business enterprise. Ideally, a business manager might wish to sit down and plan his funds source and funds allocation decisions over a long period of time, say 10, 20, or more years. This would require a great deal of foreknowledge of future events; but given this foresight, he would be able to determine the best opportunities in which to invest funds and the best sources from which these funds should come. Then he could balance this pattern in the light of the objectives of the enterprise. In reality, it is very difficult to look ahead specifically more than two or three years; consequently, our manager has to deal with relatively short periods of time within which to balance his uses and sources of funds. This means that he is dealing with a revolving "planning horizon," on which new opportunities constantly emerge, but which at the same time limits his vision. The result is that he often may have committed limited funds to current opportunities, while future better opportunities just below the horizon are not yet known to him. These might yield him greater economic returns and greater growth were he to wait and commit his funds to them. Yet he cannot wait without action, otherwise competition will pass him by. This fact of life can seriously impair the pure concept of maximizing economic returns and growth commensurate with the objectives of the enterprise that ideally could be achieved by taking the theoretical long-range look, but it cannot be circumvented.

The matching of funds uses and sources in line with the corporate objectives is generally referred to as *capital budgeting*. In its broadest sense the concept includes all funds movements in the enterprise, both short-term movements, such as operating cash flows, and long-term movements, such as investments in plant and equipment, changes in working capital levels, and capital structure planning. A somewhat narrower working definition of capital budgeting commonly refers to the process of planning the *long-term* movements of funds. These involve decisions for outlays on plant, equipment, new product lines, major changes in distribution methods, or similar long-range funds commitments made from various funds sources.

Some indications of the difficult nature of the process have been given in the preceding pages. It is not the purpose of this chapter to deal with the many policy issues, economic concepts, administrative involvements, and different schools of thought involved. In keeping with the nature of this book as a collection of major techniques of analysis, the following presentation will deal with the commoner aspects of investment analysis as one of the areas of capital budgeting where a variety of useful tools has been developed.

Before going into a description of some of these tools and the concepts underlying them, a few more comments are required to put this material in its proper perspective. The basic concept of the funds allocation process is one of *choice from among alternatives*, imperfect as it may be. There are usually more opportunities for investment than funds or manpower available for the purpose. Consequently, rational investment analysis requires the development at any one time of a list of investment opportunities ranked in order of their desirability according to some rational criterion, such as economic return, or "necessity" as expressed in terms of competitive advantage or continuity of the enterprise. Generally, the various criteria used for this process are given in terms of economic advantage (except where no economic return can be measured, such as a new cafeteria for employees), which implies the need to analyze investment opportunities from the point of view of evaluating the funds outlay required with the economic gains created thereby.

As pointed out in Chapter 5, the use of various ˙sources of funds, such as profits, new issues of capital stock, and debt financing, is not possible without incurring an economic cost. This is obvious when one thinks, for example, of debt for which interest has to be paid, or more generally, when one considers that the use of a given source of funds for one particular purpose precludes its use for some other purpose whose economic returns are thus lost. Apart from the specific method of identifying the cost of various funds sources, it can be stated that no funds are "free," and that any commitment of funds for an investment also implies an economic cost that has to be paid and which hopefully is lower than the economic return gained.

In a highly oversimplified sense one could describe the capital budgeting process as the matching of funds uses and funds sources until the economic return from additional investment is equal to the additional cost entailed in using funds for this purpose. There is a growing body of literature which engages in various attempts to grapple with the complex economic issues of capital budgeting as a complete concept, and references are provided at the end of this chapter for the interested student. For the purpose of making individual rational investment analyses as part of the overall capital budgeting process the following concepts and techniques will be useful. It must be remembered, nevertheless, that investment analysis is *only* *one* element of the broader process described.

Components of Investment Analysis

The basic process of investment analysis consists of the previously described evaluation of the investment outlay in terms of the economic gains provided by it. These can then be matched with the cost of the funds used for this purpose. This investment evaluation can be carried out in a number of ways, but it is necessary to define in greater detail the components going into this process. The investment outlay is represented by the *net investment* required for the proposition, while the economic benefits are represented by the *operating cash flows* generated by the investment. Another important element is the time period during which the investment will be made and its benefits realized. The nature of these components and the estimates underlying them must be examined and established before the various techniques of analysis can be applied to derive measures of relative desirability.

a) *Net Investment*. The first element to be analyzed is the concept of net investment in a specific investment project. Normally, this refers to the amount of funds committed to the investment, which might involve building a plant, buying a machine, or, in this connection, an increase in the level of working capital required to support larger operations. In these straightforward cases the investment in the project is equal to the cost of the capital assets (including installation, start-up costs, and similar outlays) plus any increase in working capital required. A common misconception arises, however, should a given project result in the replacement of an existing capital asset which has not been fully depreciated. There is a temptation to include the remaining "value" of the old asset in the amount of the investment, especially if the old asset is still almost new. The book value of the asset so replaced, however, is of no consequence to the investment analysis, as it represents a *sunk cost* attributable to a previous decision which turned out to be inferior to current opportunities. The only relevant quantity for analysis of the new project is any salvage value received for the old asset. Such a cash inflow from the old asset is a reduction of the investment required for the new project, inasmuch as the funds tied up in the old asset have been freed by the new project. In contrast, the book value of the old asset is the result of the method of depreciation chosen at the time of acquisition of the asset, and is not necessarily related to its economic value. Finally, any salvage value that can be estimated for the new project at the end of its useful life can, under certain conditions, be considered a reduction in the original investment outlay.

In this connection it is important to point out that a basic maxim of rational investment analysis is to use *cash flows* instead of accounting *allocations*. Depreciation is such an accounting allocation (see Chapter 1), and therefore not relevant in the sense described above. In determining the size of the investment for a given project, it is necessary to pose the following question: What are the *net* cash outflows (commitments) of this investment alternative in contrast to other alternatives? Since the most obvious alternative to an investment project is that of doing nothing, it is useful to ask what *cash* movements will have to take place if the project is taken up as contrasted to the status quo. This will also lead to the consideration of salvage values or tax benefits received from old equipment retired. If there are alternative ways of achieving the same purpose, each should normally be compared with the status quo to determine its unique investment requirements.

b) Operating Cash Flows. Once the size of the investment has been determined, the second step required is to define the relevant economic benefits of the project, normally found as recurring cash inflows provided by the investment. Here it is useful to consider the major types of investment projects generally handled. One of the commonest classes of capital expenditure contains those outlays made to *reduce costs* of operations currently carried on, that is, for replacement or modernization of plant and equipment. For such investment projects, the relevant operating cash flows will consist of the *differential* costs saved by instituting the project in lieu of the old way of doing things—in other words, the net improvement in the actual costs incurred in the operation.

A second major class of capital expenditures consists of investment projects whose purpose is to provide *additional profits*, such as expansion of existing facilities, the addition of new products, or a major advertising campaign designed to increase sales. In such cases, the relevant operating cash flows will consist of the *net cash inflow* resulting from the difference between the additional revenue generated and the additional expenses incurred.

Finally, a considerable number of investment projects either cannot be readily analyzed in their *economic effects* upon the enterprise, or are so *obviously desirable* that detailed analysis is unnecessary. Among the former are such outlays as employee parking lots, reception rooms for customers, and recreational facilities, whose benefits must be established purely on the basis of management judgment. Among the latter are such necessary outlays as a washed-out railroad bridge, without which the railroad could not run, or the replacement of a power transformer, without which the plant could not operate. In such circumstances, the economic benefits gained from the investment are in fact the restitution of the profits of the enterprise as a whole, not to speak of the social considerations involved. Generally, there is no question about the desirability of making the investment without further analysis.

The problem in cases warranting detailed analysis of operating flows, thus, is to make sure that all relevant cash flows are considered by analyzing the *changes* in operating cash flows brought about by the investment project. In this connection it is crucial that the analysis be made strictly on the basis of questioning every revenue and expense category involved as follows: Will the investment truly result in increasing or decreasing this revenue item? Will the investment eliminate this expense item; will it add this expense item to operations? It is important to remember every step of the way that the analysis must focus on the eventual cash differences involved. For example, an increase or decrease in sales dollars received is a relevant factor, as would be an increase or decrease in materials used in the production process, or an increase or decrease in the payroll required.

Difficulties arise when accounting allocations such as overhead costs are considered, or when the improvement in labor or space requirements caused by an investment cannot in effect be utilized. Accounting allocations are irrelevant unless there is a change in the cash flows. To illustrate, a new assembly line may require a lesser amount of overhead cost in the form of supervision and indirect labor. If it is not possible to reduce *in fact* the number of supervisors and indirect laborers, because part of their services is required in other areas of the plant, and if their time freed by the investment cannot be used productively elsewhere, no cash saving has been achieved and the investment project should not be credited with any reduction in these expenses. Similarly, if an investment frees a fraction of a production worker's time, or releases some floor space in the plant, but no productive use can be made of either, then no operating savings has been realized. On the other hand, if increased floor space is required, there is a cost only if its use results in the loss of an opportunity to derive from it an economic benefit, such as rent or the profits from another activity.

Consequently, the analysis of operating cash flows involves a step by step questioning of every revenue and expense category affected by the investment, with the critical query: Will I really have eventually more (or less) cash in my pocket because of the changes brought about by the investment? Not only must immediate cost differences be considered, but also the lost or gained opportunities for cash flow caused by the investment.

Another aspect of the operating cash flow analysis must be considered, namely, the impact on income taxes. Presumably, most investment projects will, in one way or another, increase the profits of the enterprise or at least maintain its profitability, as otherwise they would be difficult to justify. Inasmuch as increased profits normally mean increased federal income taxes, these additional taxes have to be considered as a relevant cash flow. It is therefore necessary to calculate the additional taxes due because of the operating savings or the additional profits generated by an investment project. Since we have calculated the economic gains from an investment project in the form of operating *cash flows*, a complication arises, as taxes are paid normally on the basis of *accounting profits*. The difference between cash flows and accounting profits, of course, is found in accounting allocations such as depreciation and amortization of various kinds of assets. These do not represent cash outlays, but are merely allocations of past expenditures (see Chapter 1). For purposes of calculating the additional taxes caused by the investment project, we must show the impact of the investment project on the taxable accounting profits, and we must consider depreciation and amortization as part of our operating picture *insofar as they affect* taxes. This is done quite easily, as is shown in the accompanying simple illustration, which pictures a replacement situation:

COMPARISON OF OLD AND NEW METHOD OF PRODUCING PRODUCT A

	Old Machine	New Machine	Difference
Annual Cash Flows:			
Materials actually used	$1000	$ 950	$ 50
Labor actually used	2000	1200	800
Supplies actually used	100	120	(20)
Repairs expense	300	100	200
All other expenses are the same	750	750	—
Total Pre-tax Operating Cash Flows	$4150	$3120	$1030
Noncash Elements (for tax purposes only):			
Depreciation	$ 500	$ 600	(100)
Taxable Accounting Profit			$ 930
Tax Adjustment:			
Tax at 48% (Relevant for cash flow purposes)			446
After-tax Accounting Profit...............			$ 484
Relevant Cash Flows:			
Pre-tax operating cash flows			$1030
Additional tax due (see above)			446
After-tax Operating Cash Flow			$ 584

In our hypothetical example, the differential cash flows attributable to the investment in the new machine are reduced by the actual tax payable based on the difference in accounting profits, and the final $584 figure becomes the relevant annual economic gain to be compared to the investment outlay involved in buying the new machine. The cash character of the analysis has been preserved by simply considering the federal taxes due as another cash expense of the enterprise once taxes have been calculated according to the rules prescribed by accounting convention and by law. This is also true of taxes on capital gains and losses which may arise from certain investments.

The use of accelerated depreciation methods complicates the analysis only insofar as the annual depreciation charges are not uniform. Apart from this problem the impact of accelerated depreciation on the cash flow analysis is again measured only in terms of the effect on the taxes to be paid from year to year which are figured on the reported profit, of which depreciation is a factor.

c) The Nature of Estimates. The concepts of net investment and operating cash flows described above are complicated by the fact that investment decisions deal with future events, and for all practical purposes estimates have to be used in analyzing the economic impact of the investment decision. It is usually less difficult to determine the amount of the investment required, since bids and estimates of builders and suppliers of capital equipment can be solicited for a fairly close estimate of the amount of funds to be committed. Complexities arise when an investment proposition calls for a certain outlay now, with additional investments to be made in future years. The farther away from the present, the more difficult it becomes to ascertain a good approximation of the funds needed.

The economic justification of an investment through operating cash flow analysis is even more fraught with possibilities of error. Operating savings or additional profits related to an investment are estimates, prior to the decision, and only the actual operation of the investment can prove or disprove the estimators' figures. Thus it is important to look to past experience with similar operations or to other companies' experiences with investments of this type, insofar as this is possible. Even then, however, estimates of future conditions must be made, and the difficulty of doing so must not be underrated. In order to avoid gross error it is sometimes useful to establish a range of estimates for certain operating costs or revenues, such as the most likely figure, the highest, and the lowest possibilities, in order to see whether the investment proposal has merit even if unfavorable conditions develop.

It is even possible to use judgmental weights for the range of possible outcomes by applying *probability* factors and calculating the weighted value of the cash flow pattern, called *expectation*.[1] For example, let us assume that a particular investment proposal is hoped to provide cash inflows annually which are estimated to range from a maximum of $50,000 to a minimum of $15,000 per year. After careful analysis and consultation the best judgments available in the company considering the investment indicate the following probabilities of the likely outcomes:

PROBABILITY PATTERNS OF
CASH INFLOWS AND
CALCULATION OF EXPECTATION

Possible Outcomes	Probability Estimate (Factor)	Weighted Outcomes
$15,000	0.10	$ 1,500
$20,000	0.15	3,000
$25,000	0.20	5,000
$30,000	0.20	6,000
$35,000	0.10	3,500
$40,000	0.10	4,000
$45,000	0.10	4,500
$50,000	0.05	2,500
	1.00	Expectation $30,000

The result shows that the weighted outcome or expectation is $30,000, even though it is just as likely that the outcome may be $25,000 as $30,000, and there is some chance that it may go as high as $50,000. The calculation has simply considered as possible all likely outcomes and we obtained a weighted figure based on the best judgments as to the likelihood of occurrence. The analyst can then take this weighted figure and use it in the calculations of desirability of the investment. Clearly, there are many more aspects to the approach just shown, and the student is cautioned to acquire the theoretical foundation necessary to

[1] See Neil E. Harlan, Charles J. Christenson, and Richard F. Vancil, *Managerial Economics* (Homewood, Ill.: Richard D. Irwin, Inc., 1962), section III.

deal with probability analysis and its many complications. A reference for further reading is included at the end of this chapter.

As can readily be appreciated, the problem of dealing with the uncertainty of estimates and the risk to the investor posed thereby is complex and calls for sound reasoning and the proper approach. In recent years there have been many developments in the theory of investment analysis with particular attention to this problem. To deal with the different theoretical concepts proposed goes beyond the nature of this basic book, nor have many of these approaches been translated into readily usable techniques applicable in the business environment. Much development needs to take place to bridge the gap between theory and practice.

Not all investment propositions will be equally difficult to estimate, inasmuch as the nature of the uncertainty surrounding a given investment varies tremendously between, say, a new untried product on the one hand, and an improved machine acquired to reduce costs of familiar operations on the other. It is necessary that the analyst as well as management interpreting the analysis are aware of these uncertainties.

d) Time Patterns.   So far it was tacitly assumed that operating cash flows could be derived as equal annual differences between the status quo and the investment alternatives. Quite often, however, it is found that the economic benefits gained from an investment project are patterned unevenly over time. The introduction of a new product, for example, may show slowly rising cash inflows from year to year, or even an initial period of zero inflows until momentum is gained. A machine replacement investment may produce declining cost savings over the years, as the effectiveness of the machine declines and the costs to keep it in good repair increase. Other types of investments may show completely irregular gains over the years, depending on the character of the proposition.

As will be discussed later, the pattern of cash flows can make quite a difference in the relative desirability of the investment, depending on the method of calculating the measure of desirability. It is, however, useful for the analyst under most circumstances to identify the time dimension of the investment opportunity. For this purpose he can draw up a time scale where the present is represented by 0, the first operating year (or period) is represented by the space from time 0 to time 1, the second year from time 1 to time 2, and so on. On the basis of this scale the analyst can identify investment outlays (cash outflows) as to their immediate (time 0) impact, or their future incidence in a particular future period, while operating cash inflows can be recognized both as to size and timing. As shown in the following table, such a recognition of the time dimension can lead to a graphic picture of the expectations about an investment proposition, which will be especially useful when the concept of present value is used to analyze the desirability of the investment, as will be discussed later:

TIME PATTERN OF HYPOTHETICAL INVESTMENT IN NEW PRODUCT

Time Period	Investments (Cash Outlay)		Operating Cash Inflows	
0	$100,000	(Immediate investment in new tooling)		
1	30,000	(Investment in working capital)	$ 5,000	(1st year's cash inflow)
2			10,000	(2d year's cash inflow)
3	20,000	(Additional investment in working capital)	25,000	(3d year's cash inflow)
4			40,000	(4th year's cash inflow)
5			50,000	(5th year's cash inflow)
6			50,000	(6th year's cash inflow)
7			50,000	(7th year's cash inflow)
8			25,000	(8th year's cash inflow)
9			25,000	(9th year's cash inflow)
10	(60,000)	(Recovery of working capital and $10,000 salvage value of tooling)	10,000	(10th year's cash inflow)

e) Economic Life. A final criterion of investment desirability to be built into our analysis, and which is implied by the table above, is the life of a given investment project. It is important to differentiate between the *physical* life of a plant or equipment, the period over which *depreciation* is figured for tax and accounting purposes, and the period of *economic usefulness* of the project. These periods can be quite different, yet the only period which has relevance in investment analysis is the period of *economic* usefulness, or *economic* life. It will make quite a difference whether a plant or machine costing a certain amount will yield economic benefits over one year or a 10-year period. Investments are made for the economic benefits to be derived, and the longer these benefits can be received, the better off is the investor. At the same time, it is of little consequence whether the machine or plant is physically perfect, if no economic benefits can be obtained from its operation. Similarly, the way an asset is depreciated for tax or accounting purposes is often a decision quite separate from the economic picture presented by the asset. For example, an obsolete machine, or a plant turning out an unsalable product, has exhausted its economic life, even though it may not have been fully depreciated on the books of the company.

Thus the period during which the investment is expected to yield the economic benefits for which it was made is the period over which the analysis should be carried out. Complications arise when alternatives being compared have different economic lives, but such problems will be taken up later.

Measures of Relative Desirability

Once one has determined what net funds outlay is required for an investment project, what its operating cash flows will be, what pattern these flows will assume, and what the economic life of the investment is, one has to try and combine these data into rational measures of relative desirability or investment worth. Two main approaches are commonly taken to attack this problem: rules of thumb, or rough guides on the one hand, and attempts to derive more exact economic yardsticks on the other. The rules-of-thumb category contains the widely used "payback period" (in a phrase: "How long does it take me to get my money back from the project?")and simple "return on investment," which at times can be an approximation of the economic yield of the investment. The category of economic measures utilizes the concepts of the time value of money ("a dollar received today is worth more than a dollar received a year from now"), to derive either the "present value" or the "yield" ("rate of return") of an investment as a criterion of judging its acceptability.

To take up the great number of variations on these basic concepts in detail would go beyond the scope of this book. All of the measures, however, have the basic purpose of being criteria for selection. Each has definite disadvantages as well as advantages, depending on the circumstances under which it is used.

a) *Payback Period and Simple Return on Investment.* The most commonly used method of obtaining a measure of project desirability is the "payback period," payoff period, payout, or simply payback. Its greatest merit, and probably the reason for its popularity, is the great ease of calculation. The underlying concept of this measure is the simple question: "How many years will it take me to recover my investment through the average cash flows generated by the project?" Consequently, the payback period measures the speed with which funds will be returned from a project, to be used elsewhere, as is shown in this illustration:

$$\text{Payback} = \frac{\text{Net investment}}{\substack{\text{Average annual operating} \\ \text{cash flow}}} = \frac{\$10,000}{\$\ 2,500} = 4 \text{ years}$$

The question immediately arises whether the speed of "getting your money out" is in fact the proper criterion to use in determining the relative worth of investment propositions. As will be seen later, when measures of an economic return on the investment are discussed, the factors of importance in determining investment desirability are not limited to the size of the cash flow. They include the length of time during which the cash flow is generated (the economic life of the project) and the specific pattern of cash flows, that is, whether these flows are even during the life of the investment or whether they occur unevenly. Thus the economic worth of a project is the balanced result of all these factors, while the payback device averages the cash inflows regardless of the economic life, and compares this average annual cash flow to the net investment. To illustrate this relationship is very simple. From a common sense point of view, the answer to the following hypothetical example is almost obvious:

	Project A	Project B	Project C
Net investment	$10,000	$10,000	$10,000
Average annual operating cash flow	$ 2,500	$ 2,500	$ 3,333
Project life	5 years	8 years	3 years
Total operating cash flow during life	$12,500	$20,000	$10,000
Payback	4 years	4 years	3 years

Assuming similar risks in the three projects, Project B is clearly superior to A and C, as it provides a total cash flow of $20,000 during its lifetime. The reading from the payback measure, however, points to Project C, even though this investment just returns the capital outlay over the three years of its life, with no excess receipts over and above this investment. This is like depositing $10,000 in a savings account, taking out $3333 for three years, and not receiving a single penny in interest for the period during which all or part of the money is invested. Projects A and B do, on the other hand, provide some return over and above the repayment of the investment, inasmuch as the cash flow in those cases exceeds the original investment. (The complexities of discounting are ignored at this point.) The payback measure, however, does not differentiate between Projects A and B, even though Project B is clearly better in terms of overall desirability.

From this illustration it can be seen that the payback measure must be used with great caution. It will give a satisfactory ranking or project desirability only where the economic lives of the projects are equal or close, and where the pattern of operating cash flows is similar or uniform. Any serious imbalance in the operating cash flows, such as a steep increase from year to year (for example, as a new product is exploited) or a steady decline in cash flows (as found in the declining efficiency of certain machine operations), or completely irregular flows will tend to blur the reading from the payback measure, since it does make a difference to the investing person or company whether cash inflows are large right away or only in the distant future. When average annual operating cash flows are employed, the payback measure ignores these refinements and can therefore be only a rough guide or screening device at best.

An outgrowth of the payback approach is a simple so-called rate of return which is really the reciprocal of the payback. The net investment is divided into the average annual operating cash flow to obtain a percentage return, which is then used as a ranking device. For example, an illustration would be as follows:

$$\text{Rate of return} = \frac{\text{Average annual operating cash flow}}{\text{Net investment}} = \frac{\$\ 2{,}500}{\$10{,}000} = 25 \text{ percent}$$

All of the shortcomings mentioned above apply to this device as well, since it is based on the same data which composed the payback measure. This rate of return is at best an approximation of the conceptually superior devices taken up in the next section, even though it can be shown that for investments with very long lives (15 years and above) the ranking obtained from this rate of return will come very close to that from the other methods. For most investments commonly encountered the distortion can be quite sizable, however.

A commonly used modification of the simple return or investment is the so-called accounting return, which is derived from the accounting profits less depreciation, divided by either the net investment or the average investment for the period. As was true of the payback reciprocal, this method is prone to produce serious distortions in the selection of investment alternatives, except where the alternatives are similar in cash flow patterns and economic lives. Ease of calculation and explanation are the major advantages of these yardsticks.

b) Methods Utilizing the Time Value of Money. Reference was made earlier to the fact that no investor will be indifferent to the choice between investments with all characteristics the same except for the economic life of the project. In the interest of maximizing the benefits from investment opportunities, the choice will fall on the longer lived projects, as common sense would dictate. A similar commonsense condition holds when an investor is faced with a choice between receiving a certain cash flow from an investment now or 10 years later. The obvious decision is in favor of obtaining the cash flow now, since the money thus obtained can be put to use elsewhere for profit. Waiting 10 years for the cash flow would mean loss of these extra profits. Stated another way, money has value in distinct relationship to the timing of its possession. For instance, $1000 put in a savings bank today will earn up to 5 percent per annum. Thus, the deposit will have grown to $1050 at the end of the first year (ignoring quarterly compounding). If the investor is forced to wait one year before being able to invest $1000 in the savings bank, he will clearly not be as well off. In terms of the present, the $1000 he can invest in the bank now is worth more to him than the $1000 for which he has to wait one year. To be more specific, the delayed $1000 will be worth only $\frac{\$1000}{\$1050}$, or $952.38, to him since this is the amount he would have to invest today at 5 percent to have $1000 a year from now. Similarly, over a three-year period, the $1000 investment made now would grow to $1157.62, while today's worth of $1000 received in three years would be only $\frac{\$1000}{\$1157.62}$, or $863.84. The growth of an investment on the basis of a periodic interest payment is, of course, the process of *compounding*, while the reduction in value of a future investment ("bringing back" the investment to a prior date) is called *discounting*.

It can now be argued that a manager looking at capital investment decisions should similarly value investment outlays and cash inflows according to the timing of each element. To him investment outlays to be made in future years should be less costly than ones to be made right away, since he has presumably the opportunity to put such funds to use in the company at a profit before committing them to the project, or he can save the cost of funds to be raised for the purpose of deferring the act of financing until the funds are actually needed. Cash flows received presently will be more valuable than ones received in future years, since management has the opportunity to put these funds to profitable use earlier.

c) *Net Present Value Method.* Once the concept of the time value of money has been established in relation to the profit opportunities available, it is possible to devise methods of ranking the desirability of investment projects which employ this characteristic. One basic device rests on the assumption that a company has the opportunity of earning a certain average rate of profit, say 15 percent after taxes, on investments made in the course of its operations. This may be an average return actually obtained in the past, or the future return expected by management, or it may be based on other facts or opinions. A company's "cost of capital" can be used here, where this cost of capital represents the "compensation" to all contributors of capital to the company, in line with the risk pattern experienced in the company (see Chapter 5). If the rate of return or the cost of capital represents the expectations of management, however defined, each prospective investment of management can be evaluated by determining the *present value* of all cash inflows and outflows connected with it. For instance, the amount of funds to be invested now would be a cash outflow whose present value would be the full value so committed. The operating cash inflow to be received within the first year of operations would have a present value somewhat smaller than the absolute dollars received, inasmuch as management had to wait for these funds before being able to use them, as was described earlier. The reduced value would then correspond to the value of the fraction $\frac{1}{1+i}$ (where i is the rate of interest or opportunity rate that management determines for its operations), which, when multiplied with the amount of cash received, yields the present value of this sum. Thus, if management expects a 15 percent rate of return, the present value of cash inflows received one year from the present would be $\frac{1}{1.15}$, or 0.86957 times the dollars received.

Cash inflows received two years from the present would be valued at $\frac{1}{(1.15)^2}$, or 0.75614 times the absolute dollars received, and so on. Consequently, it is possible to value each individual component in the pattern of cash flows presented by an investment in terms of its present value, given an opportunity rate of return (or desired rate of return) as stipulated by management. The cash outflows and inflows so valued can be netted out to yield the present value of the investment as a whole. This concept represents nothing more difficult than a way of saying: If management can generally put its money to use at a given rate of return, the desirability of a given investment to management is found by determining the value *today* of all the present and future cash movements connected with the project. The investment with the biggest present value will be the most desirable one, for we have in effect transformed the expectations about each investment into their cash value today. Naturally we shall choose the investment with the largest value, just the same as we would take the $100 bill if we had the choice between it and a $10 bill.

Note that this device builds into the evaluation yardstick not only the time value of money, but also the economic life and the exact pattern of the cash flows, since the analysis was made by discounting during the economic life of the investment all forecasted cash flows, in or out, based on the rate of return stipulated by the investing company or person. In order to be able to compare directly investment projects of greatly different sizes and economic lives, it is often useful to derive a "present value index," or ratio of the present value of the investment and the present value of the operating cash flows. The ratio

$$\frac{\text{PV of operating cash flow}}{\text{PV of net investment}}$$

can then be the ranking device.

Before the present value criterion is discussed, a number of additional points about the mechanics of the time value approach are in order. The idea of the time value of money is not new. Banks, insurance companies, and similar financial institutions in particular have always utilized the concept of adjusting monetary values by the timing of their incidence. Compound interest and discounting are the mathematical outgrowths of this time adjustment, and a variety of available tables contain the adjustment factors described earlier. A selection of such tables is found at the end of this chapter. Table 6–1, for instance, shows the present value of $1 received anywhere from 1 to 50 years in the future, at interest rates ranging from 1 percent to 50 percent. With the help of this table it is possible to transform annual cash outlays or receipts of any type or size into their present value equivalent simply by multiplying the actual dollars spent or received each year by the proper factor selected from the table. Table 6–3 represents a refinement of Table 6–1 by assuming that the cash flows are not received at the end of a given year, but rather in 12 monthly installments throughout a given year, which is more akin to the pattern shown by many business investments where benefits accrue continuously rather than in fixed annual installments.

Further to ease the task of calculation, it is possible to derive the present value of a whole stream of equal annual cash flows (called an annuity) by finding a single factor which, when multiplied with the annual cash flow, will yield the present value of the whole pattern. This process has long been applied to finding the present value of contracts for future payments, and Tables 6–3 and 6–4 contain a wide range of factors useful for this process. Again, Table 6–2 shows the present value of one dollar received *annually*, while Table 6–4 has the additional refinement of dividing the annual cash flows into 12 equal monthly installments to simulate more closely the incidence of benefits from many types of business investments. Many other variations of tables exist, with different assumptions built in. A particularly detailed and useful set of tables is listed among the references at the end of this chapter.

The method of calculation to determine the present value of an investment with an assumed pattern of cash flows is shown below. Tables 6–3 and 6–4 with monthly discounting are employed under the assumption that the investment represents an outlay for machinery to make a new product, whose sales are continuous during the period under consideration. All figures have been simplified to focus attention on the process and not on the realism of the example.

Time Period	Cash Outflows— Investment	Operating Cash Inflows	Present Value Factors—15%*	Net Present Value
Present	$10,000	—	1.00	($10,000)
Year 1	—	$3000⎫		
Year 2	—	3000⎬	2.436	7,308
Year 3	—	3000⎭	(Table 6–4)	
Year 4	—	2500	0.610	1,525
Year 5	—	2000	0.531	1,062
Year 6	⎰(2,000)	1000	0.461	461
	⎱		0.432	864
	(Recovery of working capital and salvage value of machinery)		(Table 6–1)	$1,220

Present Value Index: $\dfrac{10,356\dagger}{10,000 - 864} = \underline{\underline{1.13}}$

* Table 6–3, except where noted differently.
† 7308 + 1525 + 1062 + 461.

Several points should be noted here. First of all, since the initial three years of operating cash flows were assumed to be equal, Table 6–4 could be employed to find the present value of a stream of $3000 for three years at 15 percent, thus saving two multiplications. Second, the factors for the operating cash flows for years 4 through 6 were taken from Table 6–3 individually. Third, in year 6 it was assumed that $2000 of working capital and salvage value of the machinery will be recovered. Since this presumably will be more in the nature of a lump sum at the end of the period (even though working capital might be released slowly over some months), Table 6–1 was used here to reflect the present value of cash received at the end of the period. Finally, the inflows and outflows were offset to yield the net present value of the project. The present value index was derived by relating the present values of the operating cash flows and the net investment.

Had there been an initial investment of only $10,000 and six equal annual operating cash flows of $3000 per year, the calculation would have been much quicker, inasmuch as Table 6–4 would have shown a factor of 4.038 for a six-year flow at 15 percent to be multiplied by the $3000 operating cash flow, yielding a present value of the inflows of $12,114. The net present value would have been $2114. When tackling problems under the present value method it is therefore useful to look wherever possible for a simplification of the calculation by utilizing the annuity approach when the data permit.

The meaning of the resulting figure, net present value, is that this sum represents the value of the investment opportunity over and above the stipulated rate of return which was used in its calculation. The reason is that an investment whose net present value is zero at a given rate of return will exactly yield this rate on a compound basis *and* return the original investment to the investor. This must be so since the net present value figure was obtained by subtracting from the total present value of all operating cash inflows (discounted at the given rate of return) the present value of the investment outflows. In other words, the amount invested was offset by the value of the receipts time-valued at the assumed interest rate, which is the same concept employed when saying that one is willing to pay $864 for $1000 to be received in three years, if money can be invested at 5 percent per annum. Such an investment of $864 made now will yield exactly 5 percent, and the net present value will be exactly zero if the outlay and the future receipt are discounted at 5 percent.

Because of these relationships this particular measure of the relative desirability of investment opportunities serves a dual purpose. It tells us when a project is not desirable at all in terms of the stipulated rate of return, since the net present value of an investment yielding less than the desired return will be negative. It further indicates the relative level of desirability by permitting a choice between absolute values of net present value or between the present value index numbers. The bigger the net present value or present value index, the higher the desirability. There are some complicating conceptual issues involved which cannot be treated exhaustively within the scope of this book.

The most important of these, however, are briefly enumerated in a later section of this chapter.

  d) Investment Yield Method. In the previous section it was shown that a zero net present value indicates that the investment is exactly yielding the rate of return used to discount both inflows and outflows to obtain the present value. Rather than stipulate a desired rate of return and determine net present values, however, it is very often a practice to rank investments by the individual yields that can be obtained from them. This method, referred to variously as the "investor's method," "discounted cash flow method," or "internal yield," uses the same basic concepts of the time value of money discussed in the earlier section. The only difference lies in the focus on the *rate of return* which yields a zero net present value. This is in contrast to the original concept of the *size* of the *net present value*, given a specified rate of return. For investments with uneven cash flows the yield must be found by trial and error; that is, starting with an assumed rate, a net present value must be determined. If the result is positive, a higher rate must be tried; if the result is negative, a lower rate is indicated. The example on page 161 can be tried as follows:

Period	Cash Flows	Present Value Factors		Present Value	
		15%	20%	15%	20%
Present	($10,000)	1.000	1.000	($10,000)	($10,000)
Year 1	3,000 ⎫				
Year 2	3,000 ⎬	2.436	2.293	7,308	6,879
Year 3	3,000 ⎭				
Year 4	2,500	0.610	0.525	1,525	1,313
Year 5	2,000	0.531	0.438	1,062	876
Year 6	⎰ 1,000	0.461	0.365	461	365
	⎱ 2,000	0.432	0.335	864	670
			Net Present Value	$1,220	$ 103

As can be seen from this illustration, the net present value is approaching zero as the interest rate is increased from 15 to 20 percent, and the investment's individual rate of return or yield therefore is slightly higher than 20 percent.

  Investments that show uniform operating cash flows during

their economic lives can be handled more simply by dividing the annual operating cash flow into the net investment to obtain the present value factor for a stream of payments. This factor can then be located in Tables 6–2 or 6–4 on the line with the proper economic life for the investment and the yield can be read off or interpolated. (The factor, incidentally, is the same as the payback factor previously discussed, but the use made of it is entirely different.) The method is not hard to understand once it is remembered that the yield rate of an investment when applied as a discount rate results in equal present values of out-flows and inflows—a net present value of zero. We therefore know the present value of the inflows since it is equal to the net investment; we also know the economic life of the investment; the only unknown is the rate of interest which will discount the annual operating cash flows to equal the present value of the investment. Since the tables are built on discount factors, we can read off the rate of interest once we know the factor and the life. Unfortunately, this quick method works only if there are *equal* annual cash inflows, if there is only an *initial* net in-vestment, and if there are *no* residual values and recoveries at the *end* of the economic life. A demonstration of the factor method of determining the yield of a project shows the follow-ing: A $10,000 investment project with an economic life of 8 years has an even annual operating cash inflow of $2000. It can be assumed that the benefits will accrue continuously, which would dictate the use of Table 6–4 with monthly figures. The factor would be derived as follows:

$$\frac{\text{Net investment}}{\begin{array}{c}\text{Annual operating}\\ \text{cash flow}\end{array}} = \frac{\$10,000}{\$\ 2,000} = 5.00$$

In Table 6–4 we look on the eight-year line until we find the factor closest to 5.00, which is 4.929. This factor represents a 14 percent return or yield, and therefore the investment's true yield will be slightly less than 14 percent. Interpolation could be used to determine a more exact figure, but it is rarely advisable to make readings so exact since, as pointed out earlier in this chapter, the nature of the estimates underlying the investments is usually so uncertain that precise figures would create a misleading air of accuracy.

The results of either the trial and error method or the factor shortcut to determine a project's yield provide the investor or manager with a reading on the relative desirability of projects in the form of a unique yield for each investment, which can then be compared to the minimum return desired, or the cost of the funds to be employed, or any other yardstick management may devise. Presumably, a ranking of investment projects by their yields should lead to a rational choice between them, since all elements of the investment analysis have been taken into account. As it turns out, the ranking by project yields is superior to ranking by payback or return on average investment; in some cases, however, it is *inferior* to the net present value method of its outgrowth, the present value index.

The basic drawback of the projects yield method is that using yield without reference to other factors may lead to disadvantageous decisions. For instance, in choosing between alternative investments, it makes quite a difference whether a 100 percent yield can be obtained on a $1000 investment, or whether a 40 percent yield can be gotten from a $500,000 investment. Looking merely at the yield, management would choose the smaller investment, but it would clearly be more advantageous to put the larger amount of funds to use at the 40 percent return, especially if the normal return on a company's investments is 15 or 20 percent. Furthermore, a 30 percent yield on a project with an economic life of three years may not be superior to a 25 percent yield on a project of similar size but with an economic life of six years. If only one of the projects can be undertaken, and if the normal expectations for future investments are only yields of 15 percent, the company would be better off investing in the lower yield project to maximize its long-term returns. The yield method in such a case would give the opposite reading from that of the net present value approach which would indicate the lower yield project as better. Conceptually, the result of the net present value approach is superior. In terms of actual use, however, the yield method is usually better understood by the people dealing with it.

Some Complications

As the preceding comments have shown, even the superior methods of analysis must be used with great caution. Investment analysis is part of the overall capital budgeting framework described in the early parts of this chapter. Consequently, the choice between individual investments must be made with an eye to the pattern of future outlays and opportunities. The net present value analysis assumes that funds can be reinvested in the company at the opportunity or minimum rate utilized for the analysis, which the investment yield method tacitly assumes that the funds returned from the project can be reinvested at the same yield as indicated by the project analysis. The latter assumption is harder to defend, and this is a major reason for different preference indications occasionally given by the two methods. The situations which cause such problems are mainly investment alternatives with different lives, and it is often necessary to consider the difference in useful lives when making investment choices, whichever method of analysis is used. This means merely that when it comes to a choice between investment alternatives, some thought must be given to the reinvestment opportunities existing at the expiration of the different economic lives of the projects. In some cases it may be necessary to make assumptions about adding another similar investment once the first investment has expired, in order to achieve an approximately correct picture of the cash flow patterns of the future. These issues, however, lead away from the techniques of analysis to the broader issue of capital budgeting as previously described, and a fuller treatment of these aspects is found in the references at the end of this chapter.

Further complications of a similar nature are introduced by replacement decisions where the life of the new machine exceeds that of the old, and where some provision has to be made in the analysis for the fact that the improvements to be gained from replacing the less efficient machine are valid only for the length of time the old equipment would have been in service. To go beyond that point is conceptually proper only if provision is made for the investment in the new machine which would have been acquired at the normal date of junking of the old machine. For example, if an old machine with a remaining productive life span of three years is to be replaced by a better machine with an economic life of seven years, the operating savings produced by the new machine can properly be considered only for three years, since at that time a replacement would have been made anyway.

There are several ways of handling such difficulties. The most obvious approach is to provide, in the analysis, for the estimated investment in a "normal" replacement machine at the end of three years, to estimate its economic life, and to estimate any differences between the operating cash flows of the immediate replacement machine on the one hand, and the normal replacement machine on the other. Since the normal replacement machine would most likely outlive the immediate replacement for the old equipment, provision must be made for replacement of the latter machine at the end of seven years, and so on. This chain of replacements could be carried to the extreme, getting further and further away from safe estimates and into vague speculation about future conditions of markets, technology, and so forth, and equality of lives would still not have been reached. While it is true that the discounting process will reduce far distant estimates to having a relatively minor impact on present value, it is nevertheless often complicated and hazardous to develop such alternative chains of investments.

A second way of handling the problem would be to cut off the analysis at a point where reasonable estimates cease to exist, and estimate the residual value of any equipment still in use as a cash inflow at that point. In general, cutting off the analysis of alternatives at a reasonable point in time and determining the residual (or disposal) value of investments still in operation is often a useful device for analyzing on a comparable basis long-lived investment alternatives with differences in economic lives, where there is some doubt under the project yield method that a correct reading can be obtained.

A third way of handling the uneven lives problem is to "annualize" the respective cash flow patterns of the alternatives under consideration. This is the most meaningful way of handling the problem, because the result of the analysis is an annual cash cost—or cash profit, as the case may be—of the alternative in question. The choice then becomes one of selecting the alternative which has the greatest annual advantage: lowest cost or highest profit.

The process of annualizing the net present value of the cash inflow or outflow of an investment proposition is very simple. It merely involves converting this present value into an annuity over the economic life of the proposal at the suitable opportunity rate. In other words, we convert a lump sum at the present into an equivalent stream of annual cash flows over a specified period—which is simply the reverse of finding the present value of an annual cash flow, a technique we acquired earlier in the chapter. The only conceptual difference is that we arrived at the present value to be annualized by first analyzing the variety of cash inflows and outflows connected with the investment over time and bringing them back to the present into one net figure. Now we will take this net figure and transform it into an annual equivalent value, which will not be like the original annual values that made up the net figure, but will be a uniform equivalent annuity over the economic life of the proposal. By treating each alternative in this fashion, we arrive at directly comparable annual values for each of them, and we can make our choice directly: Both economic life and all cash flows have been incorporated into this number.

To illustrate, take the example on page 163. The net present value of the proposal is $1220, and the economic life is six years, while the opportunity rate has been stated at 15 percent. We now have to find the six-year annuity at 15 percent which will yield a present value of $1220. In Table 6–4 we locate the present value factor 4.038 which when substituted into our formula will give us the value of the annuity:

$$\text{Present value} = \text{Factor} \times \text{annuity}$$

When we substitute the data we defined, the result is:

$$\text{Annuity} = \frac{\$1220}{4.038} = \underline{\underline{\$302}}$$

We can now state that the annualized net benefit of the project is \$302. This number could be compared directly with similar results for projects with entirely different lives and cash flow patterns. The device affords a comparison on a common denominator and goes a long way toward easing the task of capital budgeting.

An especially useful application can be made in the analysis of equipment replacement, where the question to be decided often is: "Shall we wait another year before replacing the item?" Here the problem becomes one of determining the annual cost of owning the new equipment (an annualizing process over the economic life) and finding the cost of keeping the old equipment for another year. The lower of the two costs determines the choice. Since there are a number of special considerations to be watched in this analysis, the student is referred to a more detailed description of the approach in *Managerial Economics* by Harlan, Christenson and Vancil (see references). The annualized approach is also the basis for the so-called "MAPI Method," devised by Dr. George Terborgh of the Machinery and Allied Products Institute (see references).

For mutually exclusive alternatives (with equal lives) of handling a given investment need, it will often be useful to consider an incremental analysis to arrive at the proper choice between them. For instance, if three types of machines are available to handle the production of a new product, each costing different amounts and each providing a different operating cash flow over the same period of time, it will be relevant and economical to analyze first the machine requiring the *least* capital outlay. If this investment appears reasonable under the criteria used, the next lowest capital outlay should be compared to the first in terms of the *additional* (incremental) capital required, and the additional (incremental) operating cash flow generated. If it appears that this incremental outlay is justified by the additional operating cash flow achieved, then the second machine appears to be the proper choice. The third (and any other) even costlier alternative can be handled in the same way. The advantage of this approach is that normally the first analysis will establish the desirability of the investment move per se, and further analysis is made dependent on this decision. Again, however, the decision cannot be made without reference to the whole budgeting process.

A final word about the nature of discounting and time values and their effect upon the estimating process. Inasmuch as the present value of money shrinks rapidly both as the rate of discount is increased and as the time of receipt or payment is moved farther into the future, it is often possible to disregard elements in the analysis which appear to be many years removed from the present. For instance, the salvage value of equipment to be recovered 15 years hence may not make much difference in the net present value if a fairly high rate of interest is used, such as 15 or 20 percent. Consequently, the cash flows of the final years of an investment, if sufficiently out in the future, may often be eliminated from the calculations, thereby easing the job of the analyst. This may be the more welcome, since estimates reaching this far into the future will, at best, be tenuous. It will be good practice, however, to check with rough figures the likely impact of such simplifications to be sure the distortion introduced will not be too serious. A cardinal rule of analysis to be observed is to start with the best possible, honest estimates of conditions surrounding an investment project for its full life and only thereafter to introduce simplifications which may be reasonable adjustments.

The major techniques described in this chapter, as pointed out before, are part of the capital budgeting decision, even though the approach to present value is a more universal device. In balancing the pattern of funds sources and uses in the light of corporate objectives, specific allowance must be made for risk, the cost of the funds used, and the strategic decisions to be made, as was also mentioned at the beginning of the chapter. Even though basic techniques dealing specifically with risk were mentioned and cost capital is taken up in Chapter 5, the theoretical foundation which must be laid for this purpose is so broad that the material has been excluded from this collection of techniques, and the student is again directed to the selected reference material below.

SELECTED REFERENCES

a) Components of Analysis

ANTHONY, ROBERT N. *Management Accounting*. 3rd ed. Homewood, Ill.: Richard D. Irwin, Inc., 1964, chaps. 17 and 18.

GRANT, EUGENE. *Principles of Engineering Analysis*. 3rd ed. New York: The Ronald Press Co., 1950.

HARLAN, NEIL E.; CHRISTENSON, CHARLES J.; AND VANCIL, RICHARD F. *Managerial Economics*. Homewood, Ill.: Richard D. Irwin, Inc., 1962. Section IV.

HORNGREN, CHARLES T. *Cost Accounting, A Managerial Emphasis*. Englewood Cliffs, N.J.: Prentice-Hall, Inc., 1962, chaps. 13 and 14.

MOORE, CARL D., AND JAEDICKE, ROBERT K. *Managerial Accounting*. Cincinnati, Ohio: South-Western Publishing Company, 1963, chap. 19.

b) Capital Budgeting

BIERMAN, HAROLD J., AND SMIDT, SEYMOUR. *The Capital Budgeting Decision*. New York: Macmillan Co., 1960.

DEAN, JOEL. *Capital Budgeting*. New York: Columbia University Press, 1957.

HUNT, PEARSON; WILLIAMS, CHARLES M.; AND DONALDSON, GORDON. *Basic Business Finance*. 3rd ed. Homewood, Ill.: Richard D. Irwin, Inc., 1964.

SOLOMAN, EZRA. *The Management of Corporate Capital*. New York: Free Press, 1959. (Selected articles.)

c) Special Considerations

1. The MAPI Method:
TERBORGH, GEORGE. *Business Investment Policy*. Washington, D.C.: Machinery & Allied Products Institute, 1958.

2. Tables for the Analysis of Capital Expenditures:
HARLAN, NEIL E.; CHRISTENSON, CHARLES J.; AND VANCIL, RICHARD F. *Managerial Economics*. Homewood, Ill.: Richard D. Irwin, Inc., 1962. (See Appendix.)

3. Probability Analysis:
SCHLAIFER, ROBERT O. *Probability and Statistics for Business Decisions*. New York: McGraw-Hill Book Company, 1959.

PROBLEMS

1. *a*) The XYZ Company is considering an investment of $125,000 in a promotional and advertising campaign, which is designed to increase the sales of one of its products over an estimated five-year period. At that time it is planned that a new product will be introduced. The increased annual profits expected from the outlay, which will be made over a three-month period and expensed in the current year, are $35,000 before taxes. Assume taxes are paid at the rate of 48 percent. Calculate payback, simple return on investment, net present value (the company's investment opportunities average 12 percent after taxes), the present value index, and the yield of the investment, and the annualized net present value.

b) The ABC Company is considering investing in a machine to improve the efficiency of a hitherto manual manufacturing process. The machine costs $24,200 installed, has an expected economic life of 10 years, and will also be depreciated over this period on a straight-line basis. It will qualify for the full 7 percent investment tax credit. The main operating saving to be hoped for is a reduction in labor use and materials spoilage, while there are estimated to be additional costs such as power, lubrication, and repairs. The savings are true savings, since the man-hours freed by the machine can be readily used elsewhere in the plant. The net annual savings of the machine amount to $4750 before taxes, not counting depreciation. The company pays income taxes at the rate of 48 percent. Calculate payback, simple return on investment, net present value (management insists on a return of 10 percent after taxes on capital investments), the present value index, and the yield of the investment.

c) An investor is faced with the choice between two investment opportunities of equal risk, each calling for an initial outlay of $10,000. The first alternative promises to pay $1850 at the end of each year over a seven-year period, while the other will furnish a lump-sum payment of $21,600 at the end of the 10th year. Which of the two alternatives has the higher yield? Assuming that the investor is accustomed to earning 6 percent on his money, which alternative gives him the higher present value? Taxes are to be ignored.

2. The introduction of a new product at the Blue Sky Corporation calls for an expenditure of $165,000 on new equipment (installed and net of the investment tax credit), which is to be depreciated over a 15-year period on a straight-line basis. In addition, working capital in the amount of $100,000 will be committed to the project, and it is expected that this amount will be recovered at the end of the economic life of the project, which is 10 years. It is assumed that due to slowly rising prices the undepreciated book value of the equipment will be recovered through sale at that time. Profits before taxes and depreciation will be $70,000 in the first three years, $80,000 in the following five years and $60,000 in the last two years. Taxes will be paid at the rate of 48 percent. Calculate the net present value, the present value index, and the yield of the project. The company on average earns 12 percent after taxes on new product investments.

3. After having invested one year ago in a new machine to manufacture a product more efficiently, the XYZ Corporation's management discovered that a new and much improved machine had appeared on the market which seriously competed with the performance of its currently used machine. The latter had cost $8,000 one year ago, and was being depreciated straight-line over an eight-year period. This was also its estimated useful life, at the end of which it would be scrapped. If this machine were to be sold now, about $5,000 would be received. Gains and losses on sale of capital assets affected taxes at the rate of 48 percent.

The new machine, with an estimated useful life of seven years, would cost $11,000 installed (net of the investment tax credit) and would be depreciated over that period. It could be sold at the end of its useful life for an estimated $500.

The company expected to turn out 100,000 units of its product per year for the next seven years. The current machine turned out these products at $0.14 per unit for labor, $0.10 for materials, and $0.14 in allocated overhead. The new machine would effectively reduce the labor cost to $0.12 per unit by employing lower paid operators, material cost would drop to $0.09 per unit because of less spoilage, while allocated overhead (at 100 percent of labor) would now be $0.12 per unit. All other operating characteristics, such as supplies, power, and repairs were expected to be identical. Income taxes were paid at the rate of 48 percent.

Calculate the payback period, simple rate of return, net present value, present value index, and project yield. (The company's opportunity rate is 10 percent after taxes.)

4. The Super Oil Company was considering the investment of $180,000 in drilling special development wells in an oil field. The expenditure included lifting equipment for the finished wells, which were expected to produce about 15 years. Although the reserves in the ground were fairly well determined, staff members estimated that annual production of crude oil could vary within plus or minus 20 percent of the expected level. It was hoped that the net after tax cash flow (including depreciation and depletion) from the sale of oil would be $30,000 yearly, but they thought that there was a 10 percent chance that profits would be 20 percent above this level, and a 30 percent chance that the cash flows would be 20 percent below this figure. What is the yield of this investment? If the company normally earned 8 percent after taxes on similar investments, is this a reasonable project for Super Oil Company?

Table 6-1

Present Value of $1

Periods until Payment	1%	2%	4%	6%	8%	10%	12%	14%	15%	16%	18%	20%	22%	24%	25%	26%	28%	30%	35%	40%	45%	50%
1	0.990	0.980	0.962	0.943	0.926	0.909	0.893	0.877	0.870	0.862	0.847	0.833	0.820	0.806	0.800	0.794	0.781	0.769	0.741	0.714	0.690	0.667
2	0.980	0.961	0.925	0.890	0.857	0.826	0.797	0.769	0.756	0.743	0.718	0.694	0.672	0.650	0.640	0.630	0.610	0.592	0.549	0.510	0.476	0.444
3	0.971	0.942	0.889	0.840	0.794	0.751	0.712	0.675	0.658	0.641	0.609	0.579	0.551	0.524	0.512	0.500	0.477	0.455	0.406	0.364	0.328	0.296
4	0.961	0.924	0.855	0.792	0.735	0.683	0.636	0.592	0.572	0.552	0.516	0.482	0.451	0.423	0.410	0.397	0.373	0.350	0.301	0.260	0.226	0.198
5	0.951	0.906	0.822	0.747	0.681	0.621	0.567	0.519	0.497	0.476	0.437	0.402	0.370	0.341	0.328	0.315	0.291	0.269	0.223	0.186	0.156	0.132
6	0.942	0.888	0.790	0.705	0.630	0.564	0.507	0.456	0.432	0.410	0.370	0.335	0.303	0.275	0.262	0.250	0.227	0.207	0.165	0.133	0.108	0.088
7	0.933	0.871	0.760	0.665	0.583	0.513	0.452	0.400	0.376	0.354	0.314	0.279	0.249	0.222	0.210	0.198	0.178	0.159	0.122	0.095	0.074	0.059
8	0.923	0.853	0.731	0.627	0.540	0.467	0.404	0.351	0.327	0.263	0.266	0.233	0.204	0.179	0.168	0.157	0.139	0.123	0.091	0.068	0.051	0.039
9	0.914	0.837	0.703	0.592	0.500	0.424	0.361	0.308	0.284	0.227	0.225	0.194	0.167	0.144	0.134	0.125	0.108	0.094	0.067	0.048	0.035	0.026
10	0.905	0.820	0.676	0.558	0.463	0.386	0.322	0.270	0.247	0.227	0.191	0.162	0.137	0.116	0.107	0.099	0.085	0.073	0.050	0.035	0.024	0.017
11	0.896	0.804	0.650	0.527	0.429	0.350	0.287	0.237	0.215	0.195	0.162	0.135	0.112	0.094	0.086	0.079	0.066	0.056	0.037	0.025	0.017	0.012
12	0.887	0.788	0.625	0.497	0.397	0.319	0.257	0.208	0.187	0.168	0.137	0.112	0.092	0.076	0.069	0.062	0.052	0.043	0.027	0.018	0.012	0.008
13	0.879	0.773	0.601	0.469	0.368	0.290	0.229	0.182	0.163	0.145	0.116	0.093	0.075	0.061	0.055	0.050	0.040	0.033	0.020	0.013	0.008	0.005
14	0.870	0.758	0.577	0.442	0.340	0.263	0.205	0.160	0.141	0.125	0.099	0.078	0.062	0.049	0.044	0.039	0.032	0.025	0.015	0.009	0.006	0.003
15	0.861	0.743	0.555	0.417	0.315	0.239	0.183	0.140	0.123	0.108	0.084	0.065	0.051	0.040	0.035	0.031	0.025	0.020	0.011	0.006	0.004	0.002
16	0.853	0.728	0.534	0.394	0.292	0.218	0.163	0.123	0.107	0.093	0.071	0.054	0.042	0.032	0.028	0.025	0.019	0.015	0.008	0.005	0.003	0.002
17	0.844	0.714	0.513	0.371	0.270	0.198	0.146	0.108	0.093	0.080	0.060	0.045	0.034	0.026	0.023	0.020	0.015	0.012	0.006	0.003	0.002	0.001
18	0.836	0.700	0.494	0.350	0.250	0.180	0.130	0.095	0.081	0.069	0.051	0.038	0.028	0.021	0.018	0.016	0.012	0.009	0.005	0.002	0.001	0.001
19	0.828	0.686	0.475	0.331	0.232	0.164	0.116	0.083	0.070	0.060	0.043	0.031	0.023	0.017	0.014	0.012	0.009	0.007	0.003	0.002	0.001	
20	0.820	0.673	0.456	0.312	0.215	0.149	0.104	0.073	0.061	0.051	0.037	0.026	0.019	0.014	0.012	0.010	0.007	0.005	0.002	0.001	0.001	
21	0.811	0.660	0.439	0.294	0.199	0.135	0.093	0.064	0.053	0.044	0.031	0.022	0.015	0.011	0.009	0.008	0.006	0.004	0.002	0.001		
22	0.803	0.647	0.422	0.278	0.184	0.123	0.083	0.056	0.046	0.038	0.026	0.018	0.013	0.009	0.007	0.006	0.004	0.003	0.001	0.001		
23	0.795	0.634	0.406	0.262	0.170	0.112	0.074	0.049	0.040	0.033	0.022	0.015	0.010	0.007	0.006	0.005	0.003	0.002	0.001			
24	0.788	0.622	0.390	0.247	0.158	0.102	0.066	0.043	0.035	0.028	0.019	0.013	0.008	0.006	0.005	0.004	0.003	0.002	0.001			
25	0.780	0.610	0.375	0.233	0.146	0.092	0.059	0.038	0.030	0.024	0.016	0.010	0.007	0.005	0.004	0.003	0.002	0.001	0.001			
26	0.772	0.598	0.361	0.220	0.135	0.084	0.053	0.033	0.026	0.021	0.014	0.009	0.006	0.004	0.003	0.002	0.002	0.001				
27	0.764	0.586	0.347	0.207	0.125	0.076	0.047	0.029	0.023	0.018	0.011	0.007	0.005	0.003	0.002	0.002	0.001	0.001				
28	0.757	0.574	0.333	0.196	0.116	0.069	0.042	0.026	0.020	0.016	0.010	0.006	0.004	0.002	0.002	0.001	0.001	0.001				
29	0.749	0.563	0.321	0.185	0.107	0.063	0.037	0.022	0.017	0.014	0.008	0.005	0.003	0.002	0.002	0.001	0.001	0.001				
30	0.742	0.552	0.308	0.174	0.099	0.057	0.033	0.020	0.015	0.012	0.007	0.004	0.003	0.002	0.001	0.001	0.001	0.001				
40	0.672	0.453	0.208	0.097	0.046	0.022	0.011	0.005	0.004	0.003	0.001	0.001										
50	0.608	0.372	0.141	0.054	0.021	0.009	0.003	0.001	0.001	0.001												

Source: By permission, from Robert N. Anthony, *Management Accounting: Text and Cases* (rev. ed.; Homewood, Ill.: Richard D. Irwin, Inc., 1960), p. 656.

Table 6-2

Present Value of $1 Received Annually for N Years

Years (N)	1%	2%	4%	6%	8%	10%	12%	14%	15%	16%	18%	20%	22%	24%	25%	26%	28%	30%	35%	40%	45%	50%
1	0.990	0.980	0.962	0.943	0.926	0.909	0.893	0.877	0.870	0.862	0.847	0.833	0.820	0.806	0.800	0.794	0.781	0.769	0.741	0.714	0.690	0.667
2	1.970	1.942	1.886	1.833	1.783	1.736	1.690	1.647	1.626	1.605	1.566	1.528	1.492	1.457	1.440	1.424	1.392	1.361	1.289	1.224	1.165	1.111
3	2.941	2.884	2.775	2.673	2.577	2.487	2.402	2.322	2.283	2.246	2.174	2.106	2.042	1.981	1.952	1.923	1.868	1.816	1.696	1.589	1.493	1.407
4	3.902	3.808	3.630	3.465	3.312	3.170	3.037	2.914	2.855	2.798	2.690	2.589	2.494	2.404	2.362	2.320	2.241	2.166	1.997	1.849	1.720	1.605
5	4.853	4.713	4.452	4.212	3.993	3.791	3.605	3.433	3.352	3.274	3.127	2.991	2.864	2.745	2.689	2.635	2.532	2.436	2.220	2.035	1.876	1.737
6	5.795	5.601	5.242	4.917	4.623	4.355	4.111	3.889	3.784	3.685	3.498	3.326	3.167	3.020	2.951	2.885	2.759	2.643	2.385	2.168	1.983	1.824
7	6.728	6.472	6.002	5.582	5.206	4.868	4.564	4.288	4.160	4.039	3.812	3.605	3.416	3.242	3.161	3.083	2.937	2.802	2.508	2.263	2.057	1.883
8	7.652	7.325	6.733	6.210	5.747	5.335	4.968	4.639	4.487	4.344	4.078	3.837	3.619	3.421	3.329	3.241	3.076	2.925	2.598	2.331	2.108	1.922
9	8.566	8.162	7.435	6.802	6.247	5.759	5.328	4.946	4.772	4.607	4.303	4.031	3.786	3.566	3.463	3.366	3.184	3.019	2.665	2.379	2.144	1.948
10	9.471	8.983	8.111	7.360	6.710	6.145	5.650	5.216	5.019	4.833	4.494	4.192	3.923	3.682	3.571	3.465	3.269	3.092	2.715	2.414	2.168	1.965
11	10.368	9.787	8.760	7.887	7.139	6.495	5.937	5.453	5.234	5.029	4.656	4.327	4.035	3.776	3.656	3.544	3.335	3.147	2.752	2.438	2.185	1.977
12	11.255	10.575	9.385	8.384	7.536	6.814	6.194	5.660	5.421	5.197	4.793	4.439	4.127	3.851	3.725	3.606	3.387	3.190	2.779	2.456	2.196	1.985
13	12.134	11.343	9.986	8.853	7.904	7.103	6.424	5.842	5.583	5.342	4.910	4.533	4.203	3.912	3.780	3.656	3.427	3.223	2.799	2.468	2.204	1.990
14	13.004	12.106	10.563	9.295	8.244	7.367	6.628	6.002	5.724	5.468	5.008	4.611	4.265	3.962	3.824	3.695	3.459	3.249	2.814	2.477	2.210	1.993
15	13.865	12.849	11.118	9.712	8.559	7.606	6.811	6.142	5.847	5.575	5.092	4.675	4.315	4.001	3.859	3.726	3.483	3.268	2.825	2.484	2.214	1.995
16	14.718	13.578	11.652	10.106	8.851	7.824	6.974	6.265	5.954	5.669	5.162	4.730	4.357	4.033	3.887	3.751	3.503	3.283	2.834	2.489	2.216	1.997
17	15.562	14.292	12.166	10.477	9.122	8.022	7.120	6.373	6.047	5.749	5.222	4.775	4.391	4.059	3.910	3.771	3.518	3.295	2.840	2.492	2.218	1.998
18	16.398	14.992	12.659	10.828	9.372	8.201	7.250	6.467	6.128	5.818	5.273	4.812	4.419	4.080	3.928	3.786	3.529	3.304	2.844	2.494	2.219	1.999
19	17.226	15.678	13.134	11.158	9.604	8.365	7.366	6.550	6.198	5.877	5.316	4.844	4.442	4.097	3.942	3.799	3.539	3.311	2.848	2.496	2.220	1.999
20	18.046	16.351	13.590	11.470	9.818	8.514	7.469	6.623	6.259	5.929	5.353	4.870	4.460	4.110	3.954	3.808	3.546	3.316	2.850	2.497	2.221	1.999
21	18.857	17.011	14.029	11.764	10.017	8.649	7.562	6.687	6.312	5.973	5.384	4.891	4.476	4.121	3.963	3.816	3.551	3.320	2.852	2.498	2.221	2.000
22	19.660	17.658	14.451	12.042	10.201	8.772	7.645	6.743	6.359	6.011	5.410	4.909	4.488	4.130	3.970	3.822	3.556	3.323	2.853	2.498	2.222	2.000
23	20.456	18.292	14.857	12.303	10.371	8.883	7.718	6.792	6.399	6.044	5.432	4.925	4.499	4.137	3.976	3.827	3.559	3.325	2.854	2.499	2.222	2.000
24	21.243	18.914	15.247	12.550	10.529	8.985	7.784	6.835	6.434	6.073	5.451	4.937	4.507	4.143	3.981	3.831	3.562	3.327	2.855	2.499	2.222	2.000
25	22.023	19.523	15.622	12.783	10.675	9.077	7.843	6.873	6.464	6.097	5.467	4.948	4.514	4.147	3.985	3.834	3.564	3.329	2.856	2.499	2.222	2.000
26	22.795	20.121	15.983	13.003	10.810	9.161	7.896	6.906	6.491	6.118	5.480	4.956	4.520	4.151	3.988	3.837	3.566	3.330	2.856	2.500	2.222	2.000
27	23.560	20.707	16.330	13.211	10.935	9.237	7.943	6.935	6.514	6.136	5.492	4.964	4.524	4.154	3.990	3.839	3.567	3.331	2.856	2.500	2.222	2.000
28	24.316	21.281	16.663	13.406	11.051	9.307	7.984	6.961	6.534	6.152	5.502	4.970	4.528	4.157	3.992	3.840	3.568	3.331	2.857	2.500	2.222	2.000
29	25.066	21.844	16.984	13.591	11.158	9.370	8.022	6.983	6.551	6.166	5.510	4.975	4.531	4.159	3.994	3.841	3.569	3.332	2.857	2.500	2.222	2.000
30	25.808	22.396	17.292	13.765	11.258	9.427	8.055	7.003	6.566	6.177	5.517	4.979	4.534	4.160	3.995	3.842	3.569	3.332	2.857	2.500	2.222	2.000
40	32.835	27.355	19.793	15.046	11.925	9.779	8.244	7.105	6.642	6.234	5.548	4.997	4.544	4.166	3.999	3.846	3.571	3.333	2.857	2.500	2.222	2.000
50	39.196	31.424	21.482	15.762	12.234	9.915	8.304	7.133	6.661	6.246	5.554	4.999	4.545	4.167	4.000	3.846	3.571	3.333	2.857	2.500	2.222	2.000

Source: By permission, from Robert N. Anthony, *Management Accounting: Text and Cases* (rev. ed.; Homewood, Ill.: Richard D. Irwin, Inc., 1960), p. 657.

Table 6–3

Present Value of $1/12 Received Monthly in Year N

Year (N)	1%	2%	4%	6%	8%	10%	12%	14%	15%	16%	18%	20%	22%	24%	25%	26%	28%	30%	35%	40%	45%	50%
1	0.995	0.989	0.979	0.969	0.959	0.950	0.941	0.932	0.928	0.924	0.915	0.907	0.899	0.892	0.888	0.884	0.877	0.870	0.853	0.837	0.822	0.808
2	0.985	0.970	0.941	0.914	0.888	0.864	0.840	0.818	0.807	0.796	0.776	0.756	0.737	0.719	0.710	0.702	0.685	0.669	0.632	0.598	0.567	0.539
3	0.975	0.951	0.905	0.862	0.823	0.785	0.750	0.717	0.702	0.686	0.657	0.630	0.604	0.580	0.568	0.557	0.535	0.515	0.468	0.427	0.391	0.359
4	0.965	0.932	0.870	0.814	0.762	0.714	0.670	0.629	0.610	0.592	0.557	0.525	0.495	0.468	0.455	0.442	0.418	0.396	0.347	0.305	0.270	0.239
5	0.956	0.914	0.837	0.768	0.705	0.649	0.598	0.552	0.531	0.510	0.472	0.438	0.406	0.377	0.364	0.351	0.327	0.305	0.257	0.218	0.186	0.160
6	0.946	0.896	0.805	0.724	0.653	0.590	0.534	0.484	0.461	0.440	0.400	0.365	0.333	0.304	0.291	0.278	0.255	0.234	0.190	0.156	0.128	0.106
7	0.937	0.879	0.774	0.683	0.605	0.536	0.477	0.425	0.401	0.379	0.339	0.304	0.273	0.245	0.233	0.221	0.199	0.180	0.141	0.111	0.088	0.071
8	0.928	0.861	0.744	0.644	0.560	0.488	0.426	0.373	0.349	0.327	0.287	0.253	0.224	0.198	0.186	0.175	0.156	0.139	0.104	0.079	0.061	0.047
9	0.919	0.844	0.715	0.608	0.518	0.443	0.380	0.327	0.303	0.282	0.244	0.211	0.183	0.160	0.149	0.139	0.122	0.107	0.077	0.057	0.042	0.032
10	0.909	0.828	0.688	0.574	0.480	0.403	0.339	0.287	0.264	0.243	0.206	0.176	0.150	0.129	0.119	0.110	0.095	0.082	0.057	0.041	0.029	0.021
11	0.900	0.812	0.661	0.541	0.444	0.366	0.303	0.251	0.229	0.209	0.175	0.147	0.123	0.104	0.095	0.088	0.074	0.063	0.042	0.029	0.020	0.014
12	0.892	0.796	0.636	0.510	0.411	0.323	0.271	0.221	0.199	0.180	0.148	0.122	0.101	0.084	0.076	0.070	0.058	0.049	0.031	0.021	0.014	0.009
13	0.883	0.780	0.612	0.482	0.381	0.303	0.242	0.193	0.173	0.156	0.126	0.102	0.083	0.067	0.061	0.055	0.045	0.037	0.023	0.015	0.010	0.006
14	0.874	0.765	0.588	0.454	0.353	0.275	0.216	0.170	0.151	0.134	0.106	0.085	0.068	0.054	0.049	0.044	0.035	0.029	0.017	0.011	0.007	0.004
15	0.865	0.750	0.565	0.429	0.327	0.250	0.193	0.149	0.131	0.116	0.090	0.071	0.056	0.044	0.039	0.035	0.028	0.022	0.013	0.008	0.005	0.003
16	0.857	0.735	0.544	0.404	0.302	0.227	0.172	0.131	0.114	0.100	0.076	0.059	0.046	0.035	0.031	0.028	0.022	0.017	0.009	0.005	0.003	0.002
17	0.848	0.721	0.523	0.381	0.280	0.207	0.153	0.115	0.099	0.086	0.065	0.049	0.037	0.029	0.025	0.022	0.017	0.013	0.007	0.004	0.002	0.001
18	0.840	0.707	0.503	0.360	0.259	0.188	0.137	0.100	0.086	0.074	0.055	0.041	0.031	0.023	0.020	0.017	0.013	0.010	0.005	0.003	0.001	0.001
19	0.832	0.693	0.483	0.340	0.240	0.171	0.122	0.088	0.075	0.064	0.047	0.034	0.025	0.019	0.016	0.014	0.010	0.008	0.004	0.002	0.001	0.001
20	0.823	0.679	0.465	0.320	0.222	0.155	0.109	0.077	0.065	0.055	0.039	0.028	0.021	0.015	0.013	0.011	0.008	0.006	0.003	0.001		0.001
21	0.815	0.666	0.447	0.302	0.206	0.141	0.098	0.068	0.057	0.047	0.033	0.024	0.017	0.012	0.010	0.009	0.006	0.005	0.002	0.001		
22	0.807	0.653	0.430	0.285	0.191	0.128	0.087	0.060	0.049	0.041	0.028	0.020	0.014	0.010	0.008	0.007	0.005	0.004	0.002	0.001		
23	0.799	0.640	0.413	0.269	0.176	0.117	0.078	0.052	0.043	0.035	0.024	0.016	0.011	0.008	0.007	0.005	0.004	0.003	0.001	0.001		
24	0.791	0.627	0.397	0.254	0.163	0.106	0.069	0.046	0.037	0.030	0.020	0.014	0.009	0.006	0.005	0.004	0.003	0.002	0.001			
25	0.783	0.615	0.382	0.239	0.151	0.096	0.062	0.040	0.032	0.026	0.017	0.011	0.008	0.005	0.004	0.003	0.002	0.002	0.001			
26	0.776	0.603	0.367	0.226	0.140	0.088	0.055	0.035	0.028	0.023	0.015	0.010	0.006	0.004	0.003	0.003	0.002	0.001				
27	0.768	0.591	0.353	0.213	0.130	0.080	0.049	0.031	0.025	0.019	0.012	0.008	0.005	0.003	0.003	0.002	0.001	0.001				
28	0.760	0.580	0.340	0.201	0.120	0.072	0.044	0.027	0.021	0.017	0.010	0.007	0.004	0.003	0.002	0.002	0.001	0.001				
29	0.753	0.568	0.326	0.190	0.111	0.066	0.039	0.024	0.019	0.014	0.009	0.006	0.003	0.002	0.002	0.001	0.001	0.001				
30	0.745	0.557	0.314	0.179	0.103	0.060	0.035	0.021	0.016	0.012	0.008	0.005	0.003	0.002	0.001	0.001	0.001					
40	0.675	0.457	0.212	0.100	0.048	0.023	0.011	0.006	0.004	0.003	0.001	0.001										
50	0.611	0.375	0.143	0.056	0.022	0.009	0.004	0.002	0.001	0.001												

Source: By permission, from Robert N. Anthony, Management Accounting: Text and Cases (rev. ed.; Homewood, Ill.: Richard D. Irwin, Inc., 1960), p. 658.

Table 6-4

Present Value of $1/12 Received Monthly for N Years

Years (N)	1%	2%	4%	6%	8%	10%	12%	14%	15%	16%	18%	20%	22%	24%	25%	26%	28%	30%	35%	40%	45%	50%
1	0.995	0.989	0.979	0.969	0.959	0.950	0.941	0.932	0.928	0.924	0.915	0.907	0.899	0.892	0.888	0.884	0.877	0.870	0.853	0.837	0.822	0.808
2	1.979	1.959	1.920	1.883	1.848	1.814	1.781	1.750	1.735	1.720	1.691	1.663	1.637	1.611	1.598	1.586	1.562	1.539	1.485	1.435	1.390	1.347
3	2.954	2.910	2.826	2.746	2.670	2.599	2.531	2.467	2.436	2.406	2.348	2.293	2.241	2.191	2.167	2.143	2.098	2.054	1.953	1.863	1.781	1.706
4	3.920	3.843	3.696	3.559	3.432	3.313	3.201	3.096	3.046	2.998	2.905	2.818	2.736	2.658	2.621	2.585	2.516	2.450	2.300	2.168	2.050	1.946
5	4.876	4.757	4.533	4.327	4.137	3.962	3.799	3.648	3.577	3.508	3.377	3.256	3.142	3.036	2.985	2.936	2.842	2.755	2.557	2.386	2.236	2.106
6	5.822	5.653	5.338	5.051	4.790	4.551	4.333	4.132	4.038	3.948	3.778	3.620	3.475	3.340	3.276	3.214	3.098	2.989	2.747	2.541	2.365	2.212
7	6.759	6.531	6.111	5.734	5.395	5.088	4.810	4.557	4.439	4.327	4.117	3.924	3.748	3.585	3.509	3.435	3.297	3.169	2.888	2.653	2.453	2.283
8	7.687	7.392	6.855	6.379	5.954	5.575	5.235	4.929	4.788	4.654	4.404	4.177	3.971	3.783	3.695	3.611	3.453	3.308	2.992	2.732	2.514	2.330
9	8.605	8.237	7.571	6.987	6.473	6.018	5.615	5.256	5.091	4.935	4.647	4.388	4.154	3.942	3.844	3.750	3.575	3.414	3.070	2.789	2.556	2.362
10	9.515	9.065	8.259	7.560	6.953	6.421	5.955	5.543	5.355	5.178	4.854	4.564	4.305	4.071	3.963	3.860	3.670	3.497	3.127	2.829	2.585	2.383
11	10.415	9.876	8.920	8.101	7.397	6.788	6.258	5.794	5.584	5.388	5.029	4.711	4.428	4.175	4.058	3.948	3.744	3.560	3.169	2.858	2.605	2.397
12	11.307	10.672	9.556	8.612	7.809	7.121	6.528	6.015	5.784	5.568	5.177	4.833	4.529	4.259	4.135	4.018	3.802	3.608	3.201	2.879	2.619	2.406
13	12.189	11.452	10.167	9.094	8.190	7.423	6.770	6.208	5.957	5.724	5.302	4.935	4.611	4.326	4.196	4.073	3.847	3.646	3.224	2.894	2.629	2.412
14	13.063	12.217	10.755	9.548	8.542	7.699	6.985	6.378	6.108	5.858	5.409	5.019	4.679	4.380	4.245	4.117	3.883	3.674	3.241	2.904	2.635	2.417
15	13.928	12.967	11.321	9.977	8.869	7.949	7.178	6.527	6.239	5.973	5.499	5.090	4.735	4.424	4.284	4.152	3.911	3.696	3.254	2.912	2.640	2.419
16	14.785	13.702	11.864	10.381	9.171	8.176	7.350	6.658	6.353	6.073	5.576	5.149	4.780	4.460	4.315	4.179	3.932	3.713	3.264	2.917	2.643	2.421
17	15.633	14.422	12.387	10.762	9.451	8.383	7.503	6.772	6.452	6.159	5.640	5.198	4.818	4.488	4.340	4.201	3.949	3.726	3.271	2.921	2.645	2.422
18	16.473	15.129	12.890	11.122	9.711	8.571	7.640	6.873	6.539	6.233	5.695	5.239	4.848	4.511	4.360	4.218	3.962	3.736	3.276	2.924	2.647	2.423
19	17.305	15.822	13.373	11.462	9.951	8.742	7.763	6.961	6.614	6.297	5.742	5.273	4.873	4.530	4.376	4.232	3.973	3.744	3.280	2.926	2.648	2.424
20	18.128	16.501	13.838	11.782	10.173	8.897	7.872	7.038	6.679	6.352	5.781	5.301	4.894	4.545	4.389	4.243	3.981	3.750	3.283	2.927	2.648	2.424
21	18.943	17.167	14.285	12.084	10.379	9.038	7.969	7.106	6.735	6.399	5.815	5.325	4.911	4.557	4.399	4.252	3.987	3.755	3.285	2.928	2.649	2.424
22	19.750	17.819	14.714	12.369	10.570	9.167	8.056	7.165	6.785	6.440	5.843	5.345	4.925	4.567	4.407	4.259	3.992	3.758	3.286	2.929	2.649	2.425
23	20.549	18.459	15.127	12.638	10.746	9.283	8.134	7.218	6.828	6.476	5.867	5.361	4.936	4.574	4.414	4.264	3.996	3.761	3.287	2.929	2.649	2.425
24	21.341	19.087	15.525	12.892	10.909	9.389	8.204	7.263	6.865	6.506	5.887	5.375	4.945	4.581	4.419	4.269	3.999	3.763	3.288	2.930	2.650	2.425
25	22.124	19.702	15.906	13.131	11.061	9.486	8.266	7.304	6.897	6.532	5.904	5.386	4.953	4.586	4.423	4.272	4.001	3.765	3.289	2.930	2.650	2.425
26	22.899	20.305	16.274	13.357	11.201	9.574	8.321	7.339	6.926	6.555	5.919	5.396	4.959	4.590	4.426	4.275	4.003	3.766	3.289	2.930	2.650	2.425
27	23.667	20.896	16.627	13.570	11.331	9.653	8.370	7.370	6.950	6.574	5.931	5.404	4.964	4.593	4.429	4.277	4.004	3.767	3.290	2.930	2.650	2.425
28	24.428	21.476	16.966	13.771	11.451	9.726	8.415	7.397	6.971	6.591	5.942	5.410	4.968	4.596	4.431	4.279	4.005	3.768	3.290	2.930	2.650	2.425
29	25.180	22.044	17.293	13.961	11.562	9.792	8.454	7.421	6.990	6.606	5.951	5.416	4.972	4.598	4.433	4.280	4.006	3.768	3.290	2.930	2.650	2.425
30	25.926	22.601	17.607	14.139	11.665	9.852	8.489	7.441	7.006	6.618	5.958	5.420	4.975	4.600	4.434	4.281	4.007	3.769	3.290	2.930	2.650	2.425
40	32.985	27.605	20.153	15.456	12.456	10.220	8.688	7.550	7.087	6.678	5.992	5.440	4.986	4.606	4.439	4.285	4.009	3.770	3.291	2.931	2.650	2.425
50	39.375	31.711	21.873	16.191	12.676	10.361	8.752	7.580	7.107	6.692	5.999	5.443	4.987	4.607	4.440	4.285	4.009	3.770	3.291	2.931	2.650	2.425

SOURCE: By permission, from Robert N. Anthony, Management Accounting: Text and Cases (rev. ed.; Homewood, Ill.: Richard D. Irwin, Inc., 1960), p. 659.

Formula: $\dfrac{1 - (1+i)^{-n}}{12[(1+i)^{1/12} - 1]}$. Annual discounting is assumed.

Chapter 7

MAJOR CONCEPTS OF
SECURITIES VALUATION

THIS CHAPTER brings together key concepts and techniques on the subject of valuation, which is basic to financial analysis and decisions. There is no intent to cover broadly the many aspects of value, which is interwoven with practically all areas of human thought and endeavor; rather, the focus will be on the use of economic value in assessing decisions about investing in, selling, and exchanging corporate securities. Only the major types of securities, bonds, preferred stock, and common stock will be taken up to demonstrate principal techniques of valuation. The many refinements which result from variations in the terms of the securities are left to specialized study outside the scope of this book.

Economic value is not a precise notion, nor are the techniques employed in deriving measurements of economic uniformity applicable and reliable. The market available for a good or service will influence its value; the uncertainties and risk surrounding the earnings potential of an investment will affect its value; the bargaining positions of the parties to an exchange of goods will influence the values finally set; methods of accounting and reporting earnings connected with an asset will reflect upon its value, and so on. It is understood that economic value represents the relative desirability of a goods or service based on its supply and demand—yet, the actual determination of this desirability is not clear-cut.

The student will recognize that previous chapters in this book have dealt with valuation problems, even though they were not defined as such. For instance, in Chapter 3, ratio analysis cannot be carried out without some value judgments about the components of the ratios. In Chapter 6, present value analysis was demonstrated as a technique to calculate the present worth of future cash movements connected with an investment: This is a valuation process; both in terms of dealing with the impact of timing of cash flows, and the uncertainty and risk surrounding the future cash movements. Other examples can be given, but the point has been made.

Before we present valuation techniques related to bonds, preferred stocks, and common stocks, it will be useful to add a few definitions connected with value in an economic setting. *Market value* refers to the value established by an open exchange of goods or services between parties acting without undue stress. Clearly, a myriad of conditions surrounding the nature of the marketplace, the attitudes of the parties, general economic conditions, fads and fashion, and so on will have a bearing upon market value at any particular time. *Book value* refers to the accounting concept of recorded cost less any amortization or other accounting adjustments, and it usually differs greatly from current market value. *Going concern value* refers to the economic value of an enterprise in operation as distinguished from the value of its individual parts; *liquidation value* refers to the terminal values to be obtained for the assets of a business being dissolved, which adds the element of duress in many cases. Specialized values are *assessed value*, used as the basis for taxation of property; *collateral value*, which is the basis for judging the amount of a loan secured by an asset; *reproduction value*, which is the cost of replacing existing assets of an enterprise; and *imputed value*, which is similar to *appraised* value, a judgment placing a value on an asset which cannot be measured because of the absence of a proper market. There will be elements of all of these value concepts throughout the material of this chapter.

The Valuation of Bonds

The principles and techniques of present value of Chapter 6 are readily applicable in arriving at bond values. Present value techniques deal with sums of money or annuities in a time dimension. Through the process of discounting we are able to bring back to the present future cash movements, given a rate of discount which expresses either the opportunities of the investor or the cost of committing funds to an investment in the light of experience and future opportunities. The keys to using present value analysis, then, were fairly definable cash movements on the one hand, and a reasonably acceptable rate of discount on the other. Both of these criteria exist with few exceptions in the case of bonds.

Corporation bonds typically are stated in terms of a *par value*, or *face value*, the commonest denomination of which is $1000. The issuing company promises to repay the holder of the bond at a specified time, called the maturity date. Furthermore, periodic interest payments are made by the issuer to the bondholder, usually through the use of detachable and dated coupons to collect semiannual interest due. The rate of interest, which is applied to the par value, is stated on the bond and is part of the contract between the issuer and the holder. The current or prospective bondholder thus has two elements of value to consider: One, a promise to be paid a specific sum on a specified date in the future, and two, the promise to receive semiannual interest payments in cash and of a specific amount until maturity of the bond. Should the bondholder decide to sell or trade his bond prior to maturity, he simply offers the remaining interest payments and the principal payment at maturity to the prospective bondholder in exchange for cash or other value equivalent to the sum of these future cash receipts. This is the type of problem which, because of its specific time dimensions, is readily solved through present value calculations.

As an example, consider the following bond: Par value of $1000, maturity date January 1, 1982, and a stated interest rate of 6 percent to be paid semiannually on January 1 and July 1 of each year. The current holder of the bond, or a prospective investor, would have to consider the following elements of value on, say, January 1, 1967:

> $1000 to be received in 15 years
>
> $30 every six months, for 15 years—30 payments

Ignoring for the moment that there may be a market value readily available through published quotations, which could be used as a guide, there is a key question to be asked: What is the price a prospective investor should be willing to pay for this bond on January 1, 1967, or, conversely, at what price should our bondholder currently owning this bond be willing to sell? If the bondholder or the investor can stipulate the rate of return he expects from this type of investment, the answer can be calculated very easily. It is important to remember that the bondholder or investor is asked to stipulate his *own* standard for the proper yield on the bond, which may be quite different from the coupon rate, or stated rate on the bond itself. This is the same concept which was employed throughout Chapter 6.

a) Price Derived from Required Yield

Once the investor has given us his desired yield, which for purposes of this example will be assumed at 8 percent per annum or 4 percent per period, the price he should be willing to pay as it reflects the value of the bond to him can be calculated as follows:

	Cash Flow	Present Value Factor—4%*	Present Value
Principal amount payable after 30 6-month periods	$1,000	0.308	$308.00
30 receipts of $30 each	900	17.292 (×$30)	518.76
Totals	$1,900		$826.76

* From Tables 6–1 and 6–2, Chapter 6.

The result is a present value of $826.76, which is the maximum price the investor should be willing to pay, if his expectation from this type of investment is a yield of 8 percent. The price is less than the face value of the bond, yet this is not surprising, since the expected yield is one third above the stated interest rate, and it is the lower *stated* rate at which interest payments are contracted.

Had the investor been willing to settle for a yield of 4 percent per annum or 2 percent per period, because of the extremely safe nature of the investment or because of his tax status, the calculation would appear as follows:

	Cash Flow	Present Value Factor—2%*	Present Value
Principal amount payable after 30 6-month periods	$1000	0.552	$552.00
30 receipts of $30 each	900	22.396 (×$30)	671.88
Totals	$1900		$1223.88

* From Tables 6–1 and 6–2, Chapter 6.

This time the result is $1223.88, or almost $225 over the par value of the bond. Since the investor is satisfied with a yield lower than the one built into the bond contract, the terminal receipt of $1000 and the semiannual payments at the rate of 6 percent per annum are worth a premium to him. Had his expectations about this type of investment been precisely 6 percent per annum, the maximum price he should have been willing to pay was precisely $1000. As the yield rate is varied, the present value—required price—varies, while all other elements of the calculation remain unchanged. Again, the parallel to the examples in Chapter 6 is quite apparent.

If the current bondholder had made the same stipulations as just discussed, the results of the calculations would have been the *minimum* price he would expect to receive before deciding to sell. The only difference here is that of point of view—investing versus disinvesting.

The relationship between price and yield governs the behavior of bond prices in general. As a bond approaches its maturity date, the price will tend to approximate the face value, assuming away the risk of default for the moment. During the time a bond is outstanding, its price will move inversely with changing yields. As bonds are traded in the general money market, the level of yields commanded for various types of obligations will affect the price of particular bonds according to this relationship. The only connection, then, between stated rates of interest and the yield-price relationship is the fact that interest *payments* are specified by the former.

b) Yield Derived from Quoted Price

So far the impact of the bond markets on the valuation process has been left aside, to establish the simple yield-price relationship. Now it is time to examine a second, and more frequent type of problem, the calculation of the yield of a specific bond given its quotations in the bond market. Bonds generally are quoted on a price basis, in terms of a percentage of par. Thus, a quotation of 94⅛ would correspond to a dollar price of $941.25. An investor deciding whether to purchase a bond must therefore analyze this commitment in the light of the future receipts he is purchasing with this outlay of funds. Through trial and error, using several yield rates, an approximation to the true yield can be found, as was shown in Chapter 6. There are available sets of "yield tables" which will specify the yield obtained from a specific bond for a variety of prices and a variety of periods to maturity. A reference to one of these sets of tables is given at the end of the chapter.

A short-cut method can be used, however, to determine quickly and fairly accurately for most purposes the approximate yield of a bond, given a price quotation. This method reflects the way discounts and premiums on bonds are handled for accounting purposes. The result of the first calculation under (a) will be used for this purpose. The price of the 6 percent bond due January 1, 1982, was $826.76. Our investor would obtain a discount from par of $173.24, but receive $1000 at maturity. The semiannual interest payment is $30, for a total of 30 periods. In fact, the investor is receiving more than $30 six months, since eventually he will collect $1000 for an outlay of only $826.76. When the discount is amortized over the 30 periods (as is commonly done for accounting purposes), the periodic income becomes $30 plus ⅟₃₀ of $173.24, or $30 + $5.78, which equals $35.78.

Over the period of investment, the average commitment of the investor is the average of the purchase price and the receipt at maturity, or the average of $826.76 and $1000, which equals $913.38. When we relate the adjusted periodic income to the average amount invested, the approximate yield is the result:

$$\frac{\$35.78}{\$913.38} = 3.92 \text{ percent per period or } 7.84 \text{ percent per annum}$$

The exact yield was, of course, 4 percent per period or 8 percent per annum, since the original calculation was made with this assumption. The degree of error will increase the larger the yield rates and the longer the time periods involved. A slightly more accurate result is obtained with the assumptions of the second calculation under (a), where the bond price was $1223.88 with an expected yield of 4 percent per annum. Under those conditions the result is as follows:

$$\frac{\$22.54}{\$1111.94} = 2.03 \text{ percent per period or } 4.06 \text{ percent per annum}$$

The student is invited to check the calculations and should note that the periodic income has shrunk below the stated amount because of the amortization of a premium.

As pointed out before, the use of bond tables eases the task of calculating either the yield from a price, or the price from a stated yield. Interpolation must be used in most cases since the tables provide data only in specific graduations for interest rates and time periods. Again, this is similar to the present value tables given in Chapter 6, and in fact we are dealing with a family of tables based on the discounting and compounding principles. Bond tables are but a special way of showing present value relationships. An example of these bond tables as shown below illustrates this point:

6% Bond

Maturity: Yield	13 Years (26 Periods)	13½ Years (27 Periods)	14 Years (28 Periods)	14½ Years (29 Periods)	15 Years (30 Periods)	15½ Years (31 Periods)
3.80%	1.224 043	1.230 661	1.237 155	1.243 528	1.249 782	1.255 919
3.85	1.218 284	1.224 709	1.231 012	1.237 196	1.243 263	1.249 215
3.90	1.212 559	1.218 793	1.224 907	1.230 904	1.236 787	1.242 557
3.95	1.206 868	1.212 913	1.218 841	1.224 654	1.230 354	1.235 944
4.00	1.201 210	1.207 068	1.212 812	1.218 443	1.223 964*	1.229 377
4.05	1.195 585	1.201 260	1.206 821	1.212 273	1.217 616	1.222 853
4.10	1.189 993	1.195 486	1.200 868	1.206 142	1.211 310	1.216 375
4.15	1.184 434	1.189 747	1.194 952	1.200 051	1.205 046	1.209 940
4.20	1.178 908	1.184 043	1.189 073	1.193 999	1.198 823	1.203 549
4.25	1.173 414	1.178 374	1.183 230	1.187 985	1.192 642	1.197 201

* Example used in previous section (slight difference due to rounding of present value factors).

The techniques of analyzing the cash flows of bond investments cannot, however, be divorced from the fact that these cash flows are contracted under varying degrees of uncertainty. It was pointed out in Chapter 6 that adjustments for relative risk stemming from uncertainty could be made by raising the required yield where uncertainty was greater. Usually, the stated interest rate at time of issue is a reflection of both the risk inherent in the company issuing the bonds and the general economic conditions as they are affecting the supply and demand for funds. How well a company is known and how widely its securities are traded are factors of major importance. As time passes, the risk characteristics of the issuer may change and the economic conditions may become quite different. For this reason significant deviations from par value may be observed in the bond markets, both for individual companies and for bonds in general, as conditions change over the years. The full job of analysis, then, becomes one of analyzing the likely performance of the issuing company, and an assessment of the trends in the securities and money markets prior to the decision to invest or disinvest. In the former case, techniques discussed in Chapters 1 through 5 become helpful; in the latter case, one must turn to the judgments of economists and monetary specialists. Thus, the initial indication of economic value and yield obtained through the approaches discussed here must be modified and strengthened through the broader look just implied.

One final comment on bonds should be made here. So far the discussion has dealt with "corporate bonds" as a general concept. There are many modifications in the nature and provisions of corporate bonds which call for extra care in the analysis of their value. The most important example would be *convertible* bonds, which can be exchanged for specified numbers of shares common stock during specified time periods. The debt contract thus becomes a potential ownership arrangement, which reflects upon the value of the debt instrument through the potential participation in the earnings and dividends of the corporation, and the appreciation of the value of the common stock. No hard and fast rules exist as to how this fact should be handled in the valuation process—a convertible bond is a hybrid of debt and equity with some of the advantages and disadvantages of both. Other examples are *mortgage* bonds on the one hand, and *income* bonds on the other. In the former, property is pledged as security against default, in the latter, interest has to be paid only if earned. These two types represent extremes of relative risk, and the analyst's judgment must be tempered by these provisions. Finally, to turn away from corporate bonds, there is a whole array of governmental bonds available, from the federal government down to the municipality. Again the provisions and the relative risk differ most pronouncedly—yet, the principles of analysis presented in the section apply, as long as the results are weighed against the pros and cons of the issuer, the specific purposes for which the bonds are issued, and the general economic conditions prevailing.

The Valuation of Preferred Stock

In principle, preferred stock stands between outright debt on the one hand, and ownership equity on the other. It differs from debt because there is no specific contract for repayment of the principal—in fact the stated par value of preferred stock often has little to do with the price at which it was issued or which holders expect to obtain for it at one time or another. It differs from straight common equity in that dividend payment stipulated must be made before any common dividends can be paid, and in the event of liquidation of the business preferred holders will be satisfied in their claims before the common stockholders. There are innumerable modifications in the specific provisions of preferred stock which may make it more or less attractive, but these will be ignored for the moment.

From the standpoint of valuation techniques, the only parallel to the bond techniques discussed previously is the fact that preferred stocks generally carry a fixed dividend rate, stated either in percent of par value or as a dollar amount, such as $6 per share. The holder of a share of preferred stock thus has a stream of future dividend payments to his credit, and in valuation of the stock this must be a main criterion. Since there is no maturity as such, at which the preferred holder can claim a stated principal amount, the apparent choices available are (1) to assume ownership indefinitely, or (2) to make a judgment as to the price at which the preferred stock might be disposed of at given times in the future. The first choice is unrealistic, and the second imposes another valuation problem on top of the first.

A simpler approach to the problem can be taken by relating the periodic income to the rate of return or yield which a prospective investor demands from investments of this risk category. In the case of the $6 preferred, the process would be as follows, if the investor were to consider 8 percent as a reasonable return:

$$\frac{\$6 \text{ per period}}{0.08 \text{ stipulated}} = \underline{\underline{\$75}}$$

In other words, the price per share which would correspond to the investor's expectation would be $75 per share for a preferred stock which pays $6 per share. Conversely, if the investor had expected only 5 percent per annum from an investment of this type, the price would have been calculated at $120. This process is, of course, nothing but a simple manipulation of interest rate, yield, and price, and ignores the uncertainty both of the dividend payment itself, and of the movements in the securities markets which for listed preferred stocks and those traded over the counter exert a powerful influence.

Regarding the first of these uncertainties, the dividend rate, though stipulated, is not a legally binding contract, and in some instances the dividend payments may be interrupted or suspended upon the judgment of the board of directors of the corporation. This normally does not happen unless the corporation is passing through difficult periods with low or nonexistent earnings. Thus part of the valuation problem is the appraisal of the corporation's earnings performance and its projection into the future, to ascertain how well these earnings cover the dividend and interest obligations. A discussion of this type of calculation is found in Chapter 5.

The second of the uncertainties is the nature of the securities markets, and the yields reflected for preferred stocks in relation to debt securities and equity issues. These data can be used as a general guide for appraising the value of a particular preferred stock, but in individual cases the circumstances surrounding the company and the prospective investor must be taken into account.

One additional aspect has so far been neglected. As in the case of bonds, preferred stocks are often issued with particular provisions designed to make the stock more attractive to prospective holders. One form which has gained popularity in recent years is *convertible* preferred, which as in the case of convertible bonds can be exchanged into a stipulated number of common shares during certain periods under certain conditions. The added attraction again is the possibility of participating in the apprecation of common stock values as well as common dividends and the value of the preferred thus is no longer a function of preferred dividends and their reliability, but becomes enmeshed with the valuation of the number of shares of common stocks into which conversion is possible. Connected with convertibility is a *call* provision, which sometimes appears also with regular preferred stock. This option on the part of the issuing company may affect the valuation of the preferred, since the holder can be put to the inconvenience of having to cash in his shares and must then reinvest his funds. To soften this impact, calls are usually made at more than par value, which will tend to raise the valuation of a preferred where a call is imminent. Finally, there is also a *participating* feature found at times, which simply means that the preferred holders will participate in earnings and dividends over and above those needed to satisfy common stockholders. Again, there may be additional value derived from this feature which is used to make relatively unknown or weak issues more attractive.

The Valuation of Common Stock

The problem of valuing a share of common stock causes the most difficulty among the three basic types of securities dis-

cussed here. Neither earnings nor principal of such an investment are defined in specific terms, and thus the analysis cannot
rest upon reasonably defined magnitudes but is fraught with
assumptions and judgments. Yet, the widespread ownership of
common stocks (about 20 million shareholders now exist in the
United States alone) and the importance of the issuance and
trading in common securities for the economy of any industrial-
ized nation make the valuation problem a continuously demand-
ing issue.

In the absence of specific formulae or definite techniques,
several approaches are commonly taken to obtain a range of
results which must then be interpreted under the particular circumstances and the points of view of the interested parties. The
approach most related to the previous chapter on investment
analysis is to arrive at stock values via an analysis and valuation
of the *earnings* each share of common stock represents to the
investor. Another approach is to arrive at value through the
analysis of the *assets* of the corporation against which the stockholder has the legal equity claim. Finally, the most direct but
not necessarily the most satisfactory approach is to judge stock
values via the *market values* at which the very stock analyzed
is traded, or at which similar issues are traded in the stock
market.

The earnings approach makes use of the concept of *capitalizing* the *earnings* of an investment at a suitable rate of discount,
akin to the reasoning employed in the present value analysis
presented in Chapter 6, and in the valuation of preferred stocks
earlier. The technique used is simply expressed by the formula:

$$\text{Share value} = \frac{\text{Earnings per share}}{\text{Rate of capitalization}}$$

The problem thus reduces to two basic aspects: (1) to find
a reliable expression of earnings attributable to the common
stock, and (2) to find the appropriate rate of capitalization which
the investor or other interested party will accept as an expression of the relative desirability of the earnings stream under the
uncertainties surrounding it.

It is rather difficult in practice to arrive at so-called normal earnings which can be applied in the formula just described. As we have seen in earlier chapters, earnings per share are the residue of operating, accounting and financing decisions, as well as of the economic climate in the industry and in the country. Again we are dealing with a forecast of the company's future experience extrapolated and adjusted from past history. Since it is impossible to foretell precisely what a company's earnings will be, we must deal with reasonable assumptions based on as much information as the analyst is able to obtain. Clearly, it is impossible to weigh, analyze and digest all information that conceivably can be found, and some shortcuts must normally be taken. It is common to arrive at a range of possible earnings, and even to make a probability assessment of the likely outcomes to obtain as good a figure as one can. Moreover, it would be too difficult to make a forecast on a year-by-year basis; rather, a reasonable average is taken to represent future earnings.

Part of the uncertainty surrounding earnings estimates is founded in the leeway given to management in the accounting for operations. Such choices as the capitalization or write-off of research expenditures, the recognition of installment contracts, depreciation methods, differences in tax and accounting treatment of revenues and expenses and resulting tax deferrals, and so forth, further becloud the earnings picture and the uncertainties brought about by purely economic and operating fluctuations. The point is that there is considerable risk in taking past figures and extrapolating without at least attempting to come to grips with the most important of these issues.

Once a reasonable earnings figure, or range of earnings, has been derived, the next step is to find a reasonable rate of capitalization to represent the value of the earnings stream. Here we are attempting to inject the investor's judgment as to what he considers a fair compensation for the risk to which is is exposed holding the common stock under question. Apart from the individual feelings toward risk, which only the party in question can define for us, there are some guides of a general nature which can be used to help determine this judgment. There is a

definite relationship, proportional in nature, between the relative
risk surrounding a stream of earnings and the rate of discount
(capitalization) to be applied. We have observed this before,
and this general rule applies here as well. The greater the uncertainty, and therefore the risk, the greater will be the rate of
capitalization and thus the smaller will be the value of the investment represented by the earnings. A space-age electronics
venture of uncertain success will be discounted more heavily
than a staid, conservative "widow's and orphan's" type of company in a long-established, relatively safe line of products or
services, as for instance, a public utility. This range of rates of
discount, or as it is more often expressed, the "earnings multiple"
or the "times earnings" value of the stock, is considerable. It is
not uncommon to demand 20 percent or 30 percent or more in
the form of a return or capitalization rate from a risky venture,
which would then be valued at four to five times earnings, and
on the other side of the spectrum to be satisfied with a return
or capitalization rate of 4 percent or 5 percent, that is 20 to 25
times earnings. The guide to a rough selection of such a rate
will be to some extent the experience prevailing in the industry
to which the corporation being analyzed belongs, and more
specifically, it may be useful to pay particular attention to enterprises closely resembling the company. It is, of course, never
possible to find an exact duplicate because of differences in
management, resources, products, and so on, and approximations must suffice.

We have noted here that the earnings valuation approach is
an attempt to deal with an uncertain stream of earnings discounted to find its value at the present. Care must be taken that
the risk element is not expressed in an overlapping fashion both
when the earnings are determined and when the rate of discount
is applied. In other words, there is the temptation to adjust earnings downward as uncertainty increases, and at the same time to
adjust the rate of capitalization upward. The best safeguard to
avoid dual adjustments is to try for a reasonable average of earnings and the normal range of variation expected, and then to
make the risk adjustment through the choice of the capitalization rate.

It should be pointed out that the earnings approach outlined here is not limited to valuation of common stock alone, but is one basic method of arriving at the value of going enterprises which may never have issued stock as such. Whether we use as the basis of investment a share of stock, or a valuing of the enterprise as a whole, the basic relationship of earnings, yield (capitalization), and value of the investment hold.

One aspect has not been mentioned which is particular to common stock valuation. So far we have dealt with earnings accruing to the common stockholder, but we have not taken into account the disposition of these earnings. Companies vary in their policies concerning the payout of earnings to their stockholders, and range from no cash (or stock) dividends at all to established long-run policies of paying out certain proportions of earnings, or certain per-share dividends every quarter. There is, therefore, no universal value of cash dividends to all common stockholders, in fact, there are so-called growth companies (such as Texas Instruments, IBM, and so forth) large and small, whose stockholders would prefer to see all earnings reinvested in corporate growth. In other instances, stockholders expect and demand steady dividends, and a prime example is the American Telephone and Telegraph Company. Thousands of other companies in all types of industries pride themselves in providing their stockholders with dividend income. Since dividends above a certain minimum amount are taxable to the receiver, the valuation problem is complicated by the varying circumstances of the individual stockholder looking at dividend income—apart from the fact that the relative means of investors will influence their judgment.

There is no easy formula by which the particular company's dividend policy can be built into the valuation process. Many attempts have been made, and are being made, to weigh the dividend factor in the valuation of common stock. To describe these additional approaches goes beyond the scope of this book. The most recent attempts have involved the use of electronic computers to simulate stock price behavior relative to earnings and dividends, and there is continuing work being done to quantify the valuation process. It should be noted here that dividends, where paid, have tended to influence value favorably, and the stability of dividends in companies with established dividend policies has contributed to stock value. Yet, absolute statements in this regard are not possible.

The second approach to stock values, via the assets represented on the balance sheet, does not really take into account earnings or dividends, but rather assumes that assets recorded on the books on the corporation, less claims by creditors and preferred holders, represent a fair value of the common stockholders' claims and therewith can be used as a standard of value. This assumption is rather dangerous unless there is a close correspondence between economic value of the assets on the one hand, and the economic value of the stock on the other. Economic theory ascribes value to the earnings potential of assets, and in the profit-oriented business corporation this remains the foremost criterion of value. The going concern is justified and achieves value through profitable operations.

It can be stated as a general rule that only in unusual circumstances will there be a reasonable relationship between recorded values of assets and the stocks representing them. These unusual circumstances include the point at which a corporation is just being formed, when stock is issued for tangible and intangible assets, and the point at which a corporation is being dissolved and terminated. Between those extreme events, there will be a usually growing divergence among recorded values of assets on the one hand, and the value of the stocks on the other, simply because over a period of time accounting adjustments, changes in price levels, technological progress and economic conditions force a continuous reappraisal of asset values and their earnings potential, which are *not*, however, normally reflected in the balance sheets of corporations. The only way to arrive at reasonable stock values through an asset approach would be to examine all corporate assets, revalue them in the light of changes in conditions, adjust for the fact that the intangibles such as entrepreneurship, reputation, trademarks, and so forth, of a going company make the value of the total worth more than the sum of the individual parts, and then divide the residual value after deducting creditors' claims and the claims of preferred stockholders among the common stockholders. In view of the information normally available and the difficulty of making the many judgments involved, it appears futile in most cases to arrive at an economic value via this approach.

There are a number of circumstances in which book value of common stock is used in spite of its shortcomings. Where market values do not exist and earnings approaches are difficult, book value is often used as a floor of value, adjusted for known divergences in asset values, such as intangibles or known understatements in historical costs. Too often book value per share of common stock appears as a factor in valuation without the user having pointed out the limitations of the concept. As stated before, the best application of the concept is in the initial and terminal stages of a company, with due attention to accounting practices, such as depreciation methods, inventory value adjustments, and amortization of intangibles, as well as the nonrecording of many corporate attributes which come to light when, for instance, a merger or liquidation is planned.

The third approach to valuation of common stocks is related to market value which may or may not be obtainable for a particular stock. Here a variety of circumstances enter the judgment to be made. First of all, if the common stock in question is listed on an exchange or trade "over the counter," the quotations listed reflecting transactions or offers to buy or sell can be interpreted as a standard of value. Again, there is no full reliance possible on the values thus indicated, since among the most important factors influencing the individual stock are the general trend of the stock market as a whole, the prospects for the industry and the economy in general, known facts about the particular company, and so forth. Very important also is the nature of the market for the individual security. It makes quite a difference whether trading took place among a large group of buyers or sellers, or if the market was "thin." It is possible that a large block of stocks was traded, which could temporarily depress the market quotations, or it is possible that there was speculative selling or buying which somewhat artificially influenced the market price of the stock. Earnings prospects of the company in question will influence market prices, just as will dividend changes.

The nature of the stock market itself plays a major role. The year 1966 saw record peaks in the stock averages followed by severe sell-offs and falling averages based on a mixture of political, economic and world events, and a general dampening of confidence helped to depress stock prices. Billions of dollars in market values were wiped out within months. The judgments about the market value of individual companies thus cannot be entirely separated from the general trend, even though in 1966 as in other years, there were many instances of companies whose market values did not follow the general decline.

Where there are no market quotations for a common stock, such as in closely held corporations or in newly started enterprises, market value must either be simulated or established by actual test through the sale or purchase of some shares. The concept of market value is sometimes stretched under these circumstances, since simulation is only an approximation of what might take place under real circumstances, and since a few individual sales can be a far cry from a true test in the marketplace. "Fair market value," a concept often employed in the courts, depends upon a reasonably unhurried and "arms-length" bargain between interested parties, without coercion and without undue advantage to either side. It should be obvious that such ideal conditions rarely exist, even in the organized market of the stock exchanges, and that market value again is no absolute standard.

In the absence, then, of a truly reliable market judgment we must, as in all the other approaches, resort to considerable judgment and approximation, which is highly colored in most instances by the points of view of the parties involved. Under discussions for a merger, for instance, each side will naturally interpret the known facts to best advantage, and where there is room for assumptions these again will be made to favor the party making them. Similarly, when minority stockholders wish to be bought out, the valuation process will range from market value variously interpreted to many other ways of measuring worth, depending on the relative bargaining positions.

The point of the discussion of market value, then, is that depending on the quality and breadth of the market exchanges, there may be an indication of true economic value, in part confirmed by value as determined by earnings expectations. Because of the vagaries of the marketplace, both in organized exchanges and in the individual exchange of shares, any particular quotation may be distorted and the analyst should examine trends wherever possible and try to arrive at a reasonable figure through judgment and adjustment. At any rate, the judgment of the marketplace is not as clear-cut as is often supposed.

The Valuation of Rights

As an added consideration in the discussion of valuation, some attention should be paid to the valuation of rights to purchase securities, which most commonly involve the right to purchase additional shares of common stock extended to the existing stockholders of the corporation. Usually, this right must be exercised within a specified time period, and entitles the stockholder to purchase additional shares at a price less than current market values, before new stockholders can acquire these shares. The right amounts to a chance to protect the stockholder's proportional share in the common equity of the corporation, but the rights are commonly transferable so that the stockholder not wishing to acquire the additional shares offered can dispose of this privilege for a price. The attraction to another party is, of course, the privilege to buy stock at a discount, and often an active market develops for stock rights during their period of validity.

It is of interest to determine just how valuable these rights are, and clearly this value must be related to the size of the discount given. Rights are commonly related to each old common share, and the privilege of acquiring new stock is stated in terms of how many individual rights are required to purchase one new share. As an illustration, rights may be offered to the privilege of subscribing to one new share for each 25 held, or it may be any other relationship, depending on the number of shares outstanding, and the size of the new issue. Thus, a stockholder must own 25 shares in order to buy one other; if he owns a different number, not in multiples of 25, he must either purchase additional rights, or sell excess rights before they expire. The value of the individual right thus is a function of both the number required to purchase an additional share, and the size of the discount from market at which the new share is offered.

Let us now examine the theoretical value of an individual right. If the current market value of the stock, with the right still attached (cum rights) is, say, $120, the issue price of the new stock is $100, and 25 rights are required to buy a new share, we can first determine what should happen to the market price of the stock once the rights become detached—this will give us a clue to the value attached to each right. Assuming that a stockholder owns precisely 25 shares and that he wishes to exercise his 25 rights to buy one additional share, he has the following ownership position:

Value of old shares (cum rights): 25 × $120 = $3000
Cash investment to acquire one share 100
Total investment (26 shares) $3100

The 26 shares owned represent $3100, or $119.23 per share. Thus a drop in value, attributable to the removal of the right has taken place, which would put the value of an individual right at about 77 cents. Barring any radical change in the stock market, the actual drop in the market price as the stock goes "ex rights" is usually close to the theoretical value just calculated.

These relationships are often placed into an accepted formula for the theoretical market value of one right. If we set the following definitions, the formula appears as below:

M = Market price of one share of common stock, cum rights
N = Number of old shares required
S = Subscription price
R = Theoretical value of one right

$$R = \frac{M - S}{N + 1}$$

$$= \frac{\$120 - \$100}{25 + 1} = \frac{\$20}{26} = \underline{\underline{77 \text{ cents}}}$$

There is also a formula which depends on the same factors to develop the theoretical market price (P) of the stock after the rights have been exercised. It simply expresses the calculation we have made on the previous page in a more compact form:

$$P = \frac{MN + S}{N + 1}$$

$$= \frac{\$120 \times 25 + \$100}{25 + 1} = \frac{\$3100}{26} = \underline{\underline{\$119.23}}$$

These formulae and the reasoning behind them allows the analyst to get an estimate of the likely behavior of both the stock price because of the dilution effect of introducing new shares at a discount, and of the value of a right, which represents the privilege to the investor to protect himself against this dilution. There is one more formula which gives the theoretical market value of one right *after* it has become independent of the stock to which it was attached. The relationship expressed below is simply a recognition of the relationship of rights value to the discount granted after adjustment in the market price of the stock for the detachment of the right:

$$R = \frac{P^* - S}{N}$$

$$= \frac{\$119.23 - \$100}{25} = \frac{\$19.23}{25} = \underline{\underline{77 \text{ cents}}}$$

° Here we must substitute the actual market price after the stock has gone ex rights; the result here is only approximate.

As these formulas have shown, the rights value in theory offsets dilution otherwise suffered by the stockholder through the issuance of new shares of stock. The student is advised to reexamine Chapter 5 if the concept of dilution is not clear at this point.

In practice, the rights values can differ, even significantly, depending on the success of the offering which in part is related to stock market behavior and in part to the attractiveness of the discount set. Brokerage fees and the bother of having to dispose of rights, or acquire additional ones will reduce somewhat the compensation to the existing stockholder. Among the devices for ensuring success of a rights offering is the so-called oversubscription privilege which entitles stockholders so inclined to purchase additional shares under the same terms should not all shares have been taken up during the initial offering.

Another form of stock purchase privilege extends to preferred stock, and at times bonds are offered on a rights basis. Since in either case no dilution of common equity is involved, the theoretical value of a right is simply the proportion of the discount offered on the basis of the number of shares required. Stock purchase options, on the other hand, are rights extended to specific persons, not necessarily stockholders, who have or are going to render special services to the corporation. They are not transferable and are extended usually over a fairly long term, such as five years, at a price close to or below current market value. Since in fact such warrants are compensation for value received, and tied to particular individuals, they amount to deferred dilution of existing stockholders' equity for the benefit of specified persons. Such persons can be members of management for whom an incentive is sought and who therefore may offset the dilution by the value of their services to the corporation, or they may be promoters of an enterprise who wish to take part of their compensation in the form of a guaranteed purchase price for corporate stock for the next few years—thus in fact betting on the success of the enterprise. Tax regulations limit the nature and provisions of these warrants, and regulatory agencies such as the Securities and Exchange Commission carefully check major plans for possible abuse at the expense of existing stockholders.

As we have seen throughout the chapter, the problem of valuation of securities and rights goes beyond the quantification of whatever variables can be expressed specifically. Value, even in economic terms, is a relative concept and while our structure of industry of commerce is based on the continuous exchange of values, the final settlement of valuation decisions amounts to a compromise between divergent points of view, and the collective best judgments an analysts weighing constantly changing facts, circumstances and opinions.

SELECTED REFERENCES

Valuation

BONBRIGHT, J. C. *The Valuation of Property.* 2 Vols. New York: McGraw-Hill Book Co., 1937.

CLENDENIN, JOHN C. *Introduction to Investments.* 3rd ed. New York: McGraw-Hill Book Co., 1960, chap. 4.

HELFERT, ERICH A. *Valuation; Concepts & Practice.* Belmont, Calif.: Wadsworth Publishing Co., 1966.

GRAHAM, B.; DODD, D. L.; AND COTTLE, S. *Security Analysis.* 4th ed. New York: McGraw-Hill Book Co., 1962, Part IV, esp. chap. 32.

JOHNSON, R. W. *Financial Management.* 2d ed., Boston, Mass.: Allyn & Bacon, Inc., 1962, chaps. 18 and 19.

Rights

GUTHMANN, H. G., AND DOUGALL, H. E. *Corporate Financial Policy.* 4th ed. Englewood Cliffs, N.J.: Prentice-Hall, Inc., 1962, chap. 20.

HUNT, PEARSON; WILLIAMS, CHARLES M.; AND DONALDSON, GORDON. *Basic Business Finance.* 3rd ed. Homewood, Ill.: Richard D. Irwin, Inc., 1964.

PROBLEMS

I. Major Approaches to Common Stock Valuation

As an independent observer in early 1967, you are asked to determine the value of the common stock for ABC Corporation, according to several methods, from the simplified data below:

ABC CORPORATION

BALANCE SHEET

December 31, 1966

(thousands of dollars)

Cash	$ 115	(Adequate working balance)
Marketable securities	200	(Held for possible investment)
Accounts receivable	280	(95% collectible)
Inventories	390	(Could be sold quickly at ⅔ of stated
Total Current Assets	$ 985	value)

Total Current Assets
carried forward .... $ 985

Fixed Assets	$ 830	(Can be sold for $150, replaced for $1275)
Accumulated depreciation	425	
Net fixed assets	$ 405	
Prepaid expenses	25	(Mainly insurance, taxes, licenses, not refundable)
Goodwill	100	(Know-how, reputation, and so on)
Organization expense	10	(Legal fees and taxes)
Total Assets	$1,525	
Accounts payable	$ 175	(Normal level)
Notes payable	50	(Due within 120 days)
Accrued liabilities	220	(Wages and taxes)
Total Current Liabilities	$ 445	
Mortgage payable	100	(Mortgage on all fixed assets)
Bonds	250	(Debentures)
Reserve for inventory loss	50	(Surplus reserve for changes in value)
Preferred stock	150	(6% preferred, 1500 shares)
Common stock	300	(30,000 shares)
Earned surplus	230	(Accumulated earnings less dividends)

Total Liabilities and Net Worth $1,525

Earnings History:	1962	1963	1964	1965	1966	(3/31/67)
Total profit (000) ...	$57.00	$72.00	$111.00	$96.00	$87.00	$75.00
eps	1.90	2.40	3.70	3.20	2.90	2.50
dps	1.50	1.50	2.00	2.00	2.00	2.00

Market Price:	1962	1963	1964	1965	1966	Current (3/31/67)
High	19½	26¼	46¾	38¼	29	17⅜
Low	9¾	9¼	14½	12¾	10¾	
Average	14⅝	17¾	30⅝	25½	19⅞	

Average industry P/E ratio: 8 times

Compute the following data per share of common stock (stipulate any assumptions):

1. Capitalized earnings value based on:
   a) Current and expected prices and earnings.
   b) 1966 high.
   c) 1966 low.
   d) Five-year averages of prices and earnings.
   e) Industry average.
   f) Current prices and earnings plus redundant assets (marketable securities).

2. Book value:
   a) Unadjusted.
   b) Adjusted for intangible assets.
   c) Adjusted for reserves.

3. Reproduction value.

4. Liquidation value.

5. Market value (indicate the major questions you would wish to have answered before considering the use of market value).

II. Bond Values

A) Determining Price to Produce Desired Yield

1. A $1000 bond pays interest at 5 percent per annum, payable semi-annually, and will be redeemed for $1050 at the end of 15 years. What price would yield an investor 4 percent on this investment?

2. What would be the price for the above bond if the investor desired an 8 percent return?

3. A $1000 bond pays interest at 5½ percent per annum, payable semi-annually, and is callable at 110 percent of its face value on March 1, 1982. If not called on this date, it will be redeemed at par on March 1, 1992. What price on March 1, 1967 would guarantee a yield of at least 4 percent?

4. In the above bond (3), what price on March 1, 1967, would yield at least 7 percent? (Use interpolation.)

B) Determining Yield from Price Quotations

1. A $1000 bond pays interest at 5 percent per annum, payable semi-annually on February 1 and August 1. It will be redeemed at 110 on February 1, 1977. The market quotation on February 1, 1967, is 120. What is the approximate yield if purchased on this date? What is the yield according to the relevant bond table?

2. A $1000 bond pays interest at 7 percent per annum, payable semi-annually on January 1 and July 1. It will be redeemed at par on January 1, 1982. The market quotation on July 1, 1967 is 83¼. What is the approximate yield if purchased on this date? What is the yield according to the relevant bond table?

3. A $1000 bond pays interest at 4 percent per annum, payable semi-annually on January 15 and July 15. It will be redeemed at par on July 15, 1972. The market quotation on March 15, 1967, is 106½. What is the approximate yield if purchased on this date? What is the yield according to the relevant bond table? (Bonds are quoted with the understanding that any accrued interest up to the date of sale is to be paid by the purchaser in addition to the market price, if the sale is transacted between bond interest dates.)

4. A $500 bond pays interest at 6 percent per annum, payable annually on March 1. It will be redeemed at 105 on March 1, 1990. The bond was purchased for $485 on July 1, 1967, including accrued interest. What is the approximate yield on this date? What is the yield according to the relevant bond table?

III. Rights Values

1. The ABC Corporation offered its common stockholders the right to subscribe to one share of common at 30 for each ten shares held. The market price of common at the time of the offering was 52.

Determine:

   a) The theoretical market value of the stock after exercise of the rights.

   b) The value of one right (cum rights).

   c) The value of one right (ex rights).

   d) The value of one right if the market price (ex rights) actually was 49.50.

   (Explain any differences between (b), (c), (d).)

2. The DEF Corporation was planning to offer to its stockholders the right to buy one share of 6 percent convertible preferred stock at 85 for each five shares of common stock held. Based on similar issues of preferred by other companies in the industry, a market price of 110 was expected for the preferred stock once trading began. Calculate the theoretical value of one right. What would this value be if the stockholders were entitled to buy one share of preferred for each *three* shares of common?

3. Determine the subscription price for a common stock offering via rights, if the theoretical market price after the exercise of the rights was expected to be 103, the subscription ratio 9:1, and the market price cum rights 105.

4. Determine the theoretical market price (cum rights) of a company's common stock after a rights offering if the subscription price is 33, the theoretical rights value $1 and the subscription ratio 11:1.

Chapter 8

MAJOR SOURCES OF
FINANCIAL INFORMATION

THIS CHAPTER serves as an introduction to the great variety of public and private sources of financial information about the securities markets, financial institutions, industries and individual companies. The financial manager should be familiar with these sources of data about condtions in the economy, in his industry and in the financial markets; he will find them useful in making more informed decisions regarding new financing, temporary borrowing, credit and inventory management, investments and capital budgeting in general. This discussion will not be an exhaustive treatment of all possible sources to which the financial manager or analyst may turn, rather, it will introduce the form, extent, and character of the information published daily, weekly, monthly, or annually in the most important media and reference works. Three main groupings of information sources will be presented:

I. Financial newspapers and magazines.
II. Financial services.
III. Company and supplementary data.

I. FINANCIAL NEWSPAPERS AND MAGAZINES

The two most comprehensive and detailed daily reports of financial information, quotations, and news are found in *The Wall Street Journal* and *The New York Times*. These newspapers print detailed information on the various securities and commodities markets, statistics and news on economics and business, features on business trends, company earnings reports, dividend news, management changes, and so on. Major daily newspapers across the United States also carry financial news, the extent and coverage usually diminishing with the size and importance of the newspaper.

Among the weekly publications, the *Commercial and Financial Chronicle* is the most comprehensive source of stock quotations, securities offerings, and financial, banking, industrial, commodity, and economic developments. Similarly, *Barron's* cover business trends, industries, companies, and securities, and its very extensive section "The Stock Market at a Glance" provides a detailed picture of the securities markets. *Business Week* covers a wide range of topics on business or developments of interest to business including articles on individual companies or industries, and it presents weekly index numbers on production, prices, and other economic indicators. *The Economist*, a British weekly, surveys United Kingdom and international economic developments. *Forbes*, a semimonthly publication, specializes in reports on individual companies from an investor's viewpoint.

Monthly publications include the various bulletins of commercial banks and Federal Reserve banks which carry financial, business, and economic news and analyses of national and regional scope. Examples of these are the *National City Bank Monthly Letter* (New York) and the *New England Letter* of the First National Bank of Boston. *Dun's Review* presents trade indexes, failure data, and Dun & Bradstreet's 14 financial ratios together with articles about industry and commerce. The *Federal Reserve Bulletin* provides a wealth of statistical information on business and government finances, both domestic and international. *Nation's Business*, a U.S. Chamber of Commerce publication, contains articles on general business subjects. *Survey of Current Business* covers business trends with detailed statistics. *Bank and Quotation Record* contains detailed quotations of the various stock exchanges, general quotations of stocks, bonds, and other listed or unlisted securities, foreign exchange, money rates, and so on.

The *Journal of Finance*, a quarterly publication, presents scholarly articles on investments, business finance, money and credit, and international finance.

Too numerous to mention individually are the many specialized periodicals published by banking, commercial, and industrial, associations and groups, the variety of U.S. government surveys and publications, United Nations statistical publications, and the reviews and journals of the academic world. A very good source of information on publications concerning the field of finance and on business information in general is *Sources of Business Information* by Edwin T. Coman, Jr.; and a recently compiled annotated bibliography on the area of finance has been published by the Harvard Graduate School of Business. (See the references at the end of this chapter.)

While most of the news, statistics, and analyses mentioned in the periodicals above are in the form of articles, reports, or tables, the quotations of securities transactions of securities transactions as shown on the daily financial pages and in periodic reviews are made in a special form which warrants some discussion.

Stock Quotations

Currently 19 *stock exchanges* (such as the New York Stock Exchange and the American Stock Exchange) are the organized markets for trading in securities in the United States. The picture of exchange trading is presented generally in the same form by daily and weekly newspapers, except for the number of quotations reported. The accompanying illustration, taken from *The Wall Street Journal*, November 4, 1966, demonstrates the major characteristics of reporting stock transactions:

NEW YORK STOCK EXCHANGE TRANSACTIONS

Thursday, November 3, 1966

1966 High	Low	Stocks	Div.	Sales in 00s	Open	High	Low	Close	Net Change
14	8½	Am. Motors		426	8⅛	8½	8	8⅛	...
90¾	75½	Cont. Can pf	3.75	z190	76	76	76	76	...
56½	36¼	Crown Zell	2	31	45	45¾	44¾	45¾	+ ¾
65¾	45¾	Sears Roe	1 a	168	48⅞	49⅛	48⅝	48¾	− ⅛
44½	23⅛	Studebak	.25 e	7	34½	34½	34	34	− 1

From the first two items in the first quotation we learn that during 1966 prices paid on the New York Stock Exchange for American Motors common stock ranged from a high of $14 to a low of $8.50, not including the trading of the last day reported here, November 3. We observe further that all quotations are made in units ("points") and fractions which represent *dollars and cents* prices. As we read on we are given information on the *annual* dividend rate based on the latest quarterly or semiannual dividend declaration. In the case of American Motors, no dividends have been paid during the year 1966. The next item shows us the volume of trading in American Motors stock, in units of 100 shares. These units are called "round lot" in the trade, as contrasted to "odd lot" for less than 100 shares. Consequently we see that 42,600 shares changed hands on November 3.

The next four columns contain the price at which trading in the stock began (open), the highest price reached during the day (high), the lowest price during the day (low), and the price obtained in the last sale of the day (close). The final column of the quotation shows the net change in price between the current closing price and the closing price of the *previous* trading day.

Unless otherwise designated, the quotations refer to common stocks of a company. Preferred stocks are marked by the symbol "pf" after the name of a company, as shown in the second entry of the example, Continental Can Corporation. The dividend rate for preferred stock is also quoted on an annual basis, in this case $3.75.

Many other symbols appear with stock quotations. For example, the letter "z" in the sales column, as in the case of Continental Can, refers to the fact that the figure in the column represents sales in full for the day, and not blocks of 100 shares. The dividend column often contains a variety of symbols, since the annual dividend rate does not reflect extra or special dividends. For example, "1a" for Sears, Roebuck & Co. indicates that extra dividends were paid in addition to the $1 annual rate; ".25e" for Studebaker Corporation indicates that 25 cents is the total amount so far declared or paid this year with the implication that dividends have been erratic. Other dividend information refers to stock dividends, arrearages, liquidating dividends, and so forth. All symbols are explained in footnotes at the bottom of the financial page.

Other common abbreviations found in the quotations and also explained in the footnotes are "xd" (ex dividend), "xr" (ex rights), "xw" (without warrant), "wi" (when issued), and so on.

If there were no transactions in a given security, closing quotations in the form of "bid" and "ask" prices are listed in a separate table. These quotations do not represent transactions; rather, they are indications of what buyers were willing to pay and sellers willing to accept for a particular security.

Another listing of importance is the daily volume of securities traded as an indication of the activity in the stock market. On Thursday, November 3, a total of 5,860,000 shares was traded on the New York Stock Exchange, an average volume in a generally mixed and undecided market which had seen more than a 25 percent decline from the record high price averages achieved earlier in the year. At times the daily volume had by far exceeded 10 million shares.

Listings of the most active stocks (10 in *The Wall Street Journal*) show the center of interest during the trading day. Also, a list of new highs and lows achieved during the current year further reflects the mood and direction of the market.

The trading activity of the American Stock Exchange, when reported, is presented generally along similar lines. Most large papers also carry partial or complete listings of quotations from other exchanges, such as the Midwest Stock Exchange (Chicago), the Pacific Stock Exchange (San Francisco), and the Toronto and Montreal Stock Exchanges. The quotations from these markets are generally reported in less detail and are limited to the number of shares traded, high, low, and closing prices, and the net change for each security traded. Sometimes only volume and closing prices are shown.

An important help in interpreting the behavior of the stock market as a whole are the various indexes and averages. The most well-known of these are the *Dow-Jones Averages* of 30 industrial, 20 railroad, and 15 utility stocks, as well as the composite average of these 65 stocks; the new *New York Stock Exchange Averages* of five groups: composite, industrial, utility, transportation, and financial; *The New York Times* averages of 50 stocks (25 railroad and 25 industrial stocks); and the Standard and Poor's averages (425 industrial composite, 50 utilities, 25 rails, and the "Standard 500"; these indexes closely approximate the average price level of all stocks listed on the New York Stock Exchange). The averages are calculated daily and are plotted on graphs which show the combined daily range of trading and the closing price for these groups of companies. They contain the security prices of many of the best-known companies in the United States,[1] and are adjusted for events such as stock splits and stock dividends to maintain continuity. (See references at the end of this chapter for more detailed information.)

The movements of the averages are followed very closely by analysts, investors, and financial managers alike to evaluate the strength ("bullishness") or weakness ("bearishness") of the stock market in relation to plans for investing in or selling of securities, or floating new issues to raise capital for a company. The movement of the averages, however, does not necessarily help in judging the price behavior of a particular security, since it is quite common that individual issues move independently from the average trend of the market on the strength of developments in the company or its industry, or because of speculative trading activity in the particular issue. Thus the limitations of the indexes are those of averages in general and also of those inherent in the choice of the basic group of stocks making up the index.

Most major newspapers carry weekly reviews of the stock market and also comparative statistics on the stock averages, volume of trading, highs and lows achieved, and so on.

Over-the-counter trading, which represents a huge volume of securities, is carried out not on the organized exchanges but primarily over the telephone and by wire between security dealers and individuals. The issues traded include government bonds, state and municipal bonds, corporation bonds and stocks,

---

[1] Among the 30 industrials in the Dow-Jones Average are Du Pont, General Motors, General Electric, U.S. Steel, Procter & Gamble, Woolworth, and Alcoa.

bank stocks, mutual funds shares, insurance company stocks, and issues of small size, relatively inactive demand, or very close ownership. No record of the individual transactions, number of shares traded, or overall volume is presented in the financial pages of newspapers. Only tables of quotations are printed, which are usually furnished by the National Association of Securities Dealers, Inc., or by individual dealers that "maintain a market" in certain issues (that is, they specialize in trading in the securities of the company). These quotations represent "bid" and "ask" quotations indicative of the price a dealer would have been willing to pay, and at what price he would have been willing to sell during the trading period. The spread between bid and ask prices represents the gross margin with which he must cover his expenses and profit.

The quotations are often broken down by areas, such as the National Market, Eastern Market, National Funds Market, and also by type of stocks, such as industrials, bank stocks, and insurance stocks. The more frequently traded stocks are listed on a daily basis, while less active stocks appear on weekly lists. For example, *The Wall Street Journal* of November 4, 1966, carried the following quotations as of Thursday, November 3, 1966:

Stock and Dividends		Bid	Asked	Prev. Bid
Acme Elec	.28	17¼	18	17¼
Boston Cap		5½	5¾	5½
Irwin R D	.32	31	33	30
Kaiser St pf	1.46	21	21½	21¼
Utah Constr	1 a	40	40¾	40¼
Bank America	2	51⅝	52	51
Franklin Life	.35 b	31⅝	31⅛	33¼
Boston Fd		8.95	9.78	8.97

"Asked" quotations are always above the "bid" figures, and actual transactions most likely took place within the range indicated. The "previous bid" (third column) represents the bid quotation from the previous trading period. Often the previous bid is not shown on the listings. Again many abbreviations are used, such as "pf" for preferred stock, "a" for annual dividend rate plus cash extra or extras, "b" for annual dividend rate plus stock dividend, and many more which are explained in the foot-notes to the quotation.

Foreign stock exchange quotations are carried in some of the major newspapers. These listings of trading in exchanges such as London, Paris, or Frankfort are made in the currency of the foreign country and are apt to be rather selective groupings of representative stocks. In addition, the stock averages of the country are sometimes reported.

Bond Quotations

Both the organized exchanges and the over-the-counter markets are marketplaces for many corporate (industrial, railroad, and utility) bonds, while the bulk of United States government bonds and obligations, as well as most state and municipal bonds are traded over the counter.

Domestic (except U.S. government bonds) and foreign bonds listed on the New York Stock Exchange, the American Stock Exchange, and other exchanges are quoted in *percentages of par value*, with fractions in eighths of a point. As an example, *The Wall Street Journal* of November 4, 1966, carried the following quotations as of Thursday, November 3, 1966 (New York Stock Exchange):

1966			Sales in				Net
High	*Low*	*Bonds*	*$1000*	*High*	*Low*	*Close*	*Change*
72¾	40	Boston Me 4½s 70f	1	55	55	55	+ ½
99	71⅛	Food Fair cv4s 79	30	74	72½	73	−1
23⅞	11½	vj NYNH cv 4½s22f	5	15	14½	15	+ ⅜
526	275	PanAm Air cv4⅞s79	32	298	298	298	−8½
. . .	. . .	Australia fn 4¾s 73	3	96¼	96¼	96¼	. . . .

The price of Boston & Maine Railroad 4½ percent bonds, due in 1970, ranged from a low of $400 per $1000 par value to a high of $727.50 during 1966. On November 3, 1966, $1000 of par value bonds were sold, with the price closing at $550 per $1000 par value, up $5 from the previous trading day. The extraordinarily low prices range of the Boston and Maine bonds, and especially of the New York, New Haven and Hartford Railroad bonds shown is a reflection of the poor financial condition of these eastern roads. In fact, the symbol "f" signifies that the bonds are traded "flat," which means that the price includes consideration for all unpaid accruals of interest. (Income bonds or bonds which are in default of interest and principal are traded flat.) The symbol "vj" with the NYNH bonds stands for the fact that the company is in bankruptcy or receivership, or is being reorganized under the Bankruptcy Act. The symbol "cv" with the Food Fair and Pan American Airways bonds shows that these bonds are convertible into common stock, and the extraordinarily high price range for PanAm shows the boosting effect the conversion privilege has upon bonds when the common stock into which they can be converted has a favorable price performance. Finally, the symbol "fn" with the bonds of the Australian government indicates that this is a foreign issue subject to the interest equalization tax.

Other symbols, such as "xi" (ex interest) or "nd" (next day delivery) are explained in footnotes to the bond listings on the financial pages.

U.S. government bonds, which are listed on the stock exchanges but traded mostly over the counter, are quoted in *percentages of par value*, with fractions in thirty-seconds of a point. The unit of trading is $1000 in par value. *The Wall Street Journal* cited previously contained among others the following quotations:

Treasury Bonds	Bid	Asked	Prev. Bid	Yield
5¼s, 1967 Aug. (c)	99.25	99.27	99.25	5.46
2½s, 1963-68 Dec.	94.19	94.23	94.20	5.18
5⅜s, 1971 Nov.	100.3	100.5	(z)	5.34
3s, 1995 Feb.	81.20	82.4	81.24	4.07

We find that the first bonds carry an interest rate of 5¼ percent and are payable in August, 1967. The symbol "c" stands for Certificate of Indebtedness, one of the many special forms of government obligations. The best bid received on November 3, 1966, was $99^{25}\!/_{32}$ ($997.81 per $1000 par value), while the best offer was $99^{27}\!/_{32}$ ($998.44). The bid was unchanged from the previous trading day, and the yield if held to maturity was 5.46 percent. The 2½ percent bonds listed next are due in

December, 1968, although the government can redeem them at any time between December, 1963 and December, 1968. The symbol "z" in the next quotation indicates that the information is not available. Other symbols sometimes used include "a," which indicates that ¹⁄₆₄ should be added to the price, and "b" which stands for the yield to the *call* date.

Other U.S. government obligations, such as treasury notes, treasury bills and certificates, which are relatively short term and flexible media of government financing, are also quoted on most financial pages on the basis of bid and ask quotations, and sometimes are shown with the yield to maturity as indicated above.

Bonds of states and municipalities, and those of various government agencies, such as the World Bank, and so forth, are found on many financial pages presented along the same lines. For example, *The Wall Street Journal* previously cited showed the following over-the-counter quotations for public authority bonds:

Bond	Rate	Maturity	Bid	Ask
Florida Turnpike	4¾	2001	102½	104
Mass Port Authority	4¾	1998	105	105¾
West Va Turnpike	4⅛	1989	65	69

The quotations are self-explanatory, and it should only be added here that the financial problems of the West Virginia Turnpike are reflected in the low-price levels shown here.

Similar to summaries and averages of the stock market, the bond market is interpreted and followed on the basis of daily volume reports, summaries of issues which staged advances and declines, new highs and lows for the year, and bond averages. Again the most commonly used averages are the Dow-Jones bond averages (40 bonds; 10 higher grade rails, 10 second grade rails, 10 public utilities, and 10 industrials), which are indicators of the general strength and direction of the market. These averages are calculated in terms of percentages of par, carried out to two *decimal places*, in contrast to the fractional quotations of individual bonds. Thus, on November 3, 1966, the Dow-Jones

Average of 40 Bonds stood at 81.03 ($810.30 for each $1000 of par value), up 0.02 ($0.20) from the previous trading day.

Other Financial Data

a) *Commodities:* Most financial pages contain summaries of the trading in commodities (various basic foods such as wheat, corn, coffee, and potatoes, and industrial raw materials such as rubber, cotton, copper, and lead). The trading is carried out in organized exchanges such as the Chicago Board of Trade Commodity Exchange (especially grains) and New York Cotton Exchange and is done both on a "spot" (or cash) basis for immediate delivery and on a "futures" basis for delivery at a specified future date. Spot and futures quotations are made on varying bases[2] depending on the commodity involved, but are ally presented with opening and closing transactions, highs and lows for the trading day as well as for the season, and the change from the previous trading day. Futures prices are also quoted usually presented with opening and closing transactions, highs and lows for the trading day as well as for the season, and the change from the previous trading day. Futures prices are also quoted by the month of delivery, so that on a given day there may be several quotations for each commodity at each exchange for different months. Volume reports and commodity indexes such as the Dow-Jones Spot index and the Dow-Jones Futures index, or the Reuters United Kingdom index show the trend of commodity trading and prices. These trends and developments can be of utmost importance to the financial manager of a firm utilizing any one or several commodities traded. Many firms also engage in trading activities to "hedge" against unforeseen adverse trends in the commodities market by utilizing the "futures" device. In the simplest of terms, hedging is a method of buying and selling at the same time, but for different delivery dates to achieve "price insurance." Any price changes in the period between the purchase and sale will be cushioned or even eliminated for the hedging firm, since the loss on one contract is likely

---

[2] For example, cotton is quoted in cents and hundredths of a cent per pound, wheat in cents and eighths of a cent per bushel, rubber in cents per pound.

to be offset by the gain on the other. Manufacturers often use this device to minimize speculative effects of commodity price movements, endeavoring to limit their profit performance to the results from manufacturing operations. (See references at the end of the chapter for further detail.)

b) Foreign exchange is usually quoted in terms of selling prices for bank transfers in the United States for payment abroad, in U.S. dollars.

c) Other business and economic indicators, such as freight car loadings, price indexes, car output, and steel production, and so on, are often presented in the financial pages. These general indicators are supplemented by individual corporate earnings reports (usually by quarters), dividend declarations, major corporate personnel changes, announcements of new financing or redemption of existing issues, and other company news.

II. FINANCIAL SERVICES

A variety of current services are available to the student and practitioner of finance and investment. The commonest sources of financial data about individual companies and financial entities as well as summary statistics about selected industries are listed below:

Moody's Manuals and Surveys

The annual manuals appear in five separate volumes: Industrials; Banks, Insurance, Real Estate, Investment Trusts; Public Utilities; Railroads; and Governments and Municipals. These manuals provide detailed up-to-date histories, financial statements, security prices, and dividend records of a very large number of concerns, comprising most of the publicly held corporations. Summary statistics and industry data are found in the central "blue sections." Semiweekly supplements are issued to keep the information current.

Moody's also publishes weekly stock and bond surveys which analyze market and industry conditions, a semiweekly Dividend Record, and a semimonthly Bond Record listing prices, earnings, and ratings of thousands of bonds.

Standard & Poor's Manuals and Surveys

Standard Corporation Records contain loose-leaf current financial information about a wide variety of companies which is kept up-to-date through daily supplements. Its Industry Surveys are compilations of group data on a number of individual groups of industries. Other services by Standard and Poor's include weekly forecasts of the securities markets, securities statistics, several information services on the bond market, and a Monthly Earnings and Stock Rating Guide.

Other Sources

Other services of a similar nature are provided by *Fitch's Corporation Manuals* and other manuals such as *Walker's Manual* of Pacific Coast Securities. A great deal of information is provided, mostly from an investor's standpoint, by the many individual analyses furnished periodically by the major brokerage, banking, and investment houses. Also, independent advisory services furnished to subscribers provide investment and analytical information. Among these are houses such as *United Business Service, Babson's,* and *The Value Line.*

III. COMPANY AND SUPPLEMENTARY DATA

Annual reports furnished by most corporations are an important direct source of financial information. Also, prospectuses (detailed proposals) are issued when new securities are to be floated or major changes in the corporate structure are planned, and a great deal of information can be obtained from those statements about the history of the company, its owners, its financial and operating data, products, facilities, and similar data. (The Securities and Exchange Commission has established standard requirements of disclosure of data for publicly offered securities.) Some financial data on closely held companies, or small companies not listed in any of the financial services, can often be obtained at the corporation records departments of various state governments which require the filing of financial statements from companies doing business in the state (Massachusetts is one of the states with this requirement).

The various trade associations, such as the American Iron and Steel Institute or the National Lumber Manufacturer's Association, often publish yearly industry data and statistics, which are sometimes found in special issues of the trade magazines and journals. There are listings of these sources in most major libraries.

A great wealth of information is provided by publications, reports and studies prepared by agencies of the federal government. The Department of Commerce is especially active in this regard. Some of the major government publications are the *Survey of Current Business, Facts for Industry, Industry Reports, Statistical Abstract, Census of Manufacturers, Census of Business;* the reports of the Federal Trade Commission, and hundreds more. Monthly and annual catalogs of the U.S. Superintendent of Documents are available upon request.

There are, as pointed out, a great number of periodicals dealing with the general area of finance. Some of these are highly specialized and oriented to specific subjects such as investment banking, commercial banking, and consumer finance. Also many deal with financial conditions in foreign countries and in specific areas within the United States. On the other hand, there are certain newspapers and periodicals which deal with the broad subject of business finance in this country with which students should have some familiarity. This does not mean that all or even most of them should be read on any systematic basis; rather it is important that students be aware of their existence and of what they can be expected to offer. A selected list of these publications is presented below in addition to those mentioned in the text:

The American Banker
The Bulletin of the American Institution of Banking
Journal of Commerce
The Corporate Director
Credit and Financial Management
Finance
The Financial Executive
Financial World
Fortune

Investment Dealers Digest
National Tax Journal

The manuals and services mentioned are available in most libraries, some of which carry in addition company annual reports, registration statements with the Securities and Exchange Commission, proxy statements, and so forth.

SELECTED REFERENCES

CLENDENIN, JOHN C. *Introduction to Investments.* 3d ed. New York: McGraw-Hill Book Co., 1960, chaps. 8, 9, 10 (on securities markets).

COMAN, EDWIN T., JR. *Sources of Business Information.* Rev. ed., Berkeley, Calif.: University of California Press, 1964.

Corporate and Business Finance, A classified bibliography of recent literature (Comp. by GORDON DONALDSON and CAROLYN STUBBS). Boston, Mass.: Baker Library, Harvard Graduate School of Business Administration, 1964.

FRIEND, I.; HOFFMAN, C. W.; AND WINN, W. J. *The Over-the-Counter Securities Markets.* New York: McGraw-Hill Book Co., 1958.

HAUSDORFER, W. *Handbook of Commercial, Financial, and Information Services.* Special Libraries Association, 1956.

LEFFLER, GEORGE L. *The Stock Market.* New York: The Ronald Press Co., 1951.

LYNCH, MERRILL; PIERCE; FENNER; AND SMITH, INC. "How to Hedge Commodities"; also, "How to Buy and Sell Commodities." Rev. ed., 1958.

MANLEY, MARIAN C. *Business Information: How to Find and Use It.* New York: Harper & Bros., 1955.

The New York Times. "How to Read Financial and Business News." 7th ed. New York, 1957.

Standard and Poor's Stock Price Indexes: Method of Computation shown in "Security Price Index Record." 1962 ed. Orange, N.J.: 1962.

The Wall Street Journal. "Basis of Calculation of Dow-Jones Averages." New York, 1960.

INDEX

221

This book has been set in 12 and 10 point Caledonia, leaded 2 points. Chapter numbers and titles are in 18 point Garamond. The size of the type page is 27 by 45 picas.